TYPING: TWO-IN-ONE COURSE

Typing: Two-in-One Course

Archie Drummond
Anne Coles-Mogford
Matthew Boulton Technical College
Birmingham

***with* Ida Scattergood**

McGRAW-HILL Book Company

London · New York · St Louis · San Francisco · Auckland · Bogotá · Guatemala
Hamburg · Lisbon · Madrid · Mexico · Montreal · New Delhi · Panama · Paris
San Juan · São Paulo · Singapore · Sydney · Tokyo · Toronto

Published by McGRAW-HILL Book Company (UK) Limited
Maidenhead · Berkshire · England

07 084676 6

345 NI 887

Filmset by Eta Services (Typesetters) Ltd, Beccles, Suffolk
Printed in Italy by New Interlitho

Index to Contents

Preface

Today's office technology has put the QWERTY keyboard in the spotlight because it is to be found everywhere: in the home, in the office, in the factory, in the bank, at the travel agents, etc, and, therefore, to be able to operate the keyboard efficiently is a necessity in society today. Because of the differing needs of a variety of learners, we have designed this book to cover elementary and intermediate levels. The first part develops good typing habits, keyboarding skills and basic production technique, while the remainder of the text gives guidance and practice at a higher level of vocational competence and prepares candidates for any intermediate typewriting examination.

Keyboard mastery
The keyboard approach is the popular one used in *Typing First Course*, third and fourth editions. Because of the lack of standardization in the placement of the symbols on keyboards used with electronic typewriters and word processing machines, the figures are taught as a group with the symbols presented separately in the next 3 pages. As these extra characters are now often in different positions on different keyboards, it may be necessary for the learner to locate the symbol, decide on the correct finger, and then practise the reach from the home key that is relevant on the particular keyboard. If these extra characters are closely linked with the figure keys, it will provide a learning stimulus.

A Keyboard Review containing all the alphabet keys learnt so far is given at the beginning of each new keyboarding section and, as well as the "Word families" and "Apply the keys you know" exercises, homophones have been introduced not only to aid mastery of the key reaches, but also to make the learner aware of the use of words.

Keyboarding skills
After the keyboard has been introduced, a variety of skill-building routines have been provided and practice should still be maintained on keyboarding skills throughout the course. Exercises for this purpose are given on pages 181–196. These exercises are grouped into:

Alphabetic sentences—pages 181–182
Technique and review drills—pages 183–185
Accuracy and speed paragraphs—pages 186–191
Record your progress paragraphs—pages 192–196

Plan for improving keyboarding skills

Section 26
(a) Alphabetic sentence, page 181, **2**
(b) Carriage/carrier return drill, page 183, **2**
(c) Improve your spelling skill, page 30, **1**
(d) Accuracy/speed, page 186, **7** and **8**—1 minute at 26 wpm
(e) Record your progress, page 192, **3**—1 minute

Section 27
(a) Alphabetic sentence, page 181, **3**
(b) Common word drill, page 183, **3**
(c) Improve your spelling skill, page 30, **2**
(d) Accuracy/speed, page 186, **9** and **10**—2 minutes at 26 wpm
(e) Record your progress, page 192, **4**—2 minutes

Section 28
(a) Alphabetic sentence, page 181, **4**
(b) Double letter drill, page 183, **4**
(c) Improve your spelling skill, page 30, **3**
(d) Accuracy/speed, page 187, **11** and **12**—1 minute at 27 wpm
(e) Record your progress, page 192, **5**—1 minute

Section 29
(a) Alphabetic sentence, page 181, **5**
(b) Figure key drill, page 183, **5**
(c) Improve your spelling skill, page 30, **4**
(d) Accuracy/speed, page 187, **13** and **14**—2 minutes at 27 wpm
(e) Record your progress, page 193, **6**—2 minutes

Section 30
(a) Alphabetic sentence, page 181, **6**
(b) Fluency drill, page 184, **6**
(c) Improve your spelling skill, page 30, **5**
(d) Accuracy/speed, page 187, **15** and **16**—1 minute at 28 wpm
(e) Record your progress, page 193, **7**—1 minute

Section 31 (a) Alphabetic sentence, page 181, **7**
(b) Hyphen key drill, page 184, **7**
(c) Improve your spelling skill, page 30, **6**
(d) Accuracy/speed, page 187, **17** and **18**—2 minutes at 28 wpm
(e) Record your progress, page 193, **8**—2 minutes

Section 32 (a) Alphabetic sentence, page 181, **8**
(b) Letter combination drill, page 184, **8**
(c) Improve your spelling skill, page 30, **7**
(d) Accuracy/speed, page 188, **19** and **20**—1 minute at 29 wpm
(e) Record your progress, page 193, **9**—1 minute

Section 34 (a) Alphabetic sentence, page 181, **9**
(b) One hand word drill, page 184, **9**
(c) Improve your spelling skill, page 30, **8**
(d) Accuracy/speed, page 188, **21**—2 minutes at 29 wpm
(e) Record your progress, page 193, **10**—2 minutes

Section 35 (a) Alphabetic sentence, page 181, **10**
(b) Phrase drill, page 184, **10**
(c) Improve your spelling skill, page 30, **9**
(d) Accuracy/speed, page 188, **22**—1 minute at 30 wpm
(e) Record your progress, page 193, **11**—1 minute

Section 36 (a) Alphabetic sentence, page 181, **11**
(b) Common prefix drill, page 184, **11**
(c) Improve your spelling skill, page 30, **10**
(d) Accuracy/speed, page 188, **23**—1½ minutes at 30 wpm
(e) Record your progress, page 194, **12**—1½ minutes

Section 37 (a) Alphabetic sentence, page 181, **12**
(b) Punctuation drill, page 184, **12**
(c) Improve your spelling skill, page 30, **11**
(d) Accuracy/speed, page 188, **24**—2 minutes at 30 wpm
(e) Record your progress, page 194, **13**—2 minutes

Section 38 (a) Alphabetic sentence, page 182, **13**
(b) Space bar drill, page 184, **13**
(c) Improve your spelling skill, page 30, **12**
(d) Accuracy/speed, page 188, **25**—3 minutes at 30 wpm
(e) Record your progress, page 194, **14**—3 minutes

Section 40 (a) Alphabetic sentence, page 182, **14**
(b) Shift key drill, page 184, **14**
(c) Improve your spelling skill, page 30, **13**
(d) Accuracy /speed, page 189, **26**—4 minutes at 30 wpm
(e) Record your progress, page 194, **15**—4 minutes

Section 41 (a) Alphabetic sentence, page 182, **15**
(b) Special character drill, page 185, **15**
(c) Improve your spelling skill, page 30, **14**
(d) Accuracy/speed, page 189, **27**—5 minutes at 30 wpm
(e) Record your progress, page 195, **16**—5 minutes

Section 42 (a) Alphabetic sentence, page 182, **16**
(b) Common suffix drill, page 185, **16**
(c) Improve your spelling drill, page 30, **15**
(d) Accuracy/speed, page 190, **28** and **29**—1 minute at 35 wpm
(e) Record your progress, page 195, **17**—1 minute

Section 43 (a) Alphabetic sentence, page 182, **17**
(b) Vowel drill, page 185, **17**
(c) Improve your spelling drill, page 30, **16**
(d) Accuracy/speed, page 190, **30** and **31**—2 minutes at 35 wpm
(e) Record your progress, page 195, **18**—2 minutes

Section 44 (a) Alphabetic sentence, page 182, **18**
(b) Word building drill, page 185, **18**
(c) Improve your spelling drill, page 30, **17**

(d) Accuracy/speed, page 190, **32**—3 minutes at 35 wpm
(e) Record your progress, page 195, **19**—3 minutes

Section 45 (a) Alphabetic sentence, page 182, **19**
(b) Word division drill, page 185, **19**
(c) Improve your spelling drill, page 30, **18**
(d) Accuracy/speed, page 191, **33**—4 minutes at 35 wpm
(e) Record your progress, page 196, **20**—4 minutes

Section 47 (a) Alphabetic sentence, page 182, **20**
(b) Word family drill, page 185, **20**
(c) Improve your spelling drill, page 30, **19**
(d) Accuracy/speed, page 191, **34**—5 minutes at 35 wpm
(e) Record your progress, page 196, **21**—5 minutes

For the last 8 sections individuals should choose suitable exercises depending on the speed and accuracy reached, either starting again at the beginning or repeating those drills given nearer the end.

Word errors

Written communications involve the use of words, phrases, terms and expressions in a great variety of combinations; therefore, in order to avoid errors and misunderstanding, you must have adequate basic English. You should

(a) have a good knowledge of words and their meanings,
(b) know how to spell correctly,
(c) know how to form plurals, compound words and possessives,
(d) know how to punctuate.

To help you we have included a page of words that you may find difficult to spell and, in certain exercises, you will find deliberate errors. These are referred to as "word errors" because they may be spelling errors, typing errors, etc. In the earlier production exercises, you are told the number of errors to look for, but as the course progresses no indication of the number is given.

Syllabic intensity

We believe that a controlled but random and unselected vocabulary is the most effective way of building typing skills and therefore, the difficulty of the copy in "Accuracy/speed", and "Record your progress" exercises has been graded according to the syllabic intensity. Syllabic intensity means the average number of syllables in the words of a passage.

Information processing

Word processing and data processing terminology are integrated into the text.

Technique development

The book is divided into sections which are clearly marked at the bottom of the page together with the title of the new theory presented on that page. Each new point is explained in specific steps, which are small and easy, and is followed by exercises that relate to the theory presented. These exercises are set out clearly for the learner to copy. All the theory is enclosed in coloured boxes for easy reference.

Consolidation—Production typing

There are 4 Consolidation sections (40 tasks in all) consisting of production work which enables the typist to develop a realistic approach to office-style typing and production efficiency. The aim of each task is to apply the knowledge already gained in the technique sections covered up to that point. These tasks test the learner in the display of a great variety of documents that have to be completed within a certain time and using a particular format.

Loose-leaf teaching notes and solutions

The companion volume gives detailed suggestions on how

(a) to train students to type accurately and speedily,
(b) to introduce and explain new work,
(c) to deal with production typing.

It also includes:

(d) learning objectives for the lessons,
(e) displayed solutions in what we consider to be the most acceptable form,
(f) a variety of charts and forms which may be duplicated and used in the classroom. These are referred to in *Typing: Two-in-One Course*, in the *Teaching Notes and Solutions* and in *Typing Target Practice.*

The Solutions are excellent for class teaching, particularly with mixed groups. Students should be allowed access to the Solutions after they have completed each exercise because, in this way, they will be encouraged to check their work carefully.

Additional practice material

Students who wish to have additional practice on particular documents and points of theory should use *Typing Target Practice.*

Reference is made at the bottom of the pages to relevant exercises in *Typing Target Practice.*

Acknowledgments

This book reflects the comments, suggestions and recommendations made to us by teachers and students, and we attach a great deal of value to their contributions which, over the years, have helped enormously in the effectiveness and popularity of our typing publications.

Our very sincere thanks and appreciation is extended to the editor, Kay Baxter, for her valuable advice and encouragement at all times.

We wish also to express our gratitude to Mrs Margaret Rees-Boughton for permission to use extracts from her book *Watcham's Office Practice, Book One*, and to Mr T A C Shafto for permission to use an extract from his book *Commerce: Structure and Practice.*

We also wish to thank our colleagues for their helpful advice and assistance given in copying the manuscript exercises.

Archie Drummond
Anne Coles-Mogford

MAIN PARTS OF A TYPEBAR MACHINE

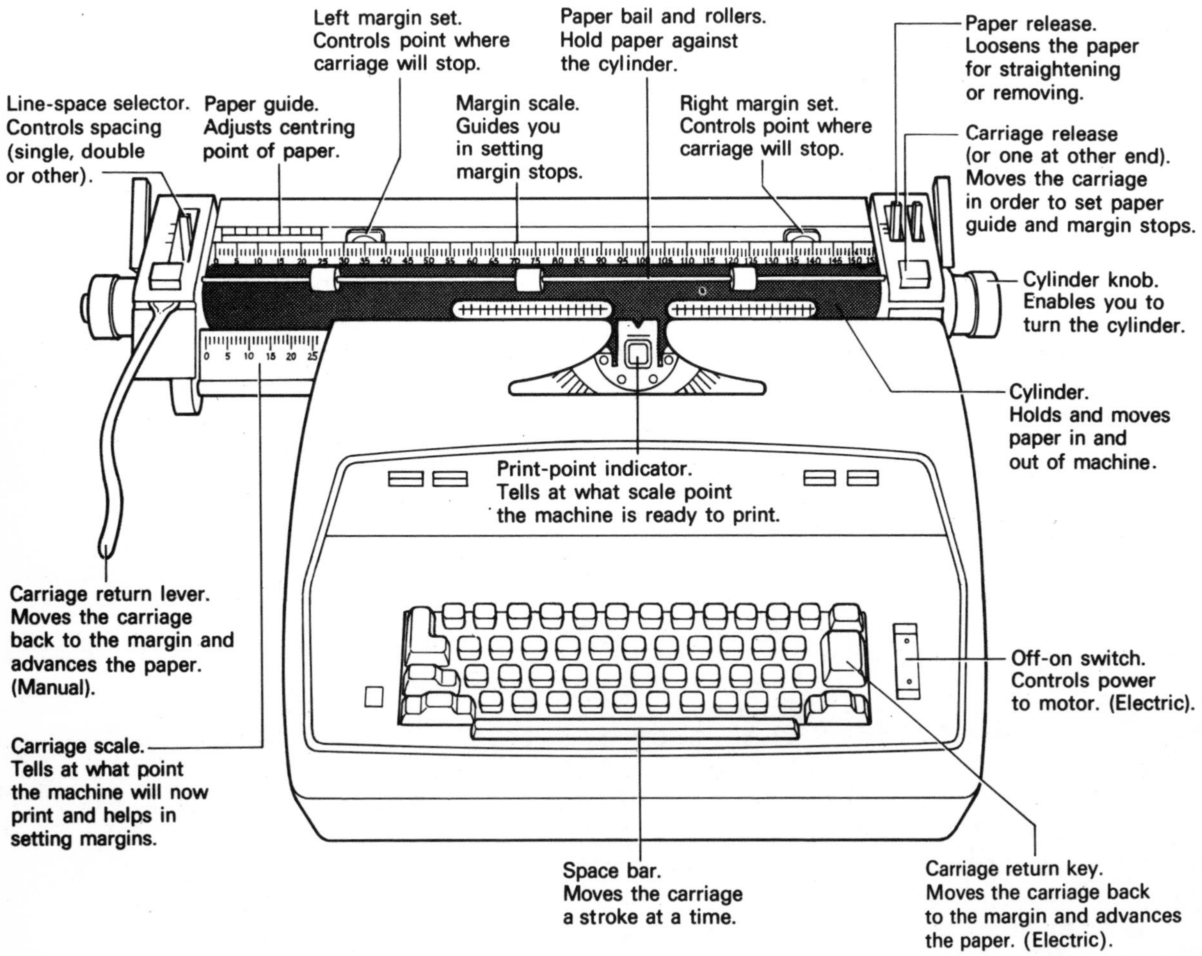

Left margin set. Controls point where carriage will stop.
Paper bail and rollers. Hold paper against the cylinder.
Paper release. Loosens the paper for straightening or removing.
Line-space selector. Controls spacing (single, double or other).
Paper guide. Adjusts centring point of paper.
Margin scale. Guides you in setting margin stops.
Right margin set. Controls point where carriage will stop.
Carriage release (or one at other end). Moves the carriage in order to set paper guide and margin stops.
Cylinder knob. Enables you to turn the cylinder.
Cylinder. Holds and moves paper in and out of machine.
Print-point indicator. Tells at what scale point the machine is ready to print.
Carriage return lever. Moves the carriage back to the margin and advances the paper. (Manual).
Off-on switch. Controls power to motor. (Electric).
Carriage scale. Tells at what point the machine will now print and helps in setting margins.
Space bar. Moves the carriage a stroke at a time.
Carriage return key. Moves the carriage back to the margin and advances the paper. (Electric).

MAIN PARTS OF AN ELEMENT MACHINE

Line-space selector. Controls spacing (single, double or other).
Paper guide. Adjusts centring point of paper.
Paper bail and rollers. Hold paper against the cylinder.
Cylinder. Holds and moves paper in and out of machine.
Paper release. Loosens the paper for straightening or removing.
Carrier. Moves the element across the paper.
Cylinder knob. Enables you to turn the cylinder.
Line scale. Numbers the spaces.
Left margin set. Controls point where carrier will stop.
Right margin set. Controls point where carrier will stop.
Off-on switch. Controls power to motor.
Carrier position indicator. Shows at what space the machine is ready to print.
Space bar. Moves the carrier a stroke at a time or, if held down, several spaces at a time.
Carrier return key. Moves the carrier back to the margin and advances the paper.

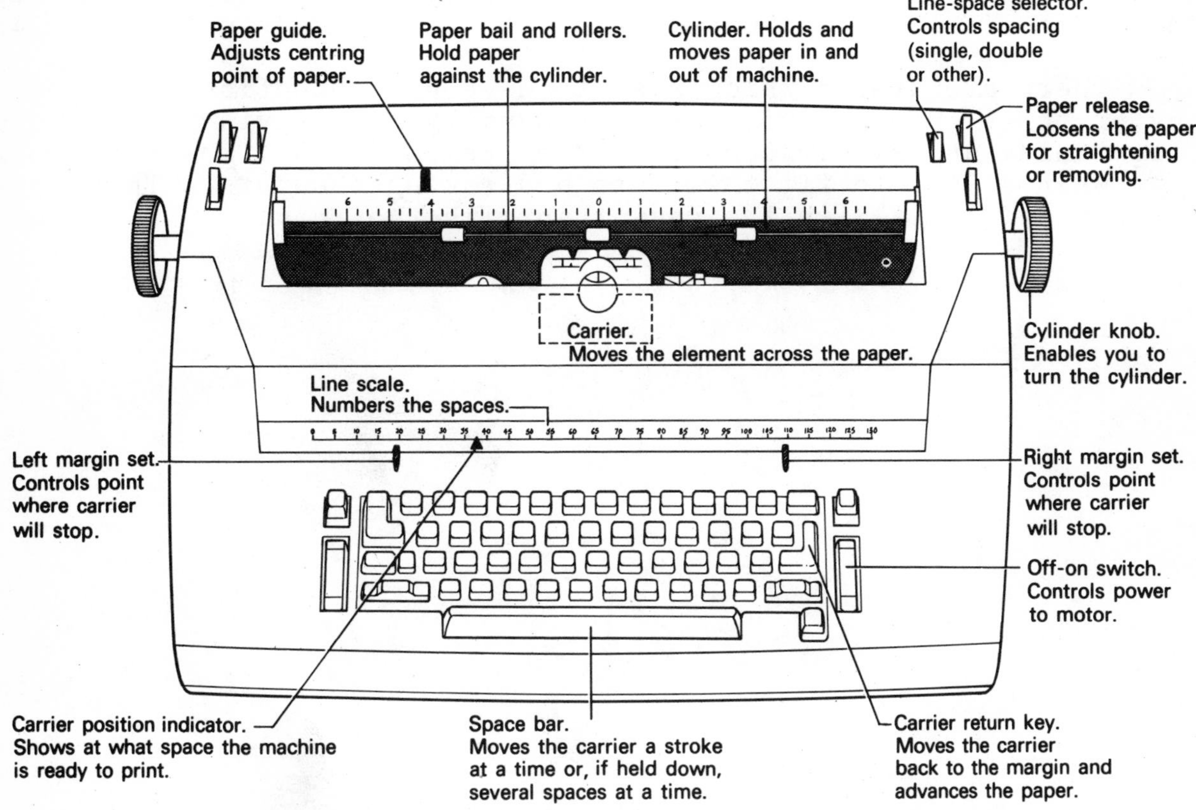

20 After exercise 33 on page 191 **4 minutes**

At the start of the year your Board was faced with a 10
strike of workers - trade union men who objected to the 21
employment by us of certain non-union men. We had to bow to 33
the wishes of the Union and accept the principle of the 44
"closed shop". Later in the year we suffered from the 55
Government's policy and from the shortage of raw materials 67
caused by the dislocation of imports. 75

From the Balance Sheet you will see that our financial 86
position is sound. During the year we offered 50,000 un- 98
issued £1 Ordinary Shares to the public; all were taken up, 109
and this provided us with capital that can now be used for 120
the future development of your Company. Bearing in mind all 132
problems, I feel sure you will be pleased with the Board's 143
recommendation that a dividend of 12½ per cent be paid to 155
holders of the 150,000 Ordinary Shares. **(SI 1.38)** 162

1 | 2 | 3 | 4 | 5 | 6 | 7 | 8 | 9 | 10 | 11 | 12 |

21 After exercise 35 on page 191 **5 minutes**

From ancient times people have attached significance to 11
dreams. Some believe that they foretell the future; others 23
suggest that they are but a recollection of the past. Which 35
view we hold must depend on our own experiences, but we must 47
agree that much depends on the kind of dream and the cause 59
of it. A dream following great mental strain is likely to 71
be due to the fact that the brain remains active after the 83
body sleeps. A nightmare dream, caused perhaps by over-eating 95
before going to bed, may be violent and rather frightening, 107
but, in view of the cause, is not likely to have any great 119
significance. The dreams we may have when we are ill, or 130
under the effect of an anaesthetic, can surely mean nothing. 142

There are dreams which seem to have no connection with 153
any of these things, and these are usually more vivid than 165
frightening and so impress us that we remember them the next 177
day, when we try to fit them into our waking thoughts. This 189
is more difficult with the past than with the future. 200
(SI 1.34)

1 | 2 | 3 | 4 | 5 | 6 | 7 | 8 | 9 | 10 | 11 | 12 |

EXAMPLE OF ELECTRONIC KEYBOARD

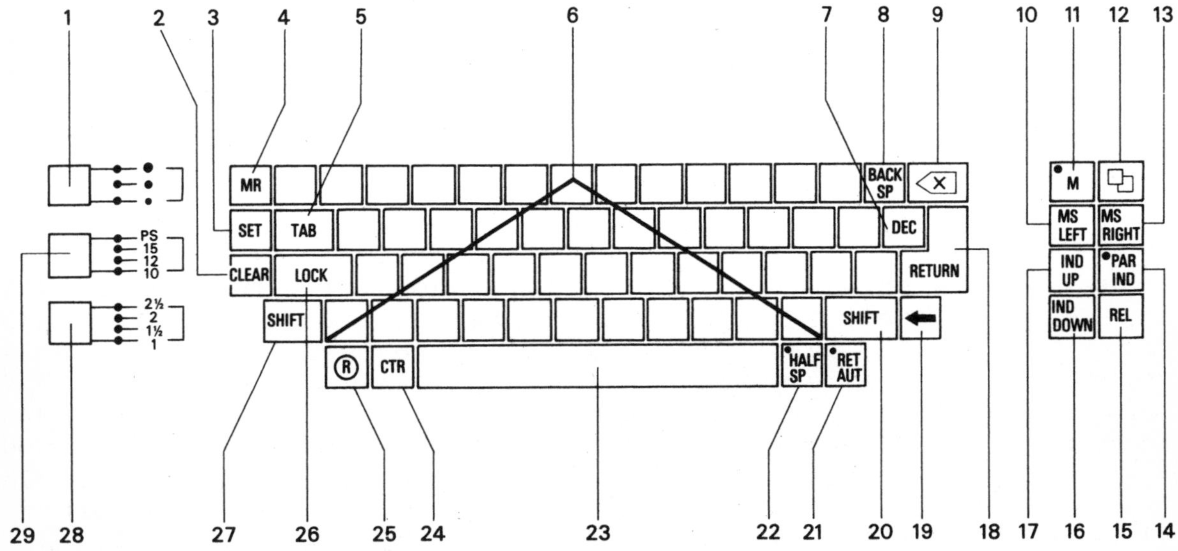

1 Impression—upper = heavy; centre = medium; lower = light.
2 Tab clear.
3 Tab set.
4 Margin release.
5 Moves carrier to tab stops.
6 Qwerty keyboard—position of special characters varies according to make of machine.
7 Decimal tab—automatically aligns decimal point at tab stop.
8 Backspace key.
9 Error correction key.
10 Sets a left margin.
11 Memory key—used to store and recall text from phrase memory.
12 Mode key—has a number of functions, including use as a second shift key for certain symbols.
13 Sets a right margin.
14 Used for paragraph indent.
15 Relocate key—used to start memory printing; used after correction has been made to return carrier to original printing point, etc.
16 Index down—moves paper down half a space (has a repeat function).
17 Index up—moves paper up half a space (has a repeat function).
18 Carrier return as for electric typewriter.
19 Express backspace—does not turn up a line space when carrier is returned.
20 Shift as for electric typewriter.
21 Automatic return—automatically returns the carrier at the end of the typing line.
22 Half space—used to move the carrier half a space to the left when typing in an extra character.
23 Space bar.
24 Centre—centres automatically between margins; when pressed after tab key, will centre between tab stops; when pressed at a given point on the page, will centre around that point.
25 Repeat key—repeats all characters.
26 Shift lock.
27 Shift key.
28 Line-space selector.
29 Pitch—PS = proportional spacing; 15 = 15 characters to the inch; 12 = 12 characters to the inch; 10 = 10 characters to the inch.

It should be noted that there are electronic typewriters with a more simple keyboard than that given above and also, that there are electronic machines with much more sophisticated keyboards.

16 After exercise 27 on page 189 **5 minutes**

Epsom is known all over the world as the place where 10
the great horse race, the Derby, is run each year, but it 22
has also given its name to the well-known Epsom Salts. 33

The small village was not known outside the immediate 43
district until early in the seventeenth century, and it is 55
said that one day a herdsman, much to his joy, found on the 66
common a water-hole which he did not know was there. He 78
hoped to water his sheep there, but they refused to drink 89
because the water was so bitter. This was at a time when it 101
was a popular habit to drink spa waters for most human ail- 113
ments. This water was soon recognized as a healing water, 124
a great blood purifier, and named Epsom Water. Soon visitors 137
flocked in from all over Europe and it was not long before 148
the craze for taking spa water was in full spate at Epsom 160
as elsewhere. Fashions change, however, and this craze died. 172
(SI 1.31)

1 | 2 | 3 | 4 | 5 | 6 | 7 | 8 | 9 | 10 | 11 | 12 |

17 After exercise 29 on page 190 **One minute**

The bright sunshine brought out more cars, thus causing 11
traffic in the narrow streets to be slowed down to a snail's 23
pace. To walk was the one sure way of getting from place to 35
place in the shortest possible time. **(SI 1.19)** 42

1 | 2 | 3 | 4 | 5 | 6 | 7 | 8 | 9 | 10 | 11 | 12 |

18 After exercise 31 on page 190 **2 minutes**

The Chairman of the Board has written to me to say that 11
Mr. T. Young has been badly hurt in an accident, and that he 23
will not be at work for at least 18 months. You are aware, 35
no doubt, of the fact that he has a large number of speaking 47
engagements in many different cities, and these will have to 59
be cancelled at once unless we are able to engage someone to 71
take over from him. I know you have heard Mr. Young speak 83
on a number of occasions and I wonder if you would take his 94
place for the time being. **(SI 1.25)** 99

1 | 2 | 3 | 4 | 5 | 6 | 7 | 8 | 9 | 10 | 11 | 12 |

19 After exercise 32 on page 190 **3 minutes**

The number of guide cards used and their arrangement 10
depend on the filing system. The purpose of the guide cards 22
is, however, the same in all systems - to guide the eye when 34
finding and filing papers, and to support the folders. Guide 46
cards can be bought in all standard sizes, as well as for 58
files. Most guide cards have a tab along the top edge, and 81
this space contains a plain and clear reference to the folder 94
behind. It is important that this reference should be easy 106
to read, and it should give clear guidance to the order of 117
the folders. **(SI 1.32)** 120

1 | 2 | 3 | 4 | 5 | 6 | 7 | 8 | 9 | 10 | 11 | 12 |

MANUAL AND ELECTRIC MACHINES (For electronic machines, see manufacturer's instruction manual)

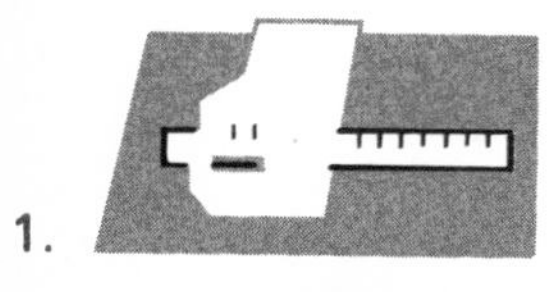

1.

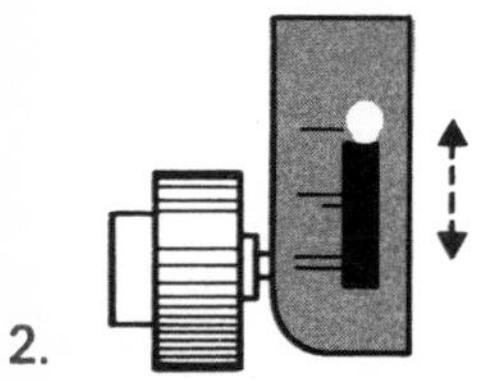

2.

1 Check the position of the paper guide
One of the marks on the paper rest shows where to set the paper guide so that the left edge of the paper will be at "0" on the carriage-position line scale. Check that the paper guide is set at that mark.

2 Set the line-space selector for single spacing
The line-space selector has a *1*, a *2*, and in some cases a *3* printed on or beside it. Adjust the selector so that it is in the *1* position. In addition, many machines are now fitted with half-line spacing to give 1½ and 2½ line-spaces. Examine your machine and check the line-spacing.

3 Set the margins as indicated in each unit or exercise

(a) On some machines you can see the margin stops on the front of the carriage or behind the paper rest. On such machines: (1) press the button on top of the stop, (2) slide the stop to the point you wish, and (3) then release the button.

(b) On other machines you cannot see the margin stops. You must use a margin-set key. You may have a separate margin-set key at each end of the carriage, or you may have one key on the keyboard for use with both stops. On such machines: (1) move the carriage to the present setting of the stop, (2) press the margin-set key while you move the carriage to the point where you want the margin and (3) then release the set key.

(c) In the keyboard learning stage (pages 6–28) only the left margin need be set. From page 32 onwards set margins at scale-points given.

As you progress through the textbook, you will find instructions such as "Use suitable margins"—in such cases you must decide what margins to use. What is important is that, in the majority of exercises other than display and tabulation, your left margin must be wider than your right margin, e.g., elite 22–82 (there are 21 clear spaces on the left and 19 clear spaces on the right).

In other cases you may be given measurements for your margins, e.g., 25 mm (one inch) on the left and 13 mm (half an inch) on the right. This would mean that, when using A4 paper, you would have margins of elite 13–94, pica 11—77. With elite type there are 12 spaces to 25 mm and with pica type there are 10 spaces to 25 mm.

4.

4 Get the paper bail out of the way
Pull the paper bail forward or up, temporarily away from the cylinder, so that you may insert paper without its bumping into the paper bail.

5 Insert a sheet of paper
Hold the sheet in your left hand. Place the paper behind the cylinder, against the raised edge of the paper guide. Turn the right cylinder knob to draw the paper into the machine.

To prevent damage to the cylinder of the typewriter, use a backing sheet such as is usually supplied in boxes of carbon paper, or use a sheet of stout paper.

5.

6.

6 Check that the paper is straight
Push the top of the paper back. If the left side of the paper, at both top and bottom, fits evenly against the paper guide, your paper is straight. If it is not straight, loosen the paper (use the paper release), straighten it, and return the paper release to its normal position.

7 Place the paper bail against the paper
Slide the rubber rollers on the bail to the right or left to divide the paper into thirds. Then, set the bail back against the paper.

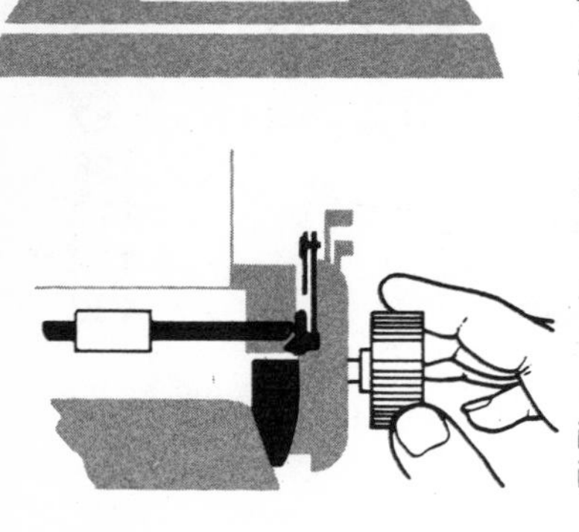

8.

8 Adjust the paper for the top margin

(a) When typing drills, turn the paper back, using the right cylinder knob, until only a small portion of paper shows above the paper bail.

(b) When typing production exercises (apart from display and tabulation) the majority of exercises typed on plain paper start on the seventh single-line space from the top edge of the paper, which means you leave 6 spaces (25 mm or one inch) clear. To do this proceed as follows:

i. Insert paper.
ii. Check to see that paper is straight. (See 6 above.)
iii. Turn paper back so that top edge is level with top edge of alignment guide.
iv. Turn up 7 single-line spaces.

12 After exercise 23 on page 188 **1½ minutes**

We have had your name and address on our list since January, 12
but although we have, from time to time, sent you details of 24
properties, we have not heard from you. If you still desire 36
to buy a country residence, please complete and return to us 48
the attached form, so that we may know what the position is. 60
(SI 1.28)

1 | 2 | 3 | 4 | 5 | 6 | 7 | 8 | 9 | 10 | 11 | 12 |

13 After exercise 24 on page 188 **2 minutes**

Since the beginning of the year we have employed about 275 12
more men then ever before, and 340 more than last year. 23
Under our new profit scheme we should like to pay 5% to the 34
workmen and 5% to the staff, and we shall require at least 46
£10,000 extra to enable us to do so. Your Board proposes 57
to add another £15,000 to the reserve fund, bringing it up 69
to £275,000. (SI 1.27) 72

1 | 2 | 3 | 4 | 5 | 6 | 7 | 8 | 9 | 10 | 11 | 12 |

14 After exercise 25 on page 188 **3 minutes**

We thank you for your request for a copy of our latest list, 12
but have to state that we do not issue a general catalogue, 24
in view of the improvements which we make in our products 35
from time to time, and we feel that any benefits should be 47
passed on at once to our customers. We are sending you a 58
few brochures which give full descriptions of some of our 70
standard lines, and also details of our prices and terms of 81
delivery. Our agent, Mr. F. A. Clarke, hopes to be in 92
Inverness from 26th to 31st May, and would be pleased to 104
call on you to help in any way he can. (SI 1.28) 112

1 | 2 | 3 | 4 | 5 | 6 | 7 | 8 | 9 | 10 | 11 | 12 |

15 After exercise 26 on page 189 **4 minutes**

We were very glad to learn from your letter of 16th July 11
that the prospects you spoke of when you called on us 3 days 23
ago are now materializing. 28

You tell us that you have bought a new truck for business 40
and that you are able to save storage charges by housing it 52
in your factory building. We are sure that you have calcu- 64
lated well and that the truck will cut down your expenses. 75

Have you had your insurance broker review your insurance? 87
We venture to suggest that you go over your policy with 98
your broker to ensure that there are no mistakes in it. 110
The fact that you have this truck in your works will change 122
the rates and may invalidate the policy. (SI 1.33) 130

1 | 2 | 3 | 4 | 5 | 6 | 7 | 8 | 9 | 10 | 11 | 12 |

SINGLE-ELEMENT TYPEWRITERS

There are now many electric/electronic typewriters with single-element heads on the market. These typewriters have no movable carriage, which also means that the cylinder is static, and there are no type bars. Instead, they have a printing head attached to a "carrier" that moves across the page from left to right, stroke by stroke. When you wish to return the carrier to the left margin, you press the return key as you would with the ordinary electric typewriter.

The printing element may be a golf ball head which whirls and tilts to make an impression on the paper, or it may be a daisy wheel which is a rapidly spinning disk of flexible arms and on the tip of each arm there is a typeface character. The required character stops at the printing point and is struck by a small hammer which impinges the image on the paper.

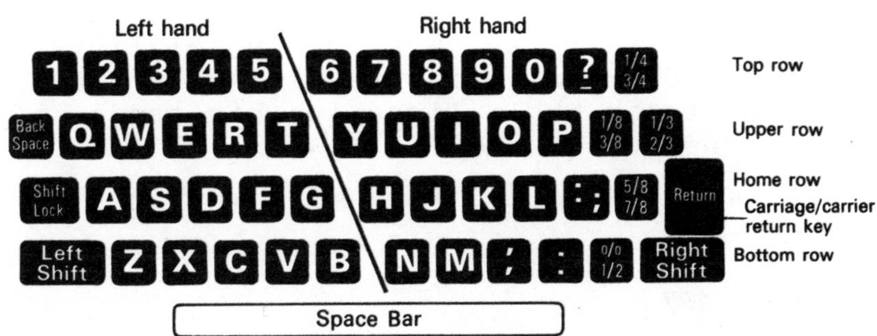

The ready-to-type position

1 Place your book on the right-hand side of your machine, or as indicated by your teacher.

2 Place your finger tips on the HOME KEYS: Left finger tips on ASDF and right finger tips on JKL; Check that you placed them correctly.

3 Keep your *left* thumb close to your left first finger.

4 Extend your right thumb so that it is slightly above the centre of the space bar.

5 Now check your posture.
Your head—hold it erect, facing the book.
Your shoulders—hold them back, and relaxed.
Your body—centre yourself opposite the J-key a hand-span away from the machine.
Your back—straight, with your body sloping slightly forward from the hips.
Arms and elbows—let them hang loosely.
Wrists—keep them low, barely clearing the machine.
Hands—close together, low, flat across the backs.
Fingers—curved as though to grasp a handle bar.
Waist—sit back in the chair.
Feet—on the floor, one foot slightly in front of the other.

Finger movement

1 Without typing, practise the finger movement for each exercise. During this preliminary practice you may look at your fingers. You will find it helpful to say the letters aloud. Continue this preliminary practice until your fingers "know" where to move from the HOME KEY. Always return finger to its HOME KEY.

2 When you are confident that your fingers have acquired the correct movement, repeat this practice *without looking at your fingers.* Keep your eyes on the copy in your book and do not strike the keys. If you hesitate in making the finger movement, repeat step one.

3 Practise the finger movement for each new key until your finger moves confidently and crisply to that key.

6 After exercise 14 on page 187 **2 minutes**

Different kinds of wild plants do not grow in the same place 12
because they need the soil and conditions to suit them, just 24
as we have our likes and dislikes. A plant which flourishes 36
in a warm, dry place will die if we move it to a place which 48
is cold and damp. It may be possible to alter its habits if 60
we do it slowly over long periods of time. **(SI 1.20)** 68

1 | 2 | 3 | 4 | 5 | 6 | 7 | 8 | 9 | 10 | 11 | 12 |

7 After exercise 16 on page 187 **One minute**

For a great number of years we have been specialists in many 12
kinds of fitted carpets - all of our selling and our fitting 24
staff having spent their whole lives in this trade. All our 36
work is done by experts. **(SI 1.24)** 41

1 | 2 | 3 | 4 | 5 | 6 | 7 | 8 | 9 | 10 | 11 | 12 |

8 After exercise 18 on page 187 **2 minutes**

Have you ever thought of taking an out-of-season holiday? A 12
winter break - in the New Year - may be just what you should 24
take. In our brochure you will find a wide choice of places 36
to which you can fly. Ask for details from: Sun Travellers, 48
Great North Road, Nottingham. Write to us straight away for 60
our new guide. **(SI 1.22)** 63

1 | 2 | 3 | 4 | 5 | 6 | 7 | 8 | 9 | 10 | 11 | 12 |

9 After exercise 20 on page 188 **One minute**

When you are asked to compile a letter, you should use short 12
words if they express clearly what you want to state. Short 24
sentences are easy to read and help the reader to understand 36
what you are trying to explain. **(SI 1.29)** 42

1 | 2 | 3 | 4 | 5 | 6 | 7 | 8 | 9 | 10 | 11 | 12 |

10 After exercise 21 on page 188 **2 minutes**

Many people who pay rent are eligible for rent allowances or 12
rebates - an allowance if you are a private tenant or rebate 24
if you are a council tenant. 29

You should write to your local council. Then they will need 41
to know your income. The bigger your family the better will 53
be your chance of getting help, and the sooner you apply the 65
more quickly will you get help. **(SI 1.36)** 71

1 | 2 | 3 | 4 | 5 | 6 | 7 | 8 | 9 | 10 | 11 | 12 |

11 After exercise 22 on page 188 **One minute**

It may be next October before I can be certain of the number 12
of guests we shall have for the Dinner. I feel sure that it 24
will be greater than it was last year as members have bought 36
a hundred or more tickets already. **(SI 1.28)** 43

1 | 2 | 3 | 4 | 5 | 6 | 7 | 8 | 9 | 10 | 11 | 12 |

Practise carriage return

1 *Manual machines*

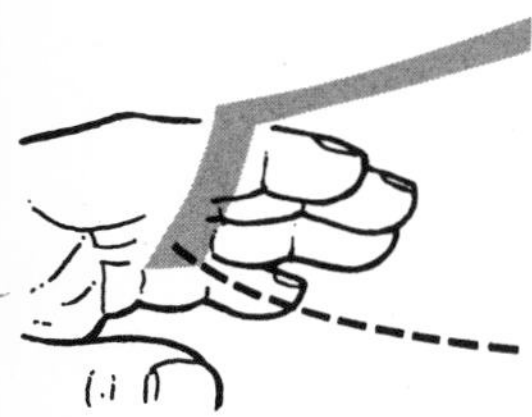

(a) Preliminary practice *without returning the carriage*. Look at the carriage return lever and raise your *left hand* and put the first finger and next finger or two against the lever. Practise the movement from the HOME KEYS to carriage return lever and back to HOME KEYS

(b) Right- and left-hand fingers on HOME KEYS

(c) Right-hand fingers remain on JKL;

(d) With eyes on textbook
 (i) raise left hand and return carriage
 (ii) return left hand to ASDF

2 *Electric/electronic machines*

(a) Preliminary practice *without returning the carriage/carrier.* Look at the carriage/carrier return key (on the right-hand side of the keyboard) and make the reach with your right-hand little finger from the semicolon to the return key and back to semicolon

(b) All fingers remain just slightly above their HOME KEY except right-hand little finger

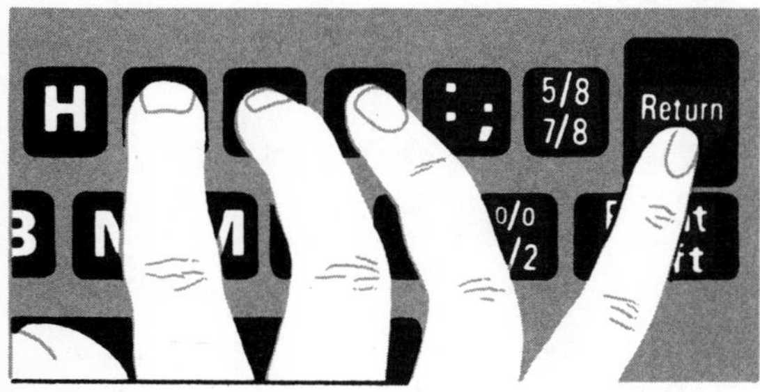

(c) With eyes on textbook
 (i) raise the little finger of the right hand and lightly press the return key
 (ii) return little finger to semicolon key immediately

Set margins, line-space selector and insert paper

1 Set left margin at 30 elite, 22 pica

2 Set line-space selector at "1"

3 Set paper guide at "O"

4 Raise paper bail bar out of the way

5 (a) Take a sheet of A4 paper in your left hand
 (b) Place the paper behind the cylinder with the left edge against the raised edge of the paper guide
 (c) With your right hand turn the right cylinder knob clockwise to draw the paper into the machine

6 Check that paper is straight by pushing the top of the paper back. If top and bottom of paper do not fit evenly against the paper guide
 (a) Use paper release to loosen paper
 (b) Straighten paper
 (c) Return paper release lever to normal position

7 Return paper bail to normal position

8 Turn the paper back, using right cylinder knob, until only a small portion of paper shows above paper bail

Striking the keys

1 Let your finger bounce off each key and return to home key

2 Reach with finger only; do *not* move wrist or arm

3 For manual machines, strike key firmly and sharply; for electric/electronic machines, stroke key

4 Strike keys, including space bar, evenly—one for each "tick" and one for each "tock" of the clock

KEYBOARDING SKILLS

Record your progress

Although not essential, it is preferable to relate the record your progress exercises to the accuracy/speed; eg, exercise 2 on this page would be typed when your accuracy/speed is approximately that required in exercises 5/6 on page 186. An indication is given before each exercise as to the stage at which it should be attempted.

Format

Follow instructions given on page 28 Margins: elite 22–82, pica 12–72.

2 After exercise 6 on page 186 **2 minutes**

```
There is still a very real risk of fire from many oil stoves  12
and lamps.  A portable oil stove must have a firm base (with  24
a guard around it) and it should always be placed out of the  36
children's reach.  Also, clothes left too near an oil stove,  48
or a gas fire that has no guard, might be set alight easily.  60
                                                     (SI 1.18)
```

1 | 2 | 3 | 4 | 5 | 6 | 7 | 8 | 9 | 10 | 11 | 12 |

3 After exercise 8 on page 186 **One minute**

```
Enclosed please find a copy of our latest price list.  After  12
you have studied its contents, please do not hesitate to let  24
us know if we can be of further help.  May we ask our agents  36
to get in touch with you? (SI 1.25)                           41
```

1 | 2 | 3 | 4 | 5 | 6 | 7 | 8 | 9 | 10 | 11 | 12 |

4 After exercise 10 on page 186 **2 minutes**

```
On sheet one we set out the pay scales agreed to at the last  12
meeting of the committee.  You will see that salaries are to  24
be increased by large amounts for all staff from the highest  36
paid to the lowest.  May we ask you to tell your staff about  48
this award when you see them next Monday.  The new rates are  60
effective from March. (SI 1.23)                               64
```

1 | 2 | 3 | 4 | 5 | 6 | 7 | 8 | 9 | 10 | 11 | 12 |

5 After exercise 12 on page 187 **One minute**

```
A thick haze covered the headland, and the wind, now at gale  12
force, was very sharp and biting.  We walked slowly and in a  24
long time we had covered only 3 miles.  We were then feeling  36
very chilly and worried. (SI 1.27)                            41
```

1 | 2 | 3 | 4 | 5 | 6 | 7 | 8 | 9 | 10 | 11 | 12 |

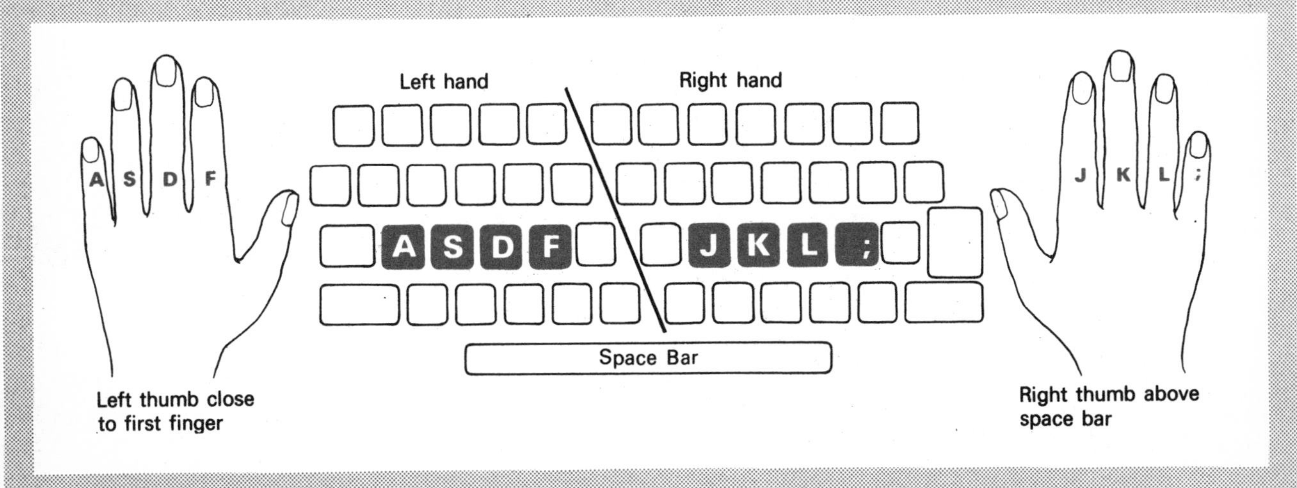

Ready-to-type position

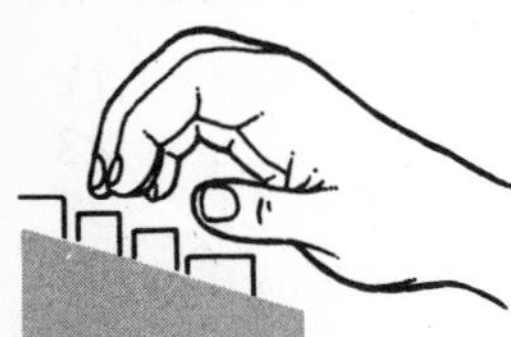

1 Place book on right-hand side of machine

2 Feet—one foot slightly in front of the other

3 Arms and elbows—let them hang loosely

4 Fingers (a) Place left-hand fingers on ASDF
(b) Right-hand fingers on JKL;
(c) Curve fingers as though to grasp a handle bar
(d) Look at the keyboard and place your fingers on the HOME KEYS—ASDF JKL;
(e) *Never* type while looking at the keyboard

5 Sit back and relax

Exercise 1

(a) See that carriage/carrier is at left margin
(b) Look at the keyboard and place your left-hand fingers on ASDF and right-hand fingers on JKL;
(c) Copy the following lines exactly as they stand—keeping eyes on textbook

```
fffjjjfffjjjfffjjjfffjjjfffjjjfffjjjfffj   return carriage/carrier
fffjjjfffjjjfffjjjfffjjjfffjjjfffjjjfffj   return carriage/carrier twice
```

(d) Sit back and relax and look at what you have typed

Space Bar

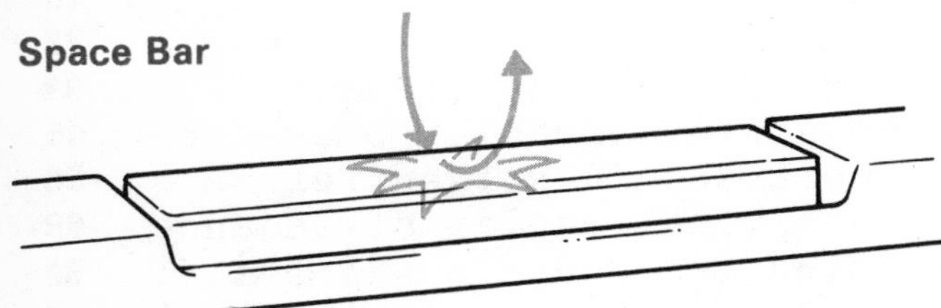

A clear space is left between each group of letters or words. This is done by striking the space bar with the *right thumb.* Keep your other fingers on the HOME KEYS as you bounce the thumb off the space bar. Practise striking space bar with right thumb

Exercise 2

(a) See that carriage/carrier is at left margin
(b) Look at the keyboard and place your left-hand fingers on ASDF and right-hand fingers on JKL;
(c) Copy the following lines exactly as they stand—keeping eyes on textbook

```
fff jjj fff jjj fjf jfj fff jjj fff fjfj   return carriage/carrier
fff jjj fff jjj fjf jfj fff jjj fff fjfj   return carriage/carrier
fff jjj fff jjj fjf jfj fff jjj fff fjfj   return carriage/carrier twice
```

(d) Sit back and relax and look at what you have typed

35 wpm **4 minutes** **Not more than 4 errors**

33 Perhaps the most lovable and desirable quality which a 11
person can have is that of tolerance. It need not be inborn 22
but it can be acquired and developed. It can be described 35
as the quality which makes us able to see the point of view 47
of the other fellow and which makes us always keep in mind 59
the fact that, however correct we may think our own opinion 71
of a thing to be, we still may be wrong. It is the decency 83
in us that concedes to others the right to have their own 94
views. It prevents us from meddling with what is no con- 105
cern of ours, and enables us to let others seek their own 116
salvation and happiness in their own way. It is a good 127
thing if you do not have tolerance to make an effort to 138
acquire it. **(SI 1.30)** 140

1 | 2 | 3 | 4 | 5 | 6 | 7 | 8 | 9 | 10 | 11 | 12 |

35 wpm **5 minutes** **Not more than 5 errors**

34 A good dictionary is the most useful reference book you 11
can have. It is a tool to help you to do your work well and 23
easily, but, like all tools, it must be handled correctly if 35
the best use is to be made of it. All words are arranged in 47
alphabetical order of the first letter of the word, and then 59
according to the second, third, and remaining letters. Thus 71
'band' will come before 'bay'. A short word always appears 83
before a longer word; thus 'bind' will come before 'binder' 94
and 'found' before 'founder'. You must be sure you know how 106
your dictionary shows and uses hyphens; take care not to mix 118
up the use of the hyphen to join compound words, and its use 130
for dividing words or syllables. Remember to keep your dic- 142
tionary always at hand, ready for use, and, when you are 153
doubtful about the spelling or meaning of a word, look it up. 165
A typist must be able to use an English dictionary. **(SI 1.33)** 175

1 | 2 | 3 | 4 | 5 | 6 | 7 | 8 | 9 | 10 | 11 | 12 |

35 wpm **5 minutes** **Not more than 5 errors**

35 Sunday is still a day of rest, but not to the extent 10
that it was years ago. In those days, because of the long 22
hours of work and the bad working conditions in industry, 33
it was necessary for workers to be given a regular break in 45
order that the standard of their work should not suffer. 56
Sunday was the obvious day to choose, and regular attendance 68
at church, being a rest for both mind and body, was greatly 80
encouraged. Gardening, walking about or sitting in the park 92
or garden, was allowed, but any form of sport or strenuous 104
exercise was frowned upon, even to the extent of laws being 116
passed against them. 120

Now, however, with the shorter working week under good 131
working conditions for the most part, the need for absolute 143
relaxation of the body is not so vital. Even the housewife 155
has had much of the drudgery removed from her work by the 166
invention of a good few labour-saving devices. **(SI 1.40)** 175

1 | 2 | 3 | 4 | 5 | 6 | 7 | 8 | 9 | 10 | 11 | 12 |

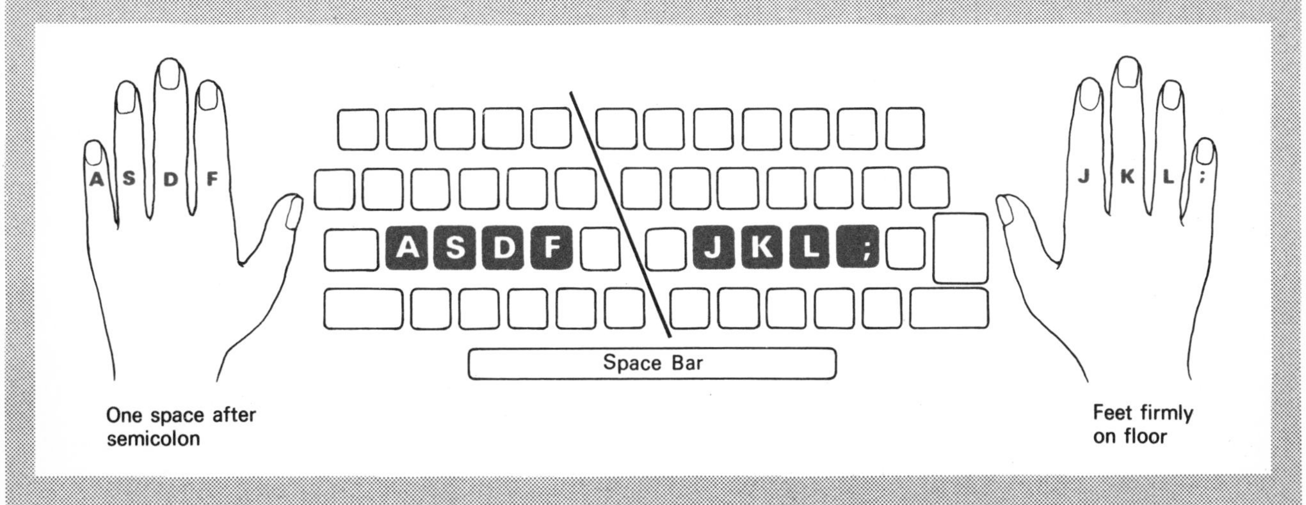

Type each line or sentence 3 times, saying the letters to yourself. If time permits, complete your practice by typing each group of lines as it appears. Keep your eyes on the copy while you type and also when returning the carriage/carrier. The carriage/carrier must be returned IMMEDIATELY after the last character in the line has been typed. Set left margin stop at 30 elite, 22 pica, and use single spacing with double between exercises.

New keys F and J
Use first fingers

1 fff jjj fjf jfj fjf jfj fff jjj fff fjfj

Turn up TWICE between exercises

New keys D and K
Use second fingers

2 ddd kkk dkd kdk dkd kdk ddd kkk dkd dkdk
3 fff jjj ddd kkk fkf kfk jdj djd fjk fdjk

New keys S and L
Use third fingers

4 sss lll sls lsl sls lsl sss lll sls slsl
5 fff jjj ddd kkk sss lll fds jkl fds jklj

New keys A and ;
Use little fingers

6 aaa ;;; a;a ;a; a;a ;a; aaa ;;; ;a; a;a;
7 f;f jaj d;d kak a;s lal aaa ;;; a;a a;a;

Word building

8 aaa lll all lll aaa ddd lad ddd aaa dad;
9 fff aaa ddd fad sss aaa ddd sad fad lad;

Apply the keys you know

10 dad fad sad lad ask all dad fad sad lad;
11 lass fall lads fads lass fall dads fads;
12 all sad lads; a sad lass; a lad asks dad
13 all sad lads ask a dad; a sad lass falls
14 as a lass falls dad falls; all lads fall

Practise space bar

Use an even stroke for space bar

15 a s d f j k l ; ; l k j f d s a a s d f;

35 wpm | One minute | Not more than one error

28 In the spring we always go to a farm, where we are made 11
most welcome. We are allowed to do more or less as we like, 23
and we have a fine time. We often wish we could live there. 35
(SI 1.11)

29 Once a month most firms send to each of their customers 11
a statement which shows how much they owe to the firm at the 23
end of the month. It also shows the trade during the month. 35
(SI 1.14)

1 | 2 | 3 | 4 | 5 | 6 | 7 | 8 | 9 | 10 | 11 | 12 |

35 wpm | 2 minutes | Not more than 2 errors

30 On checking your invoice, which has just reached us, we 11
find you have charged us the full list-price for items 4, 5 23
and 6. No doubt this is due to a mistake on the part of one 35
of the clerks in your office, because, in the past, you have 47
charged us the wholesale rates. Please check this with your 59
books, and then send us a new invoice or a credit note. 70
(SI 1.13)

31 When you walk through the woods you must look for a 11
very small plant that has green, glossy, oval-shaped leaves. 23
This plant does not grow very high. It has berries that are 35
a bright red colour and that stay there all the winter. The 47
name of this plant is the teaberry. Both berries and leaves 59
are quite pleasing to the taste, so we have been told. 70
(SI 1.17)

1 | 2 | 3 | 4 | 5 | 6 | 7 | 8 | 9 | 10 | 11 | 12 |

35 wpm | 3 minutes | Not more than 3 errors

32 The repairs to your car have been put in hand, but they 11
will take 2 or 3 weeks. In spite of this, we shall be able 23
to have the car ready for you by the date required. We have 36
no doubt that you will be quite pleased with the quality and 47
standard of the work done. 52

Your name has now been put on our mailing list, and we 63
shall send you a copy of all our leaflets. We shall also be 75
pleased to let you have any details you like regarding the 87
work we do. Please get in touch with us if you think we can 99
be of help to you in any way at all. (SI 1.14) 105

1 | 2 | 3 | 4 | 5 | 6 | 7 | 8 | 9 | 10 | 11 | 12 |

Type each line or sentence 3 times, saying the letters to yourself. If time permits, complete your practice by typing each group of lines as it appears. Keep your eyes on the copy while you type and also when returning the carriage/carrier. The carriage/carrier must be returned IMMEDIATELY after the last character in the line has been typed. Set left margin stop at 30 elite, 22 pica, and use single spacing with double between exercises.

Keyboarding review

1 aaa ;;; sss lll ddd kkk fff jjj asd jkl;
2 ask a lad; ask all lads; ask a sad lass;
3 all lads fall; dad falls; dad asks a lad

Turn up TWICE between exercises

New key E Use D finger

4 ddd eee ded ded see ded lee ded fee ded;
5 ded sea ded lea ded led ded fed ded eke;

New key H Use J finger

6 jjj hhh jhj jhj has jhj had jhj she jhj;
7 jhj has jhj had jhj she jhj ash jhj dash

Word building

8 hhh eee lll ddd held jjj aaa fff jaffas;
9 sss hhh aaa lll shall fff eee ddd feeds;

Apply the keys you know

10 see lee fee sea lea led fed eke see lee;
11 ash dash fash sash hash lash; heel shed;
12 a lass has had a salad; dad sees a lake;
13 a jaffa salad; she held a sale; he shall
14 she feeds a lad; dad has a hall; a shed;

Type the following exercise exactly as shown. Repeat the exercise 3 times.

15 as a lass
as a lass falls
as a lass falls dad falls;

Note: Speed can be built up more easily on short, simple exercises and, as we have now reached 3 minutes at 30 wpm, we suggest you use the shorter exercises on the next page for speed development. Or, if you prefer and would like to start at a lower speed, say 31 words a minute, go back to page 186 and in exercise 5 see if you can type as far as the word "can" in the third line. All the exercises on pages 186–188 can be used for a great variety of speeds.

30 wpm **4 minutes** **Not more than 4 errors**

26 Please note that as from 22 August there will be an increase **12**
of 25 per cent in air fares because of higher landing fees. **24**
You are reminded that you must comply with police and cus- **36**
toms regulations at the points of departure and arrival, and **48**
along the route. A journey may be broken at most stops with **60**
no extra charge, on condition that you complete the journey **71**
within the dates stated. As there are a number of formal- **83**
ities to be complied with, the "check-in" time quoted on the **95**
ticket is the time by which you must present yourself with **106**
your luggage - if you are late, you will miss the plane, and **118**
your holiday. **(SI 1.31)** **120**

1 | 2 | 3 | 4 | 5 | 6 | 7 | 8 | 9 | 10 | 11 | 12 |

Use indented paragraphs—set a tab stop for the indent.

30 wpm **5 minutes** **Not more than 5 errors**

27 For some reason, I have been unable to obtain any satis- **11**
faction from you in connection with the clock I left with you **23**
3 months ago to be repaired. At that time, I pointed out to **35**
you that the clock was not in first-class condition when I **47**
bought it. Right from the beginning, it has always lost about **59**
8 minutes every day. **63**

From time to time I have telephoned your company about **74**
the clock, and I usually spoke to Mr. G. Sloan. A week ago **85**
Mr. Sloan telephoned me and promised to let me know this **97**
week, without fail, what could be done to settle this matter. **109**

I do not wish to make the same complaint over and over **121**
again, but I cannot understand why a firm as large as yours **133**
should neglect to make some adjustments when one of its clocks **145**
had not been satisfactory. **(SI 1.33)** **150**

1 | 2 | 3 | 4 | 5 | 6 | 7 | 8 | 9 | 10 | 11 | 12 |

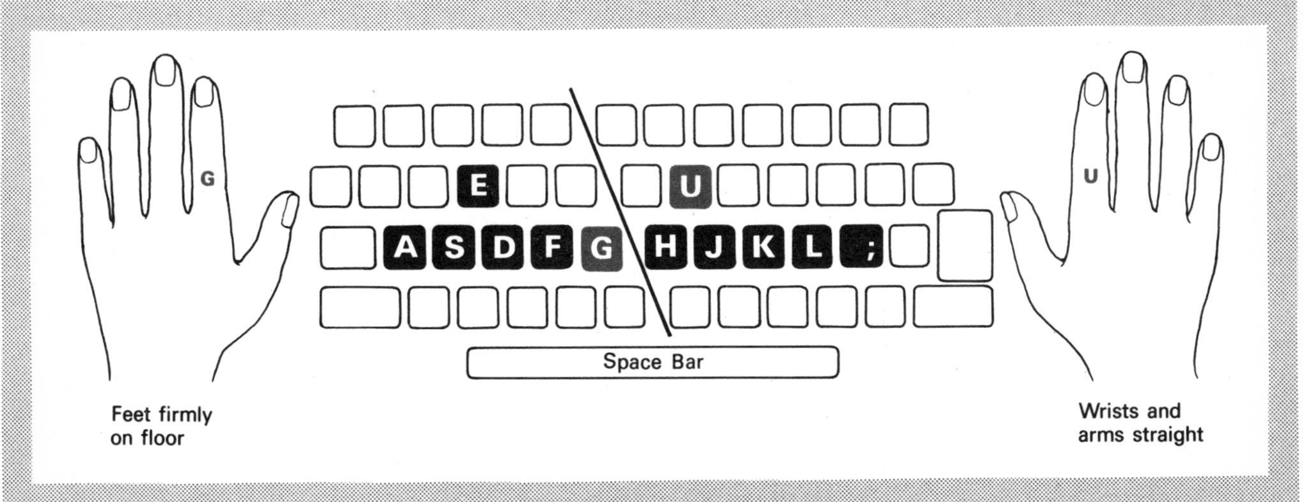

Type each line or sentence 3 times, saying the letters to yourself. If time permits, complete your practice by typing each group of lines as it appears. Keep your eyes on the copy while you type and also when returning the carriage/carrier. The carriage/carrier must be returned IMMEDIATELY after the last character in the line has been typed. Set left margin stop at 30 elite, 22 pica, and use single spacing with double between exercises.

Keyboarding review

1 asd ;lk ded jhj def khj fed has lee had;
2 add salads; a sea lake; lads feed seals;
3 add leeks; she had leeks; he has a hall;

Turn up TWICE between exercises

New key G
Use F finger

4 fff ggg fgf fgf fag fgf lag fgf sag fgf;
5 fgf jag fgf gag fgf hag fgf keg fgf leg;

New key U
Use J finger

6 jjj uuu juj juj due juj sue juj hue juj;
7 juj sug juj jug juj dug juj hug juj lug;

Word building

8 uuu sss eee ddd use uses used useful us;
9 jjj uuu ddd ggg eee judge judges judged;

Apply the keys you know

10 fag sag lag jag gag hag keg leg egg keg;
11 dues hues jugs hugs lugs suds eggs legs;
12 he had a dull glass; a judge has a flag;
13 see she has a full jug; she used jaffas;
14 dad had a full keg; he shall guess; use;

Sizes of type faces

10 Pitch	10 characters take up one inch of space
12 Pitch	12 characters take up one inch of space
15 Pitch	15 characters take up one inch of space

29 wpm — **One minute** — **Not more than one error**

19 We hear that you plan to buy new desks, chairs and files, so 12
we are sending you a copy of our price-lists which will give 24
you a wide range of choice. (SI 1.07) 29

20 In the spring we like to go to a farm where we are made most 12
welcome. We all have a very happy time as we are allowed to 24
do more or less as we like. (SI 1.14) 29

1 | 2 | 3 | 4 | 5 | 6 | 7 | 8 | 9 | 10 | 11 | 12 |

29 wpm — **2 minutes** — **Not more than 2 errors**

21 The rain poured down and it was too wet to go outside so the 12
2 girls had to play in the house, and they were quite bored. 24
At last they found a case which had no top, and they planned 36
to make a lid for it, but could not do this without a hammer 48
and nails which they could not see in the tool box. (SI 1.16) 58

1 | 2 | 3 | 4 | 5 | 6 | 7 | 8 | 9 | 10 | 11 | 12 |

30 wpm — **One minute** — **Not more than one error**

22 The weather is likely to remain mild in the south, with some 12
light rain, but in the north there may be ground frost which 24
could cause ice on some roads. (SI 1.10) 30

1 | 2 | 3 | 4 | 5 | 6 | 7 | 8 | 9 | 10 | 11 | 12 |

30 wpm — **$1\frac{1}{2}$ minutes** — **Not more than one error**

23 You will be pleased to learn that we have made more machines 12
this year than we did last year, and that we are also making 24
all vital spare parts. Over the next 12 months we shall not 36
need orders as we are to produce new models. (SI 1.18) 45

1 | 2 | 3 | 4 | 5 | 6 | 7 | 8 | 9 | 10 | 11 | 12 |

30 wpm — **2 minutes** — **Not more than 2 errors**

24 Some large offices have a pool of typists who share the work 12
to be done, but we do not know whether or not this is a good 24
plan. This is a matter which must be left to each firm to 36
decide, based on the number of jobs which have to be done 47
and on the staff employed. You may like being in a typing 59
pool. (SI 1.16) 60

1 | 2 | 3 | 4 | 5 | 6 | 7 | 8 | 9 | 10 | 11 | 12 |

30 wpm — **3 minutes** — **Not more than 3 errors**

25 When you have regular payments to make each month or each 11
quarter, as, for instance, for rent, rates, and car insur- 23
ance, there is no need for you to make out a cheque each 34
time. It will be quite simple for you to give a standing 46
order to your bank to pay such amounts on your behalf until 57
further notice, and these sums will be placed to the debit 69
of your account each month or quarter, as the case may be. 80
This method will save you a great deal of trouble. (SI 1.22) 90

1 | 2 | 3 | 4 | 5 | 6 | 7 | 8 | 9 | 10 | 11 | 12 |

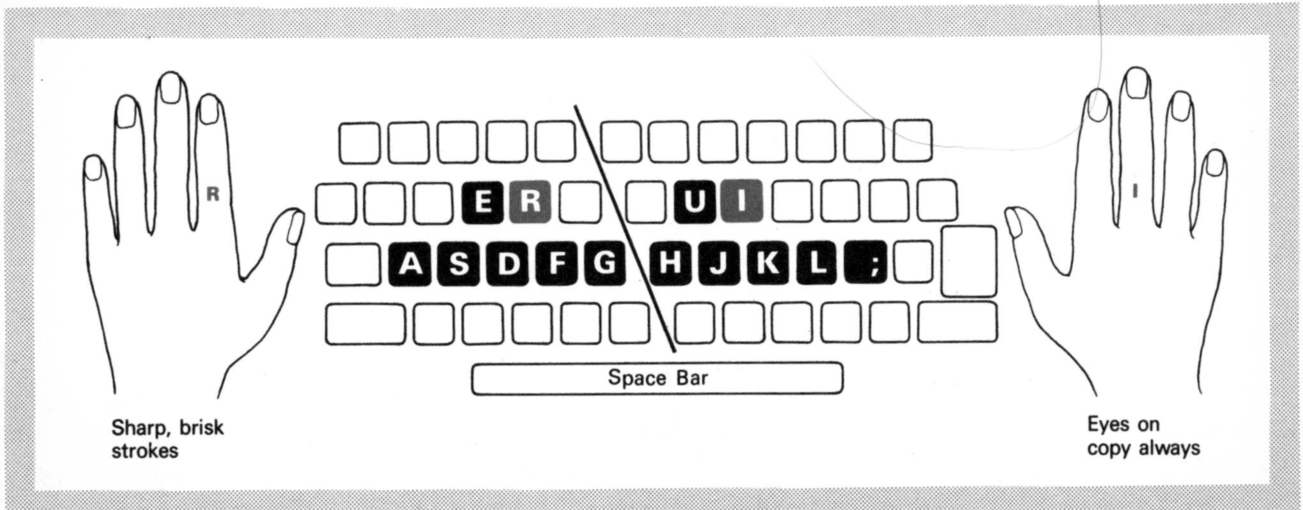

Type each line or sentence 3 times, saying the letters to yourself. If time permits, complete your practice by typing each group of lines as it appears. Keep your eyes on the copy while you type and also when returning the carriage/carrier. The carriage/carrier must be returned IMMEDIATELY after the last character in the line has been typed. Set left margin stop at 30 elite, 22 pica, and use single spacing with double between exercises.

Keyboarding review

1 fds jkl ded juj fgf jhj hag jug dug leg;
2 a lass uses a flask; all lads had a jug;
3 sell us a full keg; see she has a glass;

New key R
Use F finger

4 fff rrr frf frf jar frf far frf rag frf;
5 frf are frf ark frf red frf fur frf rug;

New key I
Use K finger

6 kkk iii kik kik kid kik lid kik did kik;
7 kik dig kik fig kik rig kik jig kik gig;

Word families

8 fill hill rill drill grill skill frills;
9 ark lark dark hark; air fair hair lairs;

Apply the keys you know

10 fill his flask; he is here; he had a rug
11 her red dress is here; she has fair hair
12 she likes a fair judge; he has dark hair
13 his lad fills a jug; she has rare skills
14 she is sure; ask her here; he likes figs

Sizes of paper

A4 $8\frac{1}{4}'' \times 11\frac{3}{4}''$ (210 × 297 mm)
A5 landscape $8\frac{1}{4}'' \times 5\frac{7}{8}''$ (210 × 148 mm)
A5 portrait $5\frac{7}{8}'' \times 8\frac{1}{4}''$ (148 × 210 mm)

27 wpm | **One minute** | **Not more than one error**

11 To give our legs a rest John and I sat down on a stone ledge 12
near the edge of the cliff. David thought he would look for 24
empty sea shells. **(SI 1.04)** 27

12 The day was sunny but cool. After we had rested and had our 12
snack, we packed our bags and set out for the distant cliffs 24
some 2 miles off. **(SI 1.15)** 27

1 | 2 | 3 | 4 | 5 | 6 | 7 | 8 | 9 | 10 | 11 | 12 |

27 wpm | **2 minutes** | **Not more than 2 errors**

13 You must not feel that your friends should sit down to write 12
to you if you do not write to them. This does not mean that 24
you must send long letters - a note will do. Would not most 36
of you rather have a note than no reply? Like us, you would 48
want to hear from your friends. **(SI 1.06)** 54

14 He said that if you want a garden then you will have to do a 12
great deal of work, but in these days you can buy many tools 24
which will be helpful for the heavy work, and thus save time 36
and effort. You would not need to employ hired help, and so 48
you could then save some money. **(SI 1.13)** 54

1 | 2 | 3 | 4 | 5 | 6 | 7 | 8 | 9 | 10 | 11 | 12 |

28 wpm | **One minute** | **Not more than one error**

15 Each year there are some new typewriters for you to use, and 12
you must know about them so that you are up to date when you 24
wish to change jobs. **(SI 1.11)** 28

16 A computer is now being made that will store voice patterns. 12
It will know your voice when you speak to it, and it will be 24
able to reply to you. **(SI 1.21)** 28

1 | 2 | 3 | 4 | 5 | 6 | 7 | 8 | 9 | 10 | 11 | 12 |

28 wpm | **2 minutes** | **Not more than 2 errors**

17 I wish you could try out our new car. It is as swift and as 12
smooth as a cloud. I am sure you will like it and will want 24
to drive it when we go on holiday to Rye. I think we should 36
leave here early and then we will be on the main road before 48
the city rush hour. Yes, we will do so. **(SI 1.09)** 56

18 When you eat your Brazil nuts at Christmas do you ever think 12
of the men who pick them and of the risks they run to do so? 24
One of the risks is the falling of nuts from the trees which 36
grow to a very great height. What we usually call nuts are, 48
in fact, really the seeds from the tree. **(SI 1.20)** 56

1 | 2 | 3 | 4 | 5 | 6 | 7 | 8 | 9 | 10 | 11 | 12 |

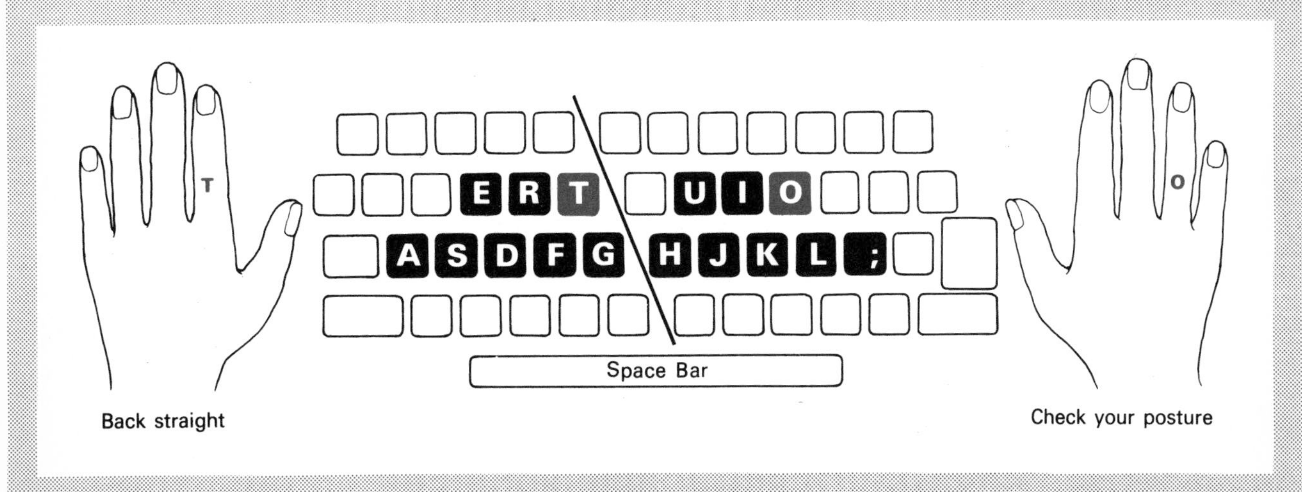

Type each line or sentence 3 times, saying the letters to yourself. If time permits, complete your practice by typing each group of lines as it appears. Keep your eyes on the copy while you type and also when returning the carriage/carrier. The carriage/carrier must be returned IMMEDIATELY after the last character in the line has been typed. Set left margin stop at 30 elite, 22 pica, and use single spacing with double between exercises.

Keyboarding review

1 fgf jhj frf juj dad kid sid did her rug;
2 his full fees; she likes a dark red rug;
3 his girl is here; he is glad she is sure

New key T
Use F finger

4 fff ttt ftf ftf fit ftf kit ftf lit ftf;
5 ftf sit ftf hit ftf sat ftf hat ftf fat;

New key O
Use L finger

6 lll ooo lol lol lot lol got lol hot lol;
7 lol rot lol dot lol jot lol tot lol sot;

Word families

8 old hold sold gold; look rook hook took;
9 let set jet get ret; rate late hate date

Homophones

Use your dictionary to check the meaning

10 see sea; here hear; tide tied; aid aide;
11 ail ale; road rode; sale sail; our hour;

Apply the keys you know

12 get her a set; he took a full jar to her
13 he had sold the gold; at this late date;
14 that old dress looks just right for her;

Practise space bar

Use an even stroke for space bar

15 a s d f g h j k l o i u t r e at it too;

Accuracy/speed practice

Format

Follow instructions on page 27 Margins: elite 22–82, pica 12–72

25 wpm **2 minutes** **Not more than 2 errors**

5 We were all happy to hear that you are now back at work, and 12
we hope that the long rest by the sea will have restored you 24
to good health. As soon as you can, please call and see us. 36
You will notice that we have moved to a new house quite near 48
the parks. **(SI 1.06)** 50

6 We have not yet been able to send the goods you ordered last 12
week as they are not stock lines, but we shall do all we can 24
to let you have some of the goods, if not all, by Tuesday of 36
next week. We trust that you will excuse the delay in send- 48
ing these. **(SI 1.12)** 50

1 | 2 | 3 | 4 | 5 | 6 | 7 | 8 | 9 | 10 | 11 | 12 |

26 wpm **One minute** **Not more than one error**

7 Tell your firm that they need not send us a cheque until the 12
tables are all sent. If it is their wish, then we will sell 24
on credit. **(SI 1.12)** 26

8 In spite of the rain all of us thought it had been an excel- 12
lent evening, but the guests could not travel till the storm 24
had passed. **(SI 1.15)** 26

1 | 2 | 3 | 4 | 5 | 6 | 7 | 8 | 9 | 10 | 11 | 12 |

26 wpm **2 minutes** **Not more than 2 errors**

9 Last May we had a chance to buy a large stock of fine cotton 12
sheets, and we are now selling these at a reduced price. If 24
your own stock of sheets is low, now is the chance to obtain 36
some of these goods at half price or less. Send an order by 48
July at the latest. **(SI 1.13)** 52

10 I hope to come and see you soon, but I fear that it will not 12
be until the end of July, as at the moment we are so busy at 24
the office that I feel it would not be wise for me to leave. 36
Next week I have to go away, but I feel sure it will be pos- 48
sible to visit soon. **(SI 1.17)** 52

1 | 2 | 3 | 4 | 5 | 6 | 7 | 8 | 9 | 10 | 11 | 12 |

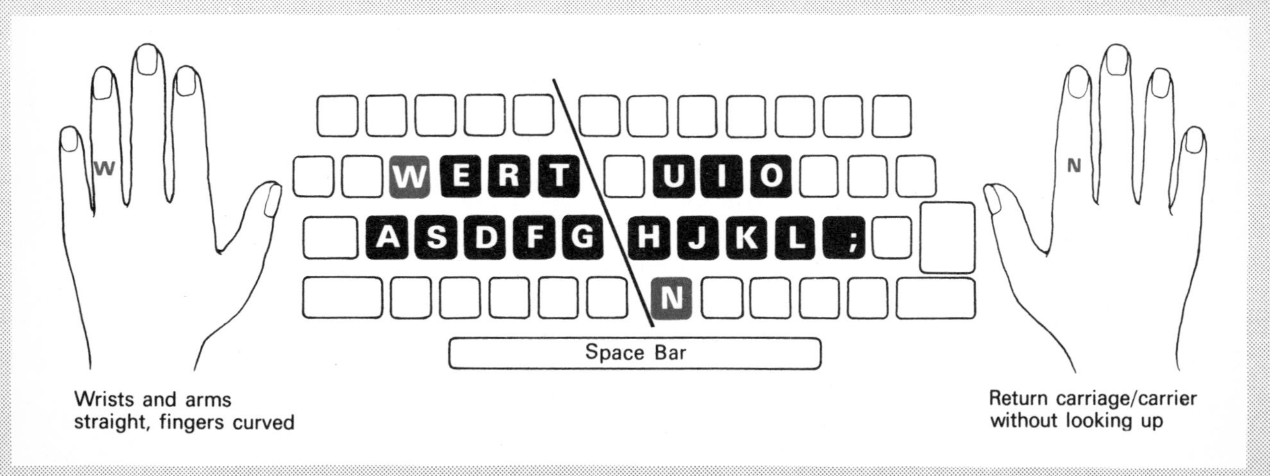

Type each line or sentence 3 times, saying the letters to yourself. If time permits, complete your practice by typing each group of lines as it appears. Keep your eyes on the copy while you type and also when returning the carriage/carrier. The carriage/carrier must be returned IMMEDIATELY after the last character in the line has been typed. Set the left margin stop at 30 elite, 22 pica, and use single spacing with double between exercises.

Keyboarding review

1 ftf lol frf juj ded kik tot out rot dot;
2 this is a red jet; the lad took the gold
3 he asked a just fee; the old folk agree;

New key W
Use S finger

4 sss www sws sws low sws sow sws row sws;
5 sws hew sws few sws dew sws sew sws tew;

New key N
Use J finger

6 jjj nnn jnj jnj fan jnj ran jnj tan jnj;
7 jnj sin jnj kin jnj din jnj lin jnj tin;

Word families

8 end send lend tend fend rend wend trend;
9 low sow how row tow saw law daw jaw raw;

Homophones

Use your dictionary to check the meaning

10 sew sow; weak week; wear ware; fair fare
11 oar ore; kneed need; not knot; loan lone

Apply the keys you know

12 we saw her look at the new gate; we know
13 he sent us a gift of red jeans last week
14 we had left a jade silk gown and the rug

Improve paper insertion

Take out the sheet of paper you are using. Put it back quickly in the machine, so that the left edge is at 0 on the carriage-position line scale, and see that the paper is straight. Repeat this drill several times daily.

15 Improve control of special characters

```
"2" 3 is/was 4 @ £5 6 & 7 "8" 9 (9 - 8) Mr & Mrs one's £102.
They asked, "Will you both come to Jim's party on March 14?"
Mr & Mrs J Burgess (address below) paid £34 for the antique.
He/She requires 20 only @ £5 each, and 18 only @ £5.50 each.
```

16 Build accuracy on common suffix drill

```
using ending asking making turning morning replying advising
comment shipment equipment settlement adjustment arrangement
We will not comment about the shipments of equipment to you.
In the morning we shall be asking him what car he is taking.
```

17 Improve control of vowel keys

```
locate unusual receiving suggestion examination distribution
assume anxious financial sufficient explanation requirements
Your suggestion has been received and we are anxious to have
an explanation of your quite unusual financial requirements.
```

18 Improve accuracy on word building drill

```
tend attend attends attended attending attendance attendants
be belie belief believe believes believed believing believer
We believe their attendance has tended to be poor this term.
The attendants believe that the attendance will now improve.
```

19 Improve control of word division

```
able, mail-able, read-able, suit-able, sens-ible, flex-ible.
so-cial, par-tial, ini-tial, finan-cial, spe-cial, pala-tial
pro-mote, pro-vided, per-mit, per-fume, pur-suit, pur-suant.
prob-able, chil-dren, knowl-edge, resig-nation, pref-erence.
```

20 Build speed on word family drill

```
look took hook book nook cook best pest rest jest west nest.
call hall fall pall wall tall will pill bill hill fill mill.
He took a look at the book and said that he would call soon.
The birds will nest in a nook of the west wall of that mill.
```

KEYS TO SPOT THE ERRORS

Page 180, No. 1: line 1—There; line 2—2 spaces after a full stop; line 3—pro-; line 4—computer; line 5—Off-line; line 6—space after comma; line 7—one space after punched; line 8—no space before and

Page 180, No. 2: line 1—John; line 2—2 spaces after full stop; line 3—cir-; line 4—full stop after action; line 5—permissible; line 6—clerks; line 7—benefited; line 8—you

Page 180, No. 3: line 1—processing; line 2—tables; line 3—edit-; line 4—and,; line 5—and; line 6—accuracy; line 7—a high degree; line 8—typewriter

Page 180, No. 4: line 1—today's; line 2—ribbon; line 3—ribbons; line 4—insufficient space for indentation of paragraph; line 5—separate; line 6—may be; line 7—space after comma; line 8—error – the; line 9—Switch

Page 180, No. 5: line 1—efficiency; line 2—perform-; line 3—space after comma; line 4—no space at beginning of the line; line 5—day-; line 6—firm's; line 7—performance; line 8—its; line 9—they

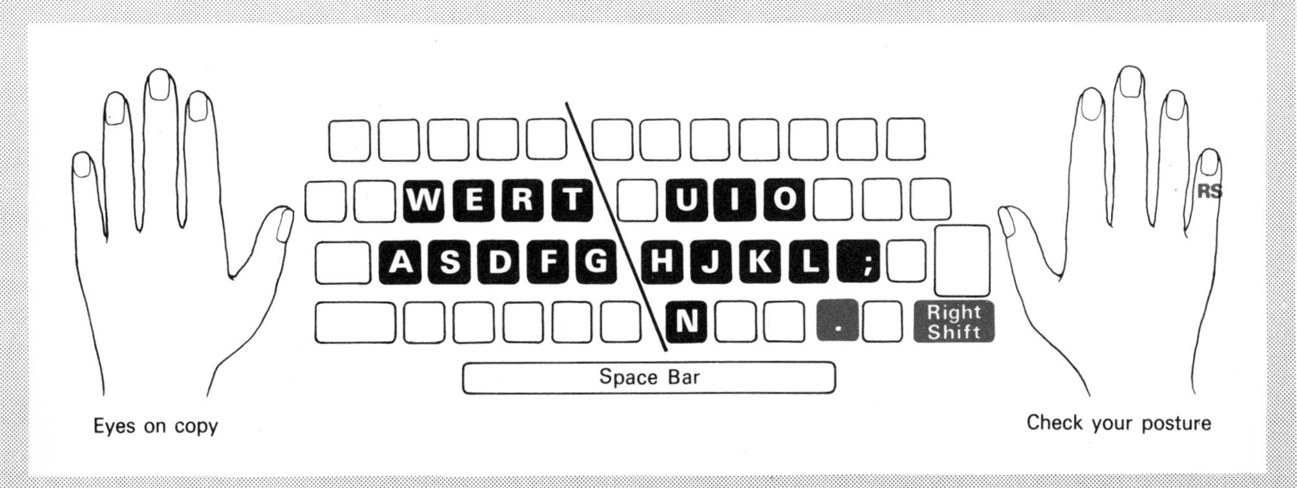

Type each line or sentence 3 times, saying the letters to yourself. If time permits, complete your practice by typing each group of lines as it appears. Keep your eyes on the copy while you type and also when returning the carriage/carrier. The carriage/carrier must be returned IMMEDIATELY after the last character in the line has been typed. Set left margin stop at 30 elite, 22 pica, and use single spacing with double between exercises.

Keyboarding review

1 sws jnj ftf lol frf jhj won win new now;
2 we do not like those jars she got for us
3 the red dogs will go for a walk just now

Capital letters

To make capitals for letters typed by the left hand:
(a) With right-hand little finger depress and hold right shift key well down.
(b) Strike left-hand capital letter.
(c) Remove finger from shift key and return all fingers to home keys.

New key Right Shift
Use right little finger

4 fF; dD; sS; aA; Ada; Sad; Dad; Fad; Wade
5 Gee; Reg; Ted; Sue; Flo; Ede; Dora; West

New key .
Use L finger

6 lll ... l.l f.l j.l Good. Dear. Ellis.

TWO spaces after full stop at end of sentence

7 Ask her. Ted is sad. Do go. She will.

Word families

8 Wee; Weed; Feed; Reed; Seed; Deed; Greed
9 And; Sand; Wand; Rand; Send; Tend; Fend;

Homophones

Use your dictionary to check the meaning

10 altar alter; guest guessed; aught ought;
11 dear deer; aloud allowed; threw through;

Apply the keys you know

12 Ask Ed Reid if we should join the Swede.
13 She was right. Dirk was jealous. Fine.
14 Flora would like to go; just state when.

Practise phrases

15 to go to us to do to see to ask to take.

6 Improve skill on fluency drill

```
she her his him are not has had any our who did but was see.
they that week know time will days this here your food when.
Your team hope that they will have much more time this week.
They know that this food must have been left here some days.
It is a busy lane to the right of a fork road by the chapel.
```

7 Review hyphen key

```
p-p; p-p; 2-9, 3-8, 4-7, 5-6, con- com- mis- pre- for- dis-.
full-time, up-to-date, blue-grey, 48-page, re-cover, co-opt.
Full-time students wore pin-striped blue-grey ties.  He con-
sidered that the up-to-date 248-page document was now ready.
```

8 Build accuracy on letter combinations

```
additional committee entitled definite credits remits visits
transport effort report inform story order work word for ore
Your committee are entitled to free transport for the visit.
Make a definite effort to prepare an additional credit note.
```

9 Build accuracy on one hand words

```
dresses nylon extra jolly great knoll agree pylon gave on my
opinion trade union aware only safe upon area joy car him at
In our opinion, you were aware of the trade union wage rate.
I agree the extra trade in nylon dresses gave him great joy.
```

10 Build speed on phrases

```
to me, to go, to do, if it, if he, if we, do we, do it, out.
and the, for the, may the, can the, you are, you can, it is.
If you are late, you can get the last train to go from town.
If he calls, do we want him to do the work for the firm now?
```

11 Build accuracy on common prefix drill

```
pro- procure profess process protect promise prolong profile
con- contain confirm condemn conceal confess consist content
Promise that you will not prolong the process.  Also confirm
that Connie will not conceal the contents of that container.
```

12 Build accuracy on punctuation review

```
"Is John - John Mann, not John Green - here, please?"  "No."
We discussed many things: the staff; an up-to-date building;
annual holidays.  "What happened then?"  "We did not agree."
I think (in fact I'm sure) that Mrs Laing will arrive today.
```

13 Improve control of space bar

```
as is so or be in am if an me go my do he by us ask may you.
It is so.  Ask me to go.  You must be in time.  I may do so.
Who is she?  He can go home on 6 May.  It is a 65-page book.
He is on the way.  I am to go to the boat in that bay.  Yes.
We will go to the park in time to see the start of the game.
```

14 Improve control of shift keys

```
Frank Jones and Denis Kelly went to the West Indies in July.
Louis Stock and Nancy Ball visited Epping Forest on 6 April.
Roger Yates joined the Aston Villa Football Club on 5 March.
Dear Sir, Yours truly, Mr J Brown, New York, Hong Kong, Miss
Adam, Olive, Frank, Lily and Ruth left Devon for York today.
```

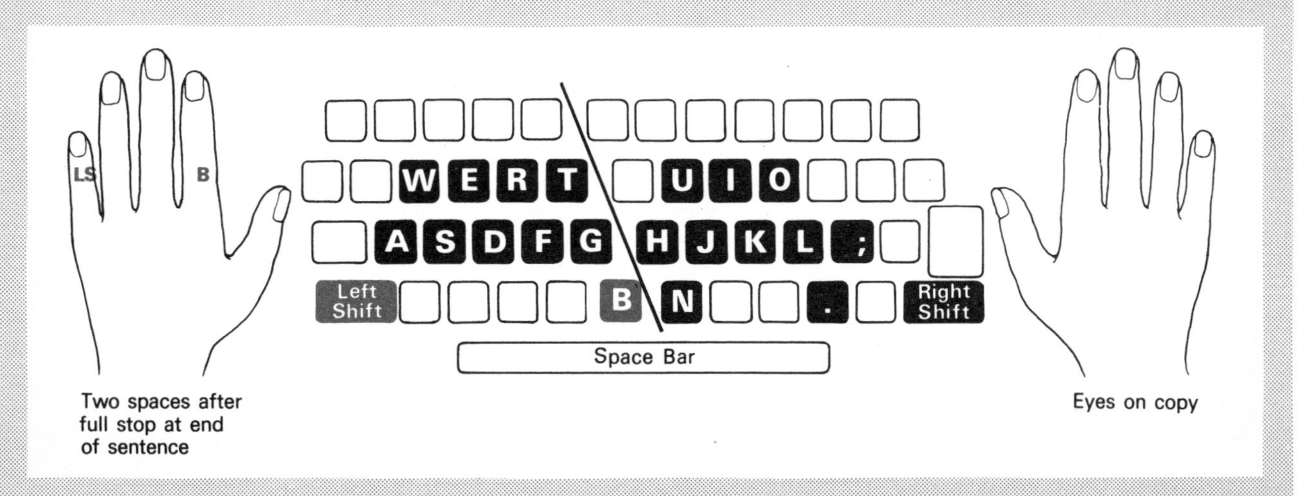

Type each line or sentence 3 times, saying the letters to yourself. If time permits, complete your practice by typing each group of lines as it appears. Keep your eyes on the copy while you type and also when returning the carriage/carrier. The carriage/carrier must be returned IMMEDIATELY after the last character in the line has been typed. Set left margin stop at 30 elite, 22 pica, and use single spacing with double between exercises.

Keyboarding review

1 aA; sS; dD; fF; wW; eE; rR; Red; Gee; As
2 Ask Flo. See Roger. Tell Fred. Go in.
3 Ede had gone. Write to us. A fake jug.

Capital letters

To make capitals for letters typed by the right hand:
(a) With left-hand little finger depress and hold left shift key well down.
(b) Strike right-hand capital letter.
(c) Remove finger from shift key and return all fingers to home keys.

New key Left Shift Use left little finger

4 jJa kKa lLa jUj kIk Judd Kidd Lode Hoad;
5 Ida Ken Len Jude Owen Hilda Oakes Usual;

New key B Use F finger

6 fff bbb fbf fbf bud fbf bus fbf but fbf;
7 fbf rob fbf sob fbf fob fbf hob fbf job;

Word families

8 Nib Jib Lib Job Lob Hob Hail Jail Nails;
9 Jill Hill Kill Lill Tall Ball Fall Wall;

Homophones

Use your dictionary to check the meaning

10 break brake; bare bear; blue blew; suite
11 sweet; whether weather; right rite write

Apply the keys you know

12 She will be taking those salads to Jane.
13 Jill knows. Kit had to bluff Bob Green.
14 Fred will ask us to do those jobs again.

Practise suffix "ing"

15 asking taking going adding owing selling

KEYBOARDING SKILLS

Techniques and reviews

Knowledge of display, of word division, and of tabulation are useless if you cannot operate the machine efficiently. Therefore, the basic need of all typing courses is the development and consolidation of good techniques.

What is meant by technique? In a general sense, it means the skills involved in the correct operation and manipulation of the machine. In a specific sense, it means the motions used in a particular operation—backspacing technique, shift-key technique, carriage/carrier return technique, etc. Good techniques are the foundation of accurate and fast typing which, in turn, are the basis of good production typing.

You should type a technique/review drill at the beginning of each lesson and you should also use the drills as remedial work; eg, if your carriage/carrier return technique is poor, drill intensively exercise 2 below.

Type each line or sentence 3 times and then type the complete exercise.

Format

Left margin: elite 20, pica 15

1 Build speed on alternate hand words

```
island visit girls lamb worn paid she hay men for but the me
formal usual their lend lame work may pen dog got did and us
The girls and the men got paid for their work on the island.
The lamb and the lame dog lay by the pen.  She may visit me.
```

2 Speed up carriage/carrier return

Type the following lines exactly as shown. Repeat the exercise 3 times.

```
I will.
I will go.
They may go today.
Ask them to go with you.
```

3 Increase speed on common word drill

```
office where files have your were know are you did the as we
looked found there idea they left that not say had but no in
We know that the files were left in your office, but, as you
say they are not there now, we have no idea where they are.
I hope you will be able to meet us when we arrive next week.
```

4 Improve control of double letter words

```
programmes possible running supply arrive proof agree added.
difficult football baggage accept excess rubber attend carry
Is it possible to supply a proof of the football programmes?
We agree that it was difficult to accept the excess baggage.
```

5 Improve control of figure keys

```
ewe 323 woe 293 our 974 rye 463 you 697 tour 5974 writ 2485.
Type 1 and 2 and 3 and 4 and 15 and 16 and 17 and 80 and 90.
Drills: 9, 29, 38, 47, 56, 234, 467, 890, 010, 343, 678, 86.
Accounts: 00-11-2345, 00-12-6789, 00-13-5858, 00-14-2679-80.
Cheque No 021048 is for £536.97 and No 0210691 is for £4.78.
```

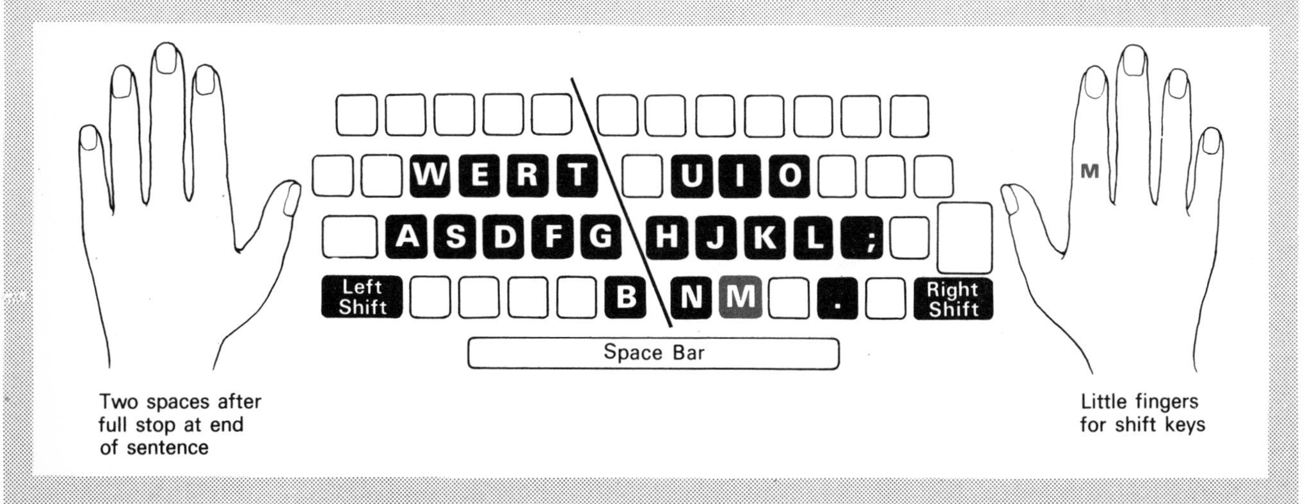

Type each line or sentence 3 times, saying the letters to yourself. If time permits, complete your practice by typing each group of lines as it appears. Keep your eyes on the copy while you type and also when returning the carriage/carrier. The carriage/carrier must be returned IMMEDIATELY after the last character in the line has been typed. Set left margin stop at 25 elite, 18 pica, and use single spacing with double between exercises.

Keyboarding review

1 fbf sws jnj ftf lol frf jhj Len Ken Hen Ian Win Go

2 Dan and Rob left. He will go just now. Ask Nell.

3 Lois and Earl will see June. Go with Fred Bolton.

New key M
Use J finger

4 jjj mmm jmj jmj jam jmj ham jmj dam jmj ram jmjmj;

5 jmj rum jmj hum jmj sum jmj mum jmj gum jmj strum;

Left and right shift keys

6 Ada Ben Dan East Fred Green Hilda Irwin James King

7 Lil Mark Nell Owen Rene Sara Todd Usher Wills Watt

Word families

8 arm farm harm warm alarm art hart tart darts mart;

9 game name dame fame same lame home dome some foam;

Homophones

Use your dictionary to check the meaning

10 there their; moan mown; air heir; eminent imminent

11 missed mist; mail male; oar ore; morning mourning;

Apply the keys you know

12 Most of the fame goes to John who had been working
hard for his father but he has now left the works.

13 I think he is now at home; I will see him tomorrow
when he is in London to attend the tennis meeting.

14 If Mark goes to the farm now, Sarah will be there.

Practise shift keys

15 Nan Owen Miss Browne Mrs Watts Mr Usher Ms Rhodes.

13 Joan Faith quickly jumped over the burning boxes, and walked away from the scene of the disaster with dazed feelings.

14 As he was at the zenith of his power, the tax official began an enquiry into the development of this joint stock company.

15 As the young musician, who wore a jacket of vivid colouring, strolled slowly round the piazza, the quaint sounds from his guitar and his relaxed manner reflected the evening calm.

Use indented paragraphs. Set a tab stop for the indent.

16 If she makes a determined and real effort, we are quite sure she will very quickly be enjoying a high place with the experts, and may win a valuable prize.

17 The Principals soon realised that extra milk would have to be requisitioned each morning for the lively young pupils in the junior school.

18 These 2 travellers were sorely vexed and puzzled by the rapturous welcome they had just been given by the quiet, but kind, official.

19 In view of the money embezzled by a junior employee, we must request you kindly to economise and avoid extravagance.

20 I expected to make just sufficient space for the quaint old table with the green baize top by removing the armchair.

21 After much coaxing, the queer-looking animal eventually was persuaded to jump over the wire on to the trapeze bars.

22 His extra blazer was made of the finely woven jet black cloth, and a quaint colourful badge adorned the pocket.

23 Marjorie had just come back from Africa and had altered considerably, being now quite unrecognisable, except for her voice.

Check your work after each exercise

After returning the carriage/carrier at the end of an exercise, check your typescript carefully and circle any errors. ALWAYS check BEFORE removing the paper from the machine.

They have to leave early.

(a) Each incorrect character is one error. — (a) Theu have to leave early.
(b) Each incorrect punctuation is one error. — (b) They have to leave early?
(c) An extra space is one error. — (c) They have to leave early.
(d) Omitting a space is one error. — (d) They haveto leave early.
(e) When using a manual machine, a raised/lowered capital is one error. — (e) They have to leave early.
(f) When using a manual machine, an uneven left margin is one error. — (f) They have to leave early.
(g) Omitting a word is one error. — (g) They have leave early.
(h) Inserting an extra word is one error. — (h) They have to to leave early.
(i) Inserting an extra letter is one error. — (i) They have to leaves early.
(j) Omitting a letter is one error. — (j) They have to lave early.

Half- or one-minute goals

1 Type the exercise. If any word causes you to hesitate, type that word 3 times.
2 Take a half- or one-minute timing.
3 If you reach the goal, or beyond, take another timing and see if you can type the same number of words but with fewer mistakes.
4 If you do not reach the goal after 3 tries, you need a little more practice on the key drills. Choose the previous exercise(s) that give intensive practice on the keys that caused difficulty.

Notes:

(a) There is little to be gained by typing any one drill more than 3 times consecutively. When you have typed it 3 times, go on to another drill; then, if necessary, go back to the original drill.

(b) At present, techniques (striking the keys evenly and sharply, good posture, eyes on copy, returning the carriage/carrier without looking up) are very important and you should concentrate on good techniques. If your techniques are right, then accuracy will follow. However, if you have more than 2 errors for each minute typed, it could mean that you have not practised the new keys sufficiently and that you should go back and do further intensive practice on certain key drills.

Measure your speed

Five strokes count as one "standard" word. In a typing line of 50 spaces there are 10 "standard" words. The figures to the right of each exercise indicate the number of "standard" words in the complete line, and the scale below indicates the number across the page. If in the exercise below you reach the word "we" in one minute, your speed is 10+6=16 words per minute. You will now be able to measure and record your speed.

Type the following exercise as instructed under Nos 1–4 of "Half- or one-minute goals". Set left margin at 25 elite, 18 pica.

Goal—8 words in half a minute   16 words in one minute

```
We will take her to see our new house on(8) the north   10
side of the new estates and we(16) shall ask George to  20
join us at that time. (SI 1.04)                         24
```

1 | 2 | 3 | 4 | 5 | 6 | 7 | 8 | 9 | 10 |

Alphabetic sentences

It is very important that you start each typing period with a "warm-up" drill and the alphabetic sentence is excellent material.

No doubt you have noticed that the pianist practises before his concert, the runner limbers up before the race, and the aeroplane warms up before take-off. Similarly, you should spend a few minutes "warming-up" before you start on other work.

Also, the alphabetic sentence gives intensive practice on the alphabet keys and, therefore, improves accuracy. Type each sentence 3 times.

Format

Left margin: elite 20, pica 15

1 Agatha Dent wears the most beautiful and exquisite
necklace of topaz and jade that Kay has ever seen.

2 The junior office clerks were then quite amazed at
the extra reward given by their generous employer.

3 The taxi driver whizzed along the busy road and a small girl
jumped quickly back to safety.

4 The bold pilot was unable to land the jet owing to extremely
thick fog which quite covered the whole zone.

5 Both the exhausted travellers, frozen by the cruel wind, and
dazed and weary from lack of rest, joined hands and squeezed
their way past the gaping chasm to safety.

6 The liquid is just what was needed; but I must criticize the
price asked and the most waxy finish which it now gives.

7 Judy was thinking of increasing the size of her antique shop
which, she said, would leave enough room for exhibits.

8 A falling off in zinc supplies in July will have been noted,
and prices may be expected to sink very quickly.

9 After all the questions had been answered, an exclamation of
joy broke out from the vast audience who had gathered around
to listen to the popular quiz.

10 The big cyclist, known as Jack, seemed quite relaxed when he
received first prize at the end of the arduous rides through
the snow and ice of the mountains.

11 Then the expert cricketer, who judged the flight precisely,
hit the ball with zest, and very quickly made a good score.

12 If he makes a determined and zealous effort, I am quite sure
Robert will very quickly join the top-ranking experts.

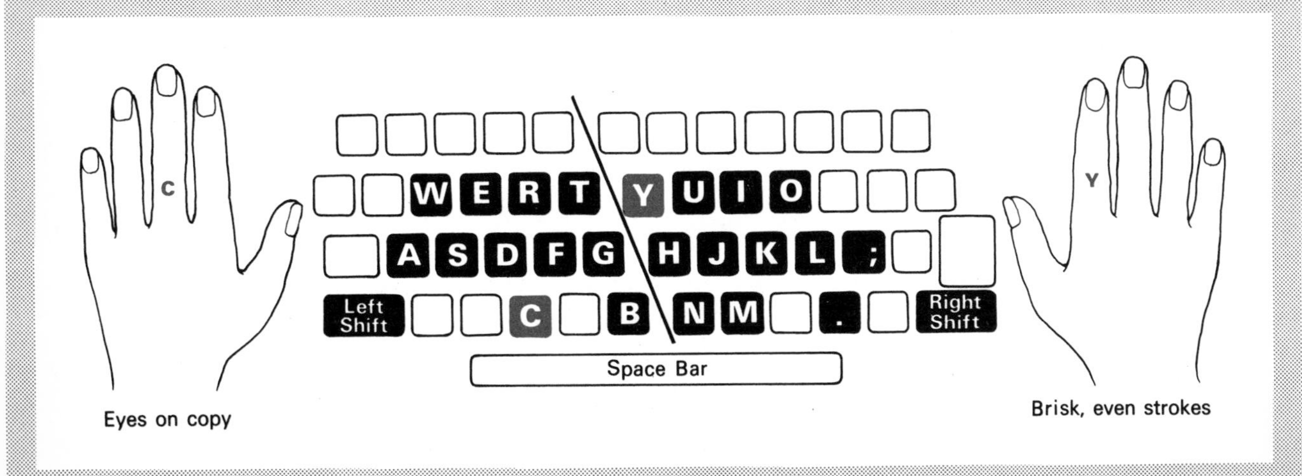

Type each line or sentence 3 times, saying the letters to yourself. If time permits, complete your practice by typing each group of lines as it appears. Keep your eyes on the copy while you type and also when returning the carriage/carrier. The carriage/carrier must be returned IMMEDIATELY after the last character in the line has been typed. Set left margin stop at 25 elite, 18 pica, and use single spacing with double between exercises.

Keyboarding review

1 jmj fmj kmk fmf lml am; Mat Tom Ham Sam Lamb Farm;

2 Mrs Lamb would like to take on the job we offered.

3 None of them would go with Job down the long road.

New key C
Use D finger

4 ddd ccc dcd dcd cod dcd cot dcd cob dcd cog dcdcd;

5 dcd cut dcd cub dcd cur dcd cud dcd cab dcd cat cd

New key Y
Use J finger

6 jjj yyy jyj jyj jay jyj hay jyj lay jyj bay jyjyj;

7 jyj say jyj day jyj ray jyj may jyj gay jyj way jj

Word families

8 sty try fry dry cry wry dice rice mice nice trice;

9 shy sky sly try sty slay stay fray gray dray stray

Left and right shift keys

10 He Ask Jon Sara Kite Dale Lord Ford Hall Iris Tait

11 Ask Miss Ford if she will see Mrs Tait in an hour.

Homophones

Use your dictionary to check the meaning

12 sealing ceiling; council counsel; strait straight;

13 stationery stationary; die dye; formerly formally;

Apply the keys you know

Goal—8 words in half a minute 16 words in one minute

14 He is not able to find a nice jacket which (8) he says 10
he lost on the way to your farm. (16) He will send you 20
his bill in a week or so. (SI 1.08) 25

1 | 2 | 3 | 4 | 5 | 6 | 7 | 8 | 9 | 10 |

Measure your speed—16 wpm

New Keys C and Y

SPOT THE ERRORS

Proofreading Target 2 minutes
Typing Target 5 minutes

At intervals throughout this book you will be referred to this page in order to improve your proofreading technique. When this occurs, read the passage carefully. Each line contains an error that may be spelling, spacing, line-end division, hyphenation, etc. When you have found and noted the errors, type the corrected passage using margins of elite 22–82, pica 12–72. Do not type the line numbers. The key is on page 185.

1 Their are 2 basic systems for keying data into a computer system: one is on-line and one is off-line. An on-line input device is connected directly to the storage or proc-essing unit of a computor system; when a key is struck, the data is instantaneously recorded and stored. Off line devices are independent of the computer in operation,and they tem-porarily store the data on punched cards, tapes, diskettes and so on.

2 Our Managing Director, Mr john R Pritchard, says it will be all right for us to buy new chairs for our typists. He is well aware that poor posture impedes breathing, hampers ci-rculation and interferes with muscular action, Therefore, it will be permissable for you to choose your own chair. He points out that many clarks in the open-plan office have benefitted from the posture chairs bought last February. If your would like to see the new chairs, ask the Office Manager.

3 Typists who are going to use word procesing equipment must be trained in setting up reports and table for all types of documents and correspondence. They must have excellent editt-ing skills and , in the first instance, be proficient in operating the typewriter at speed & with a high standard of acuracy. The skilled word processor operator will have been trained to high degree of proficiency in the use of the type writer.

4 Word processing machines and many of todays typewriters use a carbon or plastic film ribon which gives a very clear, even imprint. These ribbon can only be used once and are thus expensive.

A correction ribbon is used for correcting typing errors. This correction ribbon may be completely seperate on additional spools or it maybe the bottom half of the carbon ribbon. When you wish to correct a typing error, switch to the correction ribbon,type the same error-the correction ribbon will 'lift' the impression from the paper. Swich to normal ribbon and type correct letter(s).

5 Employee efficeincy is what every firm hopes and pays for but can never be sure it gets, unless employee performa-nce is measured or appraised,and many firms in distri-bution have no system of performance appraisal.

Informal appraisal is normally carried out on a day to-day basis, but this often falls short of a firms need for information to monitor its perfornance as a whole and plan for it's future. Also, employees need to know how well the are doing.

See Typing Target Practice, pages 15–16, for further exercises on

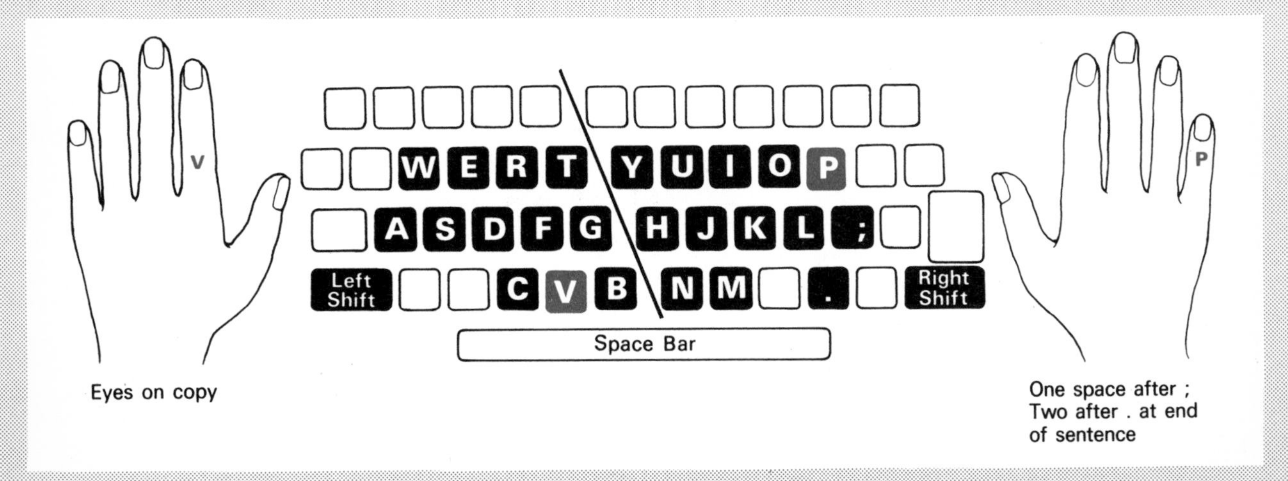

Type each line or sentence 3 times, saying the letters to yourself. If time permits, complete your practice by typing each group of lines as it appears. Keep your eyes on the copy while you type and also when returning the carriage/carrier. The carriage/carrier must be returned IMMEDIATELY after the last character in the line has been typed. Set left margin stop at 25 elite, 18 pica, and use single spacing with double between exercises.

Keyboarding review

1 dcd jyj dcd fbf jhj fgf lol yet coy yes call come.
2 Her mother had brought a new kind of jersey cloth.
3 He sent us a ticket for the jumble sale on Monday.

New key P
Use ; finger

4 ;;; ppp ;p; ;p; cap ;p; lap ;p; rap ;p; jap p;p;p;
5 ;p; pip ;p; dip ;p; sip ;p; hip ;p; lip ;p; nip p;

New key V
Use F finger

6 fff vvv fvf fvf vow fvf van fvf vat fvf vet fvfvf;
7 fvf eve fvf vie fvf via fvf very fvf give fvf live

Word families

8 tup cup pup sup lop pop fop hop cop top tops mops;
9 live jive hive dive give rave pave save wave gave;

Practise B key

10 bid but bad best both able book begin about better
11 Bob has been able to book a table for Bill and me.

Homophones

Use your dictionary to check the meaning

12 canvas canvass; reviews revues; patients patience;
13 principle principal; presents presence; cede seed;

Apply the keys you know

Goal—9 words in half a minute   17 words in one minute

14 She moved a pink jug away from the very back[9] shelf **10**
where it had been hidden from sight.[17] It now shows **20**
up better on that top shelf. **(SI 1.15)** **26**

1 | 2 | 3 | 4 | 5 | 6 | 7 | 8 | 9 | 10 |

SECTION 13

Measure your speed—17 wpm

New Keys P and V

A4 paper Typist — use the carbon copy of the form prepared in Task 20 (page 122) and type in the handwritten details below.

PROMOTION SUMMARY

1. Recommended for: Bookshop Promotion ✓..............

Library Promotion ✓..............

Direct Marketing ✓..............

2. Quarterly "New Books" Entry

Type of Entry (A, B, C): B......... Date 2nd Quarter.........

3. Other catalogue entries: Nursing General, International, British Titles.

4. Exhibitions and Conferences: Nursing Congress, Specials to Nursing Schools

5. Complimentary copies:

		Quantity			Quantity
(a)	Copyright	12	(e)	Research	–
(b)	Author	12	(f)	Reviews	40
(c)	Subsidiaries	10	(g)	Academics	150
(d)	Foreign Rights	10	(h)	Exhibitions	5

	COSTS ESTIMATED	COSTS ACTUAL
6. Advertising (in detail on separate sheets) Nursing Mirror, Nursing Times, Nursing Standard	£750.00	£600.00
7. Mail Promotion (in detail on separate sheets) Tutors, DNEs	£900.00	£892.50
8. Other (in detail on separate sheets) Stickers, Flyers, Headers	£350.00	£373.20

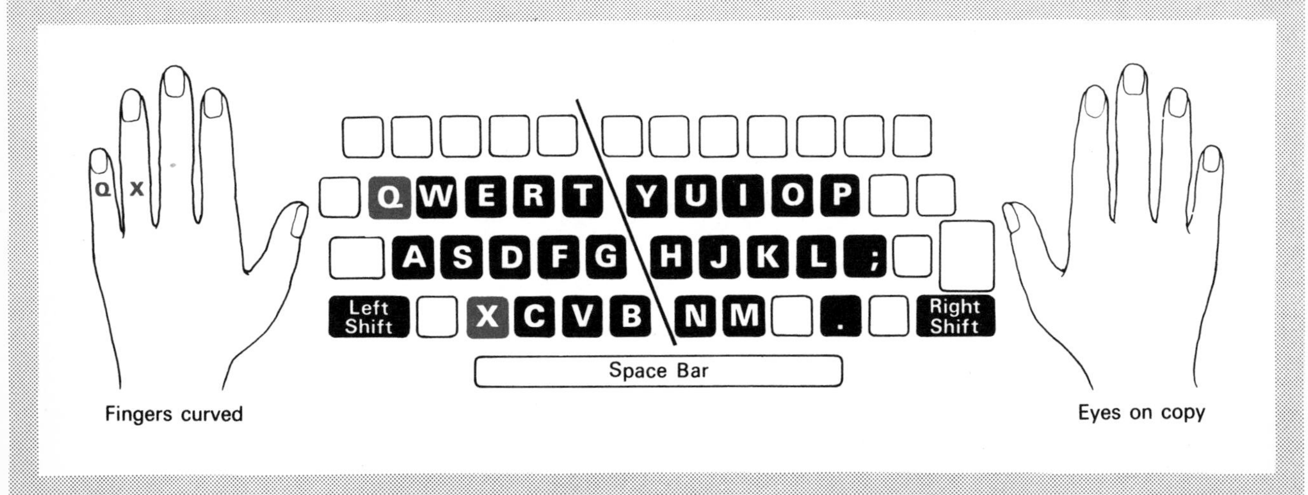

Type each line or sentence 3 times, saying the letters to yourself. If time permits, complete your practice by typing each group of lines as it appears. Keep your eyes on the copy while you type and also when returning the carriage/carrier. The carriage/carrier must be returned IMMEDIATELY after the last character in the line has been typed. Set left margin stop at 25 elite, 18 pica, and use single spacing with double between exercises.

Keyboarding review

1 ;p; fvf ftf jhj dpf apf kpf pot van cop map eve p;
2 Jack was glad my family all moved to North Avenue.
3 Daniel may have to give back a few paper journals.

New key X
Use S finger

4 sss xxx sxs sxs tax sxs lax sxs pax sxs wax sxsxs;
5 sxs sex sxs hex sxs vex sxs rex sxs cox sxs vox sx

New key Q
Use A finger

6 aaa qqq aqa aqa quad aqa aqua aqa equal aqa quick;
7 aqa quin aqa quit aqa quite aqa equal aqa query qa

Word families

8 qua quad squad quit quip quins quill quint quilts;
9 fox cox mix fix nix axe lax pax wax tax taxi taxed

Practise I and N

10 an is in into line infer night noise injure inside
11 Irene infers Nina was injured one night this week.

Homophones

Use your dictionary to check the meaning

12 accede exceed; accept except; access excess; stake
13 steak; checks cheques; choir quire; coarse course;

Apply the keys you know

Goal—9 words in half a minute 17 words in one minute

14 Joe quickly moved the gross of new boxes for[9] which 10
you had paid and then took an extra[17] box of the red 20
quilts and sheets you wanted. **(SI 1.15)** 26

1 | 2 | 3 | 4 | 5 | 6 | 7 | 8 | 9 | 10 |

Measure your speed—17 wpm

New Keys X and Q

A4 paper Minutes with side headings

Minutes of the AGM of The Gardeners' Club held at the George Hotel, Station Street, Scarborough, on 3rd July, 1985, at 7.30pm

PRESENT

Ms Hilda Baker (Chairperson)

Mrs Reneé Long
Mr Seamus Cassidy
Rev Francis de Munck
Miss Harriett Humphrey
Mr Callum Mackay
Mr Kevin Brady
Ms Fiona Vander Bilt

} Please put in alphabetical order

uc/ John Bryden (Secretary)
Plus 23 Members

1 Apologies — Apologies were received fr Ms M Brookside, Mrs G Goodlad, Mrs I Harris & Mr P Jamieson.

2 Minutes — The Secretary read the minutes of the A G Meeting held on 6 July 1984. These were signed by the Chairperson as being a correct record.

3 Matters Arising — There were no matters arising.

4 Chairperson's Report — The Chairperson spoke of the very successful yr just completed & thanked the Sect cmtee members for their help.

5 Treasurer's Report — The Treasurer presented his financial statement & answered a no. of queries.

6 Election of

(a) Officers — The following were unanimously re-elected:
Ms H Baker (Chairperson)
Mr J Bryden (Secretary)
Rev F de Munck (Treasurer)

(b) Cttee — Ms M Brookside resigned &, as no other nominations had bn rec'd, the cttee was re-elected en bloc.

7 AOB — There was no other business.

8 The Chairperson thanked the cttee & members for attending.

________________ Chairperson

________________ Date

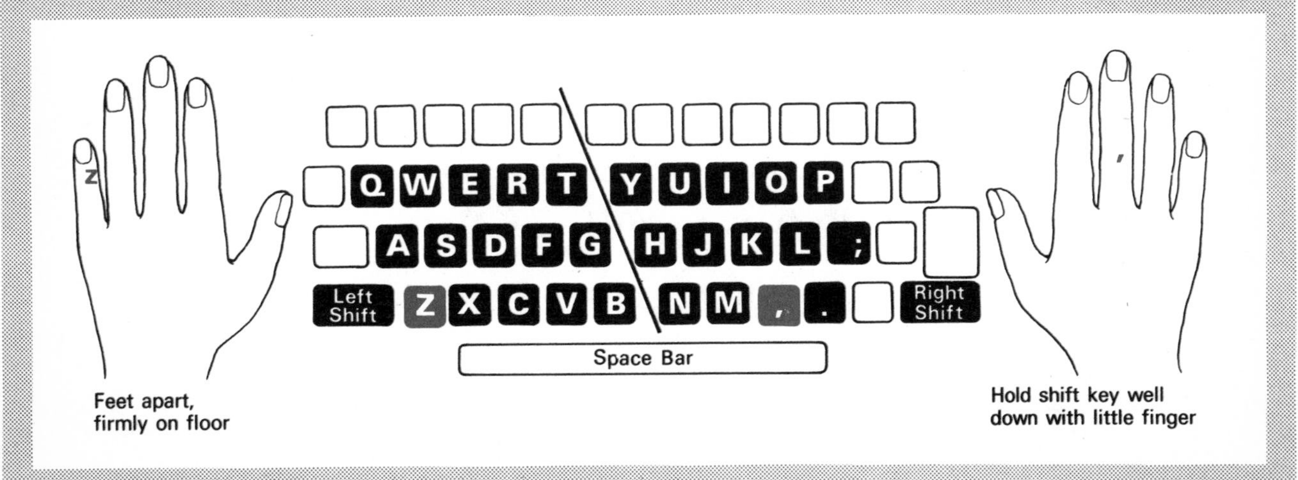

Type each line or sentence 3 times, saying the letters to yourself. If time permits, complete your practice by typing each group of lines as it appears. Keep your eyes on the copy while you type and also when returning the carriage/carrier. The carriage/carrier must be returned IMMEDIATELY after the last character in the line has been typed. Set left margin stop at 25 elite, 18 pica, and use single spacing with double between exercises.

Keyboarding review

1 axs aqa fxf fcf axs saj sex vex tax quit aqua quad

2 Just have one box of new grey mats packed quickly.

3 With extra help Clive found many quite black jugs.

New key Z
Use A finger

4 aaa zzz aza aza zoo aza zinc aza zeal aza azure za

5 aza zip aza zero aza size aza gaze aza jazz aza za

New key ,
Use K finger

6 kkk ,,, k,k k,k l,k a,k s,k j,k d,k f,k hj,k g,f,k

ONE space after a comma

7 at, it, is, or, if, one, can, yes, may, for, cross

Word families

8 daze haze gaze laze maze, lazy hazy crazy, puzzle.

9 zeal zero zest zone, size prize, buzz fuzz, azure.

Practise shift keys

10 Sal Joe Fay Ida Roy Lee Don Gay Bob Your Mary Hall

11 Tell Joe, Fay, Lee and Marie to call on Roy Young.

12 Edna Kelly and Nan Peters will visit Olive Walker.

Homophones

Use your dictionary to check the meaning

13 aloud allowed; born borne; complement compliment;

14 affect effect; higher hire; deference difference;

Apply the keys you know

Goal—9 words in half a minute 18 words in one minute

15 The whizzing of a jet plane across the sky [9] had now 10
become such a normal event that it won [18] but a quick 20
glance from the young boys in the crowd. (SI 1.14) 28

1 | 2 | 3 | 4 | 5 | 6 | 7 | 8 | 9 | 10 |

SECTION 15

Measure your speed—18 wpm

New Keys Z and Comma

Format

Output Target—12 minutes

Fully-blocked style Leave one clear space between numbered items

THE GARDENERS' CLUB
20 Manor Road Scarborough
North Yorkshire YO11 7RY

(leave 1" clear after hdg)

5 June 1985

The (AGM) in full of The Gardeners' Club wl be held /caps
at ~~in~~ the George Hotel, (on Wed, 3rd July, at
7.30 pm.) (, ~~Main~~ Station Street, Scarborough,)

AGENDA

1 Apologies

2 Minutes of last AGM

~~3~~4 Chairman's Annual Report

~~4~~5 Treasurer's Annual Report

3 Matters arising

~~6 Secretary's Annual Report~~ ꝺ

6 Election of:
(a) Officers
(b) Committee
(c) Honorary Auditor

TYPIST Please send a carbon copy to John Mackay and add the following note in brackets —(Suggested agenda — please let me know if you agree.)

7 ~~SPECIAL RESOLUTION~~ ꝺ

ꝺ ~~"As from 1 Aug 1985 the club name will be The North Yorkshire Gardeners' Club".~~

ll/ Any other Business

Type each line or sentence 3 times, saying the letters to yourself. If time permits, complete your practice by typing each group of lines as it appears. Keep your eyes on the copy while you type and also when returning the carriage/carrier. The carriage/carrier must be returned IMMEDIATELY after the last character in the line has been typed. Set left margin stop at 25 elite, 18 pica, and use single spacing with double between exercises.

Keyboarding review alphabet keys

1 You must not jeopardize the safety of the class by having those wicker chairs in the quite dark exit.

> ***Note:*** The small "L" may be used for the figure 1. However, you will find that when you type on a word processor it is essential in a number of operations to use the figure 1; in other words, if you used the small "L", the operation would not work or it would be inaccurate. If your typewriter keyboard does not have a figure 1, then you must use the small "L".

New key 1
Use A finger

2 We require 11 pairs size 11, also 11 pairs size 1.
3 Add up 11 plus 11 plus 11 plus 11 plus 11 plus 11.
4 On 11th June 11 girls and 11 boys hope to join us.
5 He left here on 1st May after being here 11 years.

New Key 2
Use S finger

6 sw2s sw2s s2ws s2ws s2s2s s2s2s s2sws s2sws 2s2ws.
7 22 sips 22 seas 22 skis 22 sons 22 spas 22 sets 2.
8 We need 2 grey, 2 blue, 2 red, and 22 orange ties.
9 The 12 girls and 12 boys won 212 games out of 222.

New key 3
Use D finger

10 de3d de3d d3ed d3ed d3d3d d3d3d d3ded d3ded 3d3ed.
11 33 dots 33 dips 33 dogs 33 dads 33 dyes 33 duds 3.
12 Send 313 only to 33 Green Road and to 3 West Road.
13 Type the numbers 3, 1, 2, 13, 31, 23, 31, 32, 313.

New key 4
Use F finger

14 fr4f fr4f f4rf f4rf f4f4f f4f4f f4frf f4frf 4f4rf.
15 44 furs 44 fish 44 firs 44 feet 44 figs 44 fans 4.
16 The 4 men, 4 women, 24 boys and 4 girls go by car.
17 We ordered 44 sets and received 4 only on the 4th.

Apply the keys you know

Follow instructions on page 16

Goal—10 words in half a minute 19 words in one minute

18 As those shoes are too small, you should take them 10
back and have them changed for the right size.[19] It 20
should not cost you any more money. **(SI 1.03)** 27

1 | 2 | 3 | 4 | 5 | 6 | 7 | 8 | 9 | 10 |

Task 39 ▶ *Format* Output Target—20 minutes

Circular letter with tear-off portion Leave room for name and address of addressee

Our Ref JWD-D/LA/CIR/BD

Please correct word errors

Today's date

Typist - one carbon copy, please.

Dear Sir/Madam

LIFE ASSURANCE

of yr assets.

l.c. It is satisfying fr time to time to be reminded th yr life Assurance fund is secure and growing. Th is why we are pleased to send you the enclosed unit allocation notice, *wh brings y up to date w the progress*

We also hv another reason f writing to y: we want to ask y to take a moment to refect on how yr needs may hv changed since y took out yr current policy, & to take the first step *today* towards ~~brubgubg tr kufe assyrabee~~ up to date w yr present requirements.

value *liability*

Yr changing family circumstances, the chahing of money, the need to minimize yr tax - all these facters and others make it essential to reveiw yr requirements regularly.

Our Insurance Advisor is ready to discuss yr presnet *ent* needs w y, & to compile yr analysis, free and w'out obligation. All y hv to do is to complete the tear-off portion at the foot of this letter and post it to us *today*.

~~Whatever your requirements, yr Insurance Advisor can provide y w a detailed analysis statement of yr little Assurance & investment needs.~~

Yrs faithfully
DAVID JESSOP (INSURANCE BROKERS) LTD

bringing yr life assurance

To: David Jessop (Insurance Brokers) Ltd
Hanbury House 20 St Mary's Street BRIGHTON BN4 2EQ

Please ask your Insurance Adviser to call and see me

on at am/pm.

SURNAME ....

FORENAME(S) ....

ADDRESS ....

.... POSTCODE ....

Type each line or sentence 3 times, saying the letters to yourself. If time permits complete your practice by typing each group of lines as it appears. Keep your eyes on the copy while you type and also when returning the carriage/carrier. The carriage/carrier must be returned IMMEDIATELY after the last character in the line has been typed. Set left margin stop at 25 elite, 18 pica, and use single spacing with double between exercises.

Keyboarding review alphabet keys

1 The quite dazzling mixture of yellow, red and dark
blue of her nylon jumper was a very good contrast.

New key 7
Use J finger

2 ju7j ju7j j7uj j7uj j7j7j j7j7j j7juj juj7j 7j7uj.
3 77 jugs 77 jars 77 jigs 77 jets 77 jags 77 jaws 7.
4 The 7 boys and 77 girls sent 77 gifts to the fund.
5 Take 4 from 47, then add 27 plus 7 and you get 77.

New key 8
Use K finger

6 ki8k ki8k k8ik k8ik k8k8k k8k8k k8kik kik8k 8k8ik.
7 88 keys 88 kits 88 kids 88 kinds 88 kilts 88 kings
8 Type 38, 83, 28, 841 and 482 with alternate hands.
9 The 8 men, 28 women, 8 boys and 78 girls are here.

New key 9
Use L finger

10 lo9l lo9l l9ol l9ol l9l9l l9l9l l9lol lol9l 9l9ol.
11 99 laws 99 logs 99 lids 99 lads 99 lots 99 laps 9.
12 Type 29, 39, 49, 927 and 939 with alternate hands.
13 Joe is 99, Bob is 89, Jim is 79, and George is 49.

New key 0
Use right little finger

14 101 201 102 301 103 401 104 701 107 801 108 90101.
15 10 left 10 look 10 last 10 lose 10 lift 10 lead 0.
16 The 40 men, 70 women, 80 boys and 90 girls remain.
17 Note the dates 10th March, 20th August, 30th June.

Apply the keys you know

Follow instructions on page 16

Goal—10 words in half a minute 20 words in one minute

18 If you are good at figures, and are keen to have a 10
job in our firm, we should like you to call on us. 20
(SI 1.06)

19 I wish that you could have been with us on Tuesday 10
to see the new office machines which were on view. 20
(SI 1.15)

1 | 2 | 3 | 4 | 5 | 6 | 7 | 8 | 9 | 10 |

AUDIO EQUIPMENT

Dictating Machines - Desk Models

Please draw a diagram 2½" (63 mm) × 1½" (38 mm)

1 Accepts standard 30, 60 & 90 cassettes
2 Built-in condenser microphone
3 Pause switch
4 One-touch recording
5 Fast & easy location of particular passages.
6 Electronic index signal

Dictating Machines - Pocket Models

Diagram please - 3" (76 mm) × 1" (25 mm)

1 Single-touch recording system
2 Electronic indexing
3 Single-touch for immediate playback
4 End-of-tape alarm

Transcribing Machines

1 Micro-cassette
2 Automatic stop function at ea. electronic index signal in rewind + fast forward movement
3 Speed control to suit the transcribing speed + this control covers playback at both 1.2 cm/s + 2.4 cm/s CM/S
4 Reverse time control for adjustment to playback - last few words are heard ea. time y. resume listening
5 Foot switch f. full remote-control transcribing
6 Power indicator lamp

Diagram - centre on typing line 5" (127 mm) × 2" (51 mm)

Type each line or sentence 3 times, saying the letters to yourself. If time permits, complete your practice by typing each group of lines as it appears. Keep your eyes on the copy while you type and also when returning the carriage/carrier. The carriage/carrier must be returned IMMEDIATELY after the last character in the line has been typed. Set left margin stop at 25 elite, 18 pica, and use single spacing with double between exercises.

Keyboarding review alphabet keys

1 A small quiet boy who lives next door to Jack came out of the gate and went down the zigzag path.

New key 5
Use F finger

2 fr5f fr5f f5rf f5rf f5f5f f5f5f f5frf frf5f 5r5rf.
3 55 fill 55 flit 55 fled 55 fail 55 flew 55 fell 5.
4 Set tab stops at 5, 15, 25, 35, 45, 55 and also 75
5 25 January 1555; 25 August 1955; 15 December 1555.

New key 6
Use J finger

6 jy6j jy6j j6yj j6yj j6j6j j6j6j j6jyj jyj6j 6j6y6j
7 66 jump 66 jerk 66 jest 66 joke 66 jilt 66 join 66
8 Bring 6 melons, 36 pears, 56 oranges and 6 lemons.
9 We need 656 green and 566 red by 16 February 1986.

New key Shift Lock
Use A finger

10 BEFORE lunch please ring me in LUDLOW next MONDAY.
11 MEETINGS held in LONDON, LIVERPOOL and MANCHESTER.
12 Both LAURA and KATHLEEN were present at the party.
13 Send 56 LARGE and 23 SMALL cartons of FRESH juice.

> PLACEMENT OF CERTAIN CHARACTERS—the location of the hyphen, question mark, underscore, etc, may vary on different makes of machines. When learning any one of these characters you should find it on the keyboard, make sure you know whether or not you have to use the shift key, decide on the correct finger, and then practise the reach from the home key and back to the home key; then type the drills given.

New key -
hyphen

NO space before or after hyphen

14 blue-grey, one-fifth, part-time, left-hand, in-out
15 Over one-third are part-time day-release students.
16 Her father-in-law asked for all-wool yellow socks.
17 Please let me have 5 up-to-date lists on Thursday.

Apply the keys you know

Follow instructions on page 16

Goal—11 words in half a minute 21 words in one minute

18 We trust that the hints we gave for the removal of 10
stains will be found to be of great help to all of 20
you. **(SI 1.09)** 21

19 We hope you will visit us now. We look forward to 10
hearing an up-to-date account about your trips out 20
East. **(SI 1.24)** 21

1 | 2 | 3 | 4 | 5 | 6 | 7 | 8 | 9 | 10 |

SECTION 18

Measure accuracy and speed—21 wpm

New Keys 5, 6, Hyphen and Shift Lock

TASK 37 Cont'd

FIXED ASSETS & DEPRECIATION

It is current policy to revalue all properties including land stet/on an ~~annual~~ yearly basis.

Properties hv bn revalued by the co's valuers, independant valuers, & by use of specific indices. Other fixed assets hv bn revalued by use of suppliers' or engineers' estimates & specific indices. Depreciation is provided for on a straight line basis ~~over the~~ over the total estimated life of the asset, any backlog depreciation on increased valuations being charged to currant cost reserve.

Our subsidary cos at 31 Dec '83, were:

INTERNATIONAL VIDEX P.L.C.
BRITISH PROPERTIES LTD.
BRITISH PACKAGING LTD.
JOHN POWELL & SON
IBA MACHINERY LTD.
BOX CONTAINERS LTD.

TYPIST: Lowercase with initial caps please

All of these cos are registered in Scotland or England.

Trs/ I enclose a copy of the /Accounts & /Report/ for the yr ended 31 Dec, '83.

Please write to me again if you feel I can be of help.

Yrs sincerely

SECRETARY

Type each line or sentence 3 times, saying the letters to yourself. If time permits, complete your practice by typing each group of lines as it appears. Keep your eyes on the copy while you type and also when returning the carriage/carrier. The carriage/carrier must be returned IMMEDIATELY after the last character in the line has been typed. Set left margin stop at 25 elite, 18 pica, and use single spacing with double between exercises. Before typing the new keys below, please see note on page 23 about PLACEMENT OF CERTAIN CHARACTERS.

Keyboarding review alphabet keys

1 In spite of the likely hazard, a decision was made to grant their request and give him the extra job.

New key [-] dash

ONE space before and after dash

2 The book - it was his first - was a great success.
3 Please see him at 8.15 - no, 9 - tomorrow morning.
4 She cannot - because of her work - join our party.
5 It is their choice - we are sure it will be yours.

New key ["] quotation marks

NO space after initial " NO space before closing "

6 "Go for 30 days." "Call at 12 noon." "Ring now."
7 "I am going," he said. "It is already very late."
8 He replied, "No, I will not do that; it is wrong."
9 She said, "Mr Bell will be there to see me leave."

New keys [(] [)] brackets

ONE space before (NO space after NO space before) ONE space after

10 (1 (2 (3 (4 (5 (6 (7 (8 (9; 10) 11) 12) 13) 14) 8)
11 (22) (23) (24) (25) (26) (27) (28) (29) (30) (31).
12 They need (a) 37 men, (b) 9 boys, and (c) 2 girls.
13 (a) 9 pots; (b) 2 pans; (c) 3 sets; (d) 7 typists.

New key [_] underscore

14 Please send them 29 only - not 9 - by air-freight.
15 John Brown, Mary Adams and Janet Kelly are coming.
16 No returns can be accepted after the end of April.
17 The car must not be sold until your uncle returns.

> Before underscoring, backspace by depressing the backspace key (see page 33). After underscoring, always tap space bar. Use shift lock when underscoring more than one character.

Apply the keys you know

Follow instructions on page 16

Goal—11 words in half a minute 22 words in one minute

18 We fear that we shall be away for some months, but 10
we shall keep in touch with you and will write you 20
very soon. **(SI 1.09)** 22

19 We want a first-class employee; one who has a good 10
knowledge of accounts. She must be able to manage 20
a section. **(SI 1.32)** 22

1 | 2 | 3 | 4 | 5 | 6 | 7 | 8 | 9 | 10 |

Measure accuracy and speed—22 wpm

A4 paper

PLEASE SEND THIS LETTER TO MRS J SEYMOUR, 27 WESTWARD RD, HADSTOCK, CAMBRIDGE, CB1 6NX. Use today's date. Take one carbon copy and address an envelope to Mrs Seymour. Correct the word errors.

Our Ref. HOF/MN

Dear Mrs Seymour

When I spoke to you at the AGM last yr, you wl remember th I said I did not expect our trade to improve during '83, &
NP/ this has proved to be the case. [Although the volume of sales does not appear to hv increased, there is an improvement on the continuous reduction we witnessed during the previous yr. Also, our operating costs hv bn helped by lower raw material costs & greater efficiency in the use of all our resources.

Profits after taxation are up (on the previous yr) & authorized share capital has bn increased to £5,000,000 to allow for future growth. I hope th the following table wl answer the last query in yr letter.

INTEREST

	1982 £000	1983 £000
Payable		
On loans repayable wholly within 5 yrs:		
Bank overdrafts	790	654
Other loans & mortgages	1,076	1,777
l.c./ On loans repayable wholly or in part after 5 yrs:		
Loan stock	1,338	891
Debenture stock	820	820
Mortgages	3,650	2,725
	7,674	6,867
Receivable		
On deposits & loans	(193)	(74)
	7,481	6,793

/Continued

Type each line or sentence 3 times, saying the letters to yourself. If time permits, complete your practice by typing each group of lines as it appears. Keep your eyes on the copy while you type and also when returning the carriage/carrier. The carriage/carrier must be returned IMMEDIATELY after the last character in the line has been typed. Set left margin stop at 25 elite, 18 pica, and use single spacing with double between exercises. Before typing the new keys below, please see note on page 23 about PLACEMENT OF CERTAIN CHARACTERS.

Keyboarding review alphabet keys

1 The boy did just give a quick answer, but he could not find words to explain the amazing story.

New key ' apostrophe

NO space before or after in middle of word

2 It's Joe's job to clean Dad's car but he's unwell.

3 Don't do that; it's bad for Mary's dog; he's nice.

4 You're told a dog's bite isn't as bad as its bark.

5 Bill's 2 vans are with John's 8 trucks at Reading.

New key £ pound sign

ONE space before £ but NO space after

6 Buy 9 at £15, 8 at £68, 17 at £415 and 30 at £270.

7 £1, £2, £3, £4, £5, £6, £7, £8, £9, £10, £20, £30.

8 You have all £1 notes; no £5 or £10 notes on hand.

9 I sent out cheques for £10, £12, £15, £16 and £20.

New key & ampersand

ONE space before and after &

10 Jones & Cutler Ltd, 67 & 68 North Street, Falkirk.

11 Mr & Mrs Weston, 18 & 19 Main Street, Cirencester.

12 Box & Cox and Jones & Green need £5 and £10 notes.

13 Mr & Mrs Ramesh Patel have a business in Stafford.

New key ? question mark

TWO spaces after ? at end of sentence

14 How? When? Where? May she? Must we? Will you?

15 Will he go? Is he going? Where is she? Will he?

16 Can you come? Do they agree? What is the matter?

17 Who said so? What is the time? Is it late? Why?

> UPPER AND LOWER CASE CHARACTERS—characters requiring use of shift key are called UPPER CASE characters. Characters not requiring use of shift key are called LOWER CASE characters.

Apply the keys you know

Follow instructions on page 16

Goal—12 words in half a minute 23 words in one minute

18 If you feel some day that you would like a trip in 10
the country, perhaps you could drive out to a farm 20
to pick fruit. **(SI 1.09)** 23

19 Do you wish to take a holiday? Now is the time to 10
take one of our out-of-season vacations. Send for 20
our brochure. **(SI 1.26)** 23

1 | 2 | 3 | 4 | 5 | 6 | 7 | 8 | 9 | 10 |

SECTION 20 New Keys Apostrophe, £ Sign, & and ?

Measure accuracy and speed—23 wpm

Typist - use suitable margins + display according to the example at the bottom of this page. Leave 1½" (38 mm) clear at the top of the first page.

PERMANENT EXHIBITIONS

BARBER INSTITUTE OF FINE ARTS

Birmingham University, Edgbaston. Permanent collection of paintings of the main European Schools ranging from 13th century to about 1900 – important drawings – sculpture – furniture – art objects – coins and medals. Open normally to individual visitors. Mon–Fri 10am–5pm and Sat 10am–1pm. Closed during University public holidays. *Parties by arrangement. Admission free.*

BILSTON MUSEUM & ART GALLERY

Mount Pleasant, Bilston. Tel: Bilston 42097. Permanent collections include the famous Bilston Enamels.

BIRMINGHAM MUSEUM & ART GALLERY

Chamberlain Square, Birmingham B3 3DH. Tel: 021–235 2834. Permanent collection contains fine paintings and drawings from 15th century to present day including large collection of works by painters of the Pre-Raphaelite School. Also Local History Gallery and sections dedicated to Archaeology, Ethnography and Natural History. Open: Mon–Sat 10am–5.30pm and Sun. 2pm–5.30pm. *Telephone for details of weekend closures. Admission free.*

BIRMINGHAM NATURE CENTRE

Pershore Road, Edgbaston, B'ham. Tel: 021–472 7775. Contains living animals of Britain and Europe; mammals, birds, fish, reptiles and amphibia. There are 6 acres of outdoor habitat with ponds, streams, beehives, butterflies and an indoor natural history museum. Open: Daily (except Tuesday) 10am–4pm. Admission – Adults 30p, children/OAPs 15p.

BIRMINGHAM RAILWAY MUSEUM

670 Warwick Road, Tyseley (A41). Tel: 021–707 4696. A working railway museum with a fully equipped workshop displaying the steam engine in its true environment. Open: Sun. 2pm–5pm all year round. Daily (escept Monday) July 6–Oct. 3, 10am–5pm. Admission – Adults 40p, children/OAPs 20p. Steam Days – First Sunday in each month (April–Dec) and Bank Holiday Mondays (higher admission charge).

BLAKESLEY HALL

Blakesley Road, Yardley. Tel: 021–783 2193. Elizabethan farmhouse built by Richard Smallbroke, incorporating period rooms and local history museum. Open: Mon–Sat 1.30pm–5.30pm. Admission – Adults 30p, children/OAPs 15p. Buses 16, 17 & 68 from City Centre or 11a and 11c Outer Circle route.

HERBERT ART GALLERY

Jordan Well, Coventry. Tel: (0203) 25555. Social history gallery, natural history section, Iliffe collection of Sutherland paintings, changing exhibitions from the permanent art collection; Weaving gallery. Open: All year Mon–Sat 10am–4pm, Sun. 2pm–5pm. *Closed Good Friday + Christmas.*

ILIFFE

```
PERMANENT EXHIBITIONS

BARBER INSTITUTE OF FINE ARTS

Birmingham University, Edgbaston.  Permanent collection of paint-
ings of the main European Schools ranging from 13th century to
about 1900 - important drawings - sculpture -
```

Type each line or sentence 3 times, saying the letters to yourself. If time permits, complete your practice by typing each group of lines as it appears. Keep your eyes on the copy while you type and also when returning the carriage/carrier. The carriage/carrier must be returned IMMEDIATELY after the last character in the line has been typed. Set left margin stop at 25 elite, 18 pica, and use single spacing with double between exercises. Before typing the new keys below, please see note on page 23 about PLACEMENT OF CERTAIN CHARACTERS.

Keyboarding review alphabet keys

1 All except the young folk were absolutely bored by the very bizarre movements of the quaint jugglers.

Review figure keys

2 were 2343 true 5473 wore 2943 writ 2485 your 6974.

3 Trains leave at 0812, 1023, 1234, 1345, 1456, 1557

4 Postal Orders needed - 9 £1, 10 £2, 11 £3 and 6 £5

5 Policy numbers 213 & 4 & 5 & 6 are dated 17 April.

New key at 

ONE space before and after @

6 f@f d@d s@s a@a 9 @ 10p; 8 @ 11p; 7 @ 12p; 3 @ 8p.

7 Please send 44 @ £5; 6 @ £7; 13 @ £8; and 28 @ £9.

8 Order 420 @ £12, 50 @ £5, 40 @ £6 and 5 @ £8 each.

New key Oblique or slash 

NO space before or after oblique

9 I can/cannot be present. I do/do not require tea.

10 The theory and/or beginners' class is on THURSDAY.

11 Jim Minett will take an aural and/or written test.

New keys %/½

12 ;½; a½a s½s d½d f½f j½j k½k 1½1 2½ 3½ 4½ 5½ 6½ 7½.

13 The prices are 2½p; 3½p; 4½p; 5½p; 6½p; 7½p; 17½p.

14 a%a s%s d%d f%f j%j k%k 1%1 ;%; 2% 3% 4% 5% 6% 7%.

15 The discount is 4% 7 days, 3% 14 days, 1% 21 days.

> In addition to the ½, most typewriters have keys with other fractions. Examine your machine to find what fractions it has. These are all typed with the ; finger. Some will require the use of the shift key. Practise the reaching movement from the home key to the fraction key you wish to type. ALWAYS return finger quickly to the home key.

Apply the keys you know

Follow instructions on page 16

Goal—12 words in half a minute   24 words in one minute

16 The account for May should now be paid, and I must 10
ask you to let me have your cheque for the sum due 20
as soon as you can. **(SI 1.04)** 24

17 When you leave the office at night you should make 10
sure that your machine is covered up and that your 20
desk is quite clear. **(SI 1.12)** 24

1 | 2 | 3 | 4 | 5 | 6 | 7 | 8 | 9 | 10 |

SECTION 21

Measure accuracy and speed—24 wpm

New Keys @ Sign, Oblique, ½ and %

2.

TIME DIFFERE<s>C</s>NCES

Country	IDD code	Time difference in hours	Directory <s>e</s>nquiries dial
Australia	010 61 (one space)	+8/10	158
Austria	010 43	+1	155
Belgium	010 32	+1	155
Canada	010 1	−3½/9	157
USA	010 1	−5/8	157
Sweden	010 41	+1	156
Denmark	010 45	+1	155
Spain	010 94	+1	156
France	010 33	+1	156
Portugal	010 351	+1	155
Hong Kong	010 852	+8	157
Germany	010 49	+1	155
Italy	010 39	+1	155

Please put countries in alphabetical order

Helping people abroad to dial you. Use the internationally agreed format for showing international tel. nos combined w national nos as follows:

National number Aberdeen (0224) 34344
International number 44* 224 34344

The initial '0' of the area code is not dialled by callers abroad.

---

* Tells callers to dial their own international prefix wh varies fr country to country.

FORMAT FOR OPEN PUNCTUATION

A number of organisations now use open punctuation in a variety of business documents. This means that the full stop is omitted from an abbreviated word (except at the end of a sentence) and is replaced by a space, eg, Mr (space) J (space) Smith, of W M Smith & Co Ltd, will discuss the terms of payments, etc, with Mrs U E St John-Browne. Where an abbreviation consists of 2 or more letters with a full stop after each letter, the full stops are omitted and no space is left between the letters but one space (or comma) after each group of letters, eg, Mrs G L Hunt, 21 South Road, will call at 7 pm today. She requires past examination papers from several bodies, eg, LCCI, RSA and UEI. Grammatical punctuation must still be used. The first part of this book is written in open punctuation, ie, no full stops are given in or after abbreviations.

IMPROVE YOUR TYPING TECHNIQUE

If your technique is faulty, check with the following list and carry out the remedial drill.

Faulty technique		**Remedy**
Manual machines		
Raised capitals caused by releasing shift key too soon.	I may go.	Drills 4–9 page 13, drills 4–9 page 15.
Uneven left margin, caused by faulty carriage return.	I may go.	Return carriage without looking up. Any "Apply the keys you know".
Heavy strokes, caused by not releasing keys quickly.	I **may** go.	Practise finger movement drills. Any "Apply the keys you know".
Light strokes, caused by not striking the keys hard enough.	I may go.	Practise finger movement drills. Any "Apply the keys you know".
Manual and electric/electronic machines	may	
Omitting or inserting words (looked up from the copy).	I go	Eyes on copy always. Page 20 lines 10 and 11 backwards.
Extra spaces caused by your leaning on the space bar.	I may go.	Right thumb slightly above space bar. Drill line 15 page 11.
Omitting spaces, caused by poor wrist position.	I maygo.	Say "space" to yourself each time you tap space bar. Drill line 15 page 11, line 15 page 13.
Fingers out of position.	I ,ay go.	Return fingers to home keys. Any "Apply the keys you know".
Turning letters around—eyes get ahead of fingers.	I may og.	Eyes on copy always. Say each letter and space to yourself as you type. Any of the preceding drills.

ACCURACY/SPEED PRACTICE—Practice routine

(a) Type a copy of the exercise.
(b) Check and circle all errors.
(c) Compare your errors with those shown above.
(d) Practise the remedial drills.
(e) Type as much of the exercise as you can in the time suggested.
(f) If you made more than the stipulated number of errors, continue with the timed practice and aim for accuracy.
(g) If your errors were below the tolerance given, type the exercise again (timed) and endeavour to type a little faster.

Accuracy/speed practice 25 wpm One minute Not more than one error

```
1 I have just moved to my new house and, when I have  10
  put it straight, I would be glad if you could then  20
  spend a few days with me.  (SI 1.00)                25

2 I am delighted to tell you that we have now joined  10
  the team.  We had hoped to do so last year, but we  20
  were then not old enough.  (SI 1.12)                25
```

1 | 2 | 3 | 4 | 5 | 6 | 7 | 8 | 9 | 10 |

INTERNATIONAL DIRECT DIALLING (IDD)

International Direct Dialling is a quick way to telephone abroad. It is available f over 98% of tels in this country to ~~over~~ to more than one hundred countries.

What to ~~ring~~ dial. Wherever y are calling, y wl hv to deal dial the complete international no. In most cases this is divided into four sections:

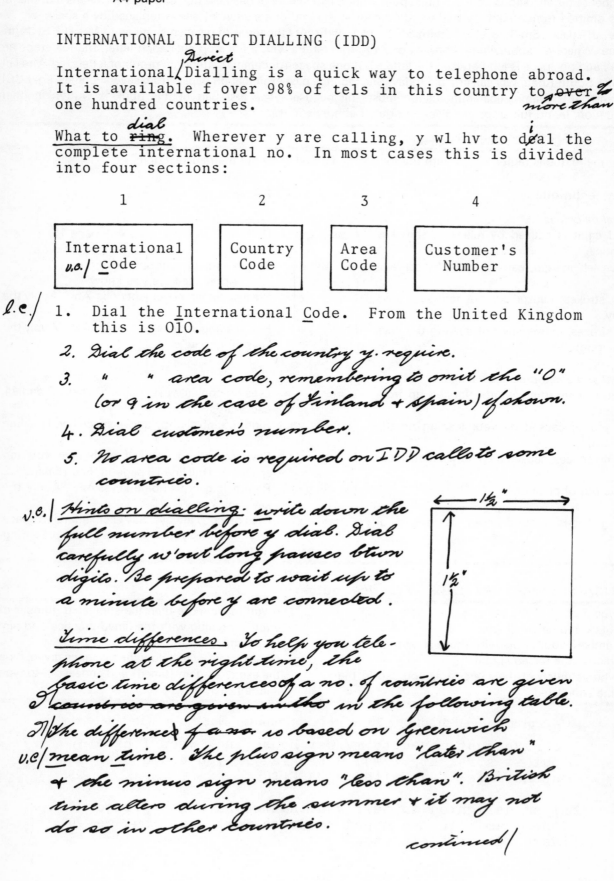

1	2	3	4
International u.c./ code	Country Code	Area Code	Customer's Number

l.c./ 1. Dial the International Code. From the United Kingdom this is 010.

2. Dial the code of the country y. require.
3. " " area code, remembering to omit the "0" (or 9 in the case of Finland + Spain) if shown.
4. Dial customer's number.
5. No area code is required on IDD calls to some countries.

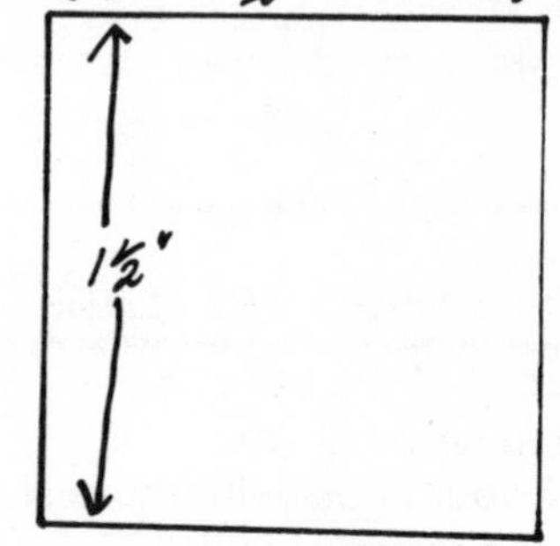

u.c./ Hints on dialling: write down the full number before y dial. Dial carefully w'out long pauses btwn digits. Be prepared to wait up to a minute before y are connected.

Time differences. To help you telephone at the right time, the basic time differences of a no. of countries are given ~~countries are given in the~~ in the following table. NP/ The difference ~~f a no.~~ is based on Greenwich u.c./ mean time. The plus sign means "later than" + the minus sign means "less than". British time alters during the summer + it may not do so in other countries.

continued/

Type each line or sentence 3 times, saying the letters to yourself. If time permits, complete your practice by typing each group of lines as it appears. Keep your eyes on the copy while you type and also when returning the carriage/carrier. The carriage/carrier must be returned IMMEDIATELY after the last character in the line has been typed. Set left margin stop at 25 elite, 18 pica, and use single spacing with double between exercises.

Keyboarding review alphabet keys

1 It was emphasized that the very young juniors need extra food which cannot be quickly obtained.

For further practice on alphabet keys, see pages 181 and 182

Fluency drill

2 the you she her did see new has had his him are an
3 they both your week that must time will days ours.
4 The man did not see the new tie she had given him.
5 Both boys said they knew that they must work hard.

For further drills see pages 183–185

New key : Use ; finger

6 ;;; ::: ;;; a:; l:; s:; k:; d:; j:; f:; h:; gf:;a;
7 Delivery Period: one month. Prices: net ex works.
8 Reference: JD; Subject: Offer; Enclosure: Invoice.

Leave ONE space after colon

Accuracy/speed practice 25 wpm 1½ minutes **Not more than 2 errors**

3 Just a year ago I said that you should be given a trial as a 12
clerk in sales and, as one of the staff will be leaving next 24
week, I would like you to take his place. Let me know if it 36
suits you. **(SI 1.11)** 38

4 There must be little imps who sleep until one begins to work 12
and then they come to our office and start to harass and try 24
us. We must all learn to keep our minds on the work that we 36
have to do. **(SI 1.13)** 38

1 | 2 | 3 | 4 | 5 | 6 | 7 | 8 | 9 | 10 | 11 | 12 |

For further accuracy/speed practice, see pages 186–191

RECORD YOUR PROGRESS

Instructions for all RECORD YOUR PROGRESS EXERCISES:

(a) Type ONCE as practice.
(b) Check for errors.
(c) With the assistance of your teacher, analyse your errors and carry out remedial work where necessary.
(d) Type as much of the passage as you can in the time allotted.
(e) Check and circle any errors.
(f) Record the number of words typed and the number of errors in the second typing. See *Teaching Notes and Solutions* for RECORD YOUR PROGRESS CHART.

Record your progress **1½ minutes**

1 Some 6 months have passed since you left the Sales Office to 12
study accounts, and we are certain it is now time to discuss 24
the future. Over the past year we have been very happy with 36
the high standard of your work and are certain you will want 48
to do well. **(SI 1.22)** 50

1 | 2 | 3 | 4 | 5 | 6 | 7 | 8 | 9 | 10 | 11 | 12 |

For further record your progress exercises, see pages 192–196

SECTION 23

Accuracy/speed—1½ minutes at 25 wpm
Record your progress—1½ minutes

New Key Colon

TASK 33 Continued PAGE 3 (leave 1" (25 mm) clear)

SWIMMING POOL
Available to guests during season from 0800-1100.

HAIRDRESSING
TYPIST: Left margin: 1" (25 mm) clear
Ask Reception to arrange an appointment.

TELEVISION
There is a colour TV in ea bedroom & one in the main lounge.

NEWSPAPERS
These wl be delivered to yr room if an order is placed w Reception.

DEPARTURE
Guests are requested to vacate their rooms by 1100 hrs on the day of departure.

TELEPHONE
lc/ Bedroom telephones are connected to the Hotel Switchboard & main post office lines. Charges for tel calls & services
NP/ are displayed at Reception. [Tel. coin boxes are located on the ground floor & are available for guests wishing to make direct calls.]

Task 34 ▶ *Format*
A5 portrait paper
Output Target—12 minutes

PLEASE WRITE A LETTER FROM THE MANAGER OF THE PHEONIX DEL MAR HOTEL – ADDRESS IN TASK 33 – TO MR J W ROBINSON, 24 LEEDS ROAD, ILKLEY, WEST YORKSHIRE, LS29 9HY; USE A SUITABLE DATE

Say,
Thank you f yr letter dated 8 May.
We are pleased to offer y 2 twin-bedded rooms for the 2 wks beginning Wed, 5 June.
The terms are: £140 per person per week for bed & Continental breakfast.
21/ Please ~~let me know if you wish~~ send a deposit of £80 if y wld like us to reserve 2 rms.
Copy of our brochure is enclosed. Yrs sincerely

(Send carbon copies to Ms C Challenor & Mr S Williams, &, of course, there will be the usual file copy)

To ensure that you produce clean, error-free transcripts, you must plan carefully. Your success will depend on:

(a) a thorough training in typing technique and acceptable display standards;

(b) your ability to read—and understand—instructions, typescript, manuscript, etc, and your capacity to produce accurate and meaningful work quickly;

(c) a good knowledge of English—spelling, punctuation, hyphenation, capitalisation, paragraphing, rules of grammar and sentence structure;

(d) your ability to organise your work area and your work habits—see that all supplies are conveniently at hand before you start. (ALWAYS read each task/exercise through CAREFULLY, altering the original where necessary, so that once you start to type a particular task you will NEVER need to restart on another sheet of paper.)

If you follow the instructions in this book and complete the exercises given, you will be well able to meet the requirements in numbers a, b and d above.

If your knowledge of words is not good and you are not sure of how to spell words in everyday use, you must make a determined effort to overcome these shortcomings.

Homophones
These are given as drills on pages 11–20. Master the meanings of the words and you will find no difficulty in deciding on the correct word to use in a particular sentence.

Spelling
A list of words that are not easy to spell are given on page 30. Type at least one exercise each time you sit down at the typewriter. Look carefully at each letter in each word and note the sequence of the letters. For example: ACCOMMODATION—2 c's and 2 m's. Listen attentively to the correct pronunciation and then pronounce it carefully. Do you say INCIDENTLY instead of INCIDENTALLY? Do you say FEBUARY instead of FEBRUARY? Keep a list of the words you habitually misspell. Review these words at least once a day, and type them whenever you have an opportunity. There are a multiplicity of rules to help you spell; look them up in a standard spelling book or in a dictionary. Certain exercises, from page 32, contain deliberate word errors. You must locate and correct these errors before typing an exercise.

Punctuation and capitalisation
Before typing, read each piece of work carefully and see that punctuation and capitalisation are correct and consistent.

Note: Books such as *Communication—A Keyboard Approach* and *Type to Spell* published by McGraw-Hill Book Company (UK) Limited will teach you communication and spelling in an easy, interesting and meaningful way.

Folded leaflet A4 paper

(LEAVE 1½" (38 mm) clear at top)

FRONT PAGE

WELCOME TO ← SPACED CAPS & centre

THE PHOENIX DEL MAR HOTEL
East Cliff
Bournemouth BH1 3EQ
Centre

(Leave 1½" (38 mm) clear)

l.c.

Leave left margin of 1" (25 mm) clear

The Phoenix Del Mar Hotel stands in its own grounds on the East Cliff, facing south.
It has 120 bedrooms with:

private bathrooms
colour TV
telephone
tea and coffee making facilities
central htg.

In addition there are:

3 lounges
games rooms
cocktail bar
conference rooms.

PAGE 2

(LEAVE 2" (51 mm) clear at top)

Meal times in Restaurant
Breakfast 0800-0945
Luncheon 1230-1400
Dinner 1830-2030
Centre ea line

Leave left margin of 1" (25 mm) clear

Afternoon tea is served in the lounges between 1600 & 1700.
Packed lunches are available instead of lunch, & shld be ordered fr the Head Waiter not later than 2000 hrs on the evening before.
Early morning tea. Facilities f making tea are provided free of charge in all bedrooms

(Leave 1" (25 mm) clear)

Other activities. Reservations may be made at Reception for horse riding, pony trekking, sailing, windsurfing, water skiing, golf & squash facilities.

Type each line of an exercise 3 times, then type the complete exercise once. Set the left margin at elite 20, pica 15.

1 view until merge awful chaos quiet forty really absorb centre
2 lose occur gauge audio among video weird choice losing prefer

3 paid guard media input recur queue depot canvas govern pursue
4 quay basic alter diary truly lying reign height eighth ascend

5 cheque usable cursor buffet unique wholly mislaid acknowledge
6 debtor tariff fulfil coming friend humour leisure undoubtedly

7 hungry murmur choose format argues misuse omitted immediately
8 modern cancel except access genius serial console transferred

9 mislaid relying dismiss useless forceful privilege stationery
10 editing college twelfth benefit February principal admissible

11 liaison minutes cursory woollen harassed Wednesday difference
12 usually grammar centred certain achieved dependent receivable
13 movable pastime synonym justify withhold perceived compliment

14 arguing marriage valuable omission function parallel envelope
15 develop exercise physical planning expenses guardian pleasant

16 believe courtesy received decision occasion familiar definite
17 pitiful forcible sentence transfer separate reducing feasible
18 proceed exercise physical hardware expenses guardian pleasant

19 knowledge agreeable competent underrate absorption colleagues
20 vaccinate committee benefited possesses accessible accidental

21 technical recognize inoculate recommend courageous wraparound
22 recipient erroneous transient emphasize especially repetition
23 courteous aggravate aggregate competent enthusiasm pagination

3. Classified business directories and 'Yellow Pages' These important supplementary directories list commercial and professional subscribers under types of business or trade. These are arranged alphabetically. The individual members of the various trades or professional groups, such as doctors, furniture manufacturers, solicitors, and so on, have their names arranged alphabetically within their respective group.

4. Directory Enquiries If the caller requires the number of a subscriber outside the area covered by the directories, Directory Enquiries is called.

u/s. 2. Code books and telephone directories Only the latest editions shd be used.

4.1 The number of this service is listed in the Telephone dialling codes for yr area. Given the name + address of any subscriber (firm or person), the operator . . . appropriate directory. v.c./

4.2 When dialling Directory Enquiries y wl be asked first of all: "Which town, please?" So be ready . . . about whom y wish to enquire . . . fr Directory Enquiries.

5. The operator—dial 100 If difficulty is experienced in obtaining a call, first check that you have dialled the correct number; if you are sure of this and the number is still unobtainable, ask the operator for help.

6. Notebook

6.1 Keep a notebook + pencil nr the telephone. A notebook w. the spine at the top instead of the side is more convenient. When starting

6.2 ea day, date the notebook at the foot of the page.

6.3 A rubber band round the used pages helps to locate quickly the next available page.

6.4 One message to ea. page reduces page turning when talking over the telephone.

6.5 Immediately the conversation has finished, write or type the necessary information on the tel. message pad.

6.6 Keep the information in date order, so th it can be instantly referred to, rather than on scraps of paper wh are soon discarded.

6.7 If a caller telephones again, it is unnecessary to request further full particulars, as the details of the previous call can be referred to in the notebook. trs

(1) From Watcham's Office Practice, Book One, 3/e, by Margaret Rees-Boughton adapted by Elizabeth Taylor [TAYLOR]

Published by McGraw-Hill Book Company (UK) Limited

STANDARD SIZES OF PAPER

In the office you will have to use different sizes of paper. The standard sizes are known as the "A" series and are shown below. The most common of these sizes are: A4, A5 and A6.

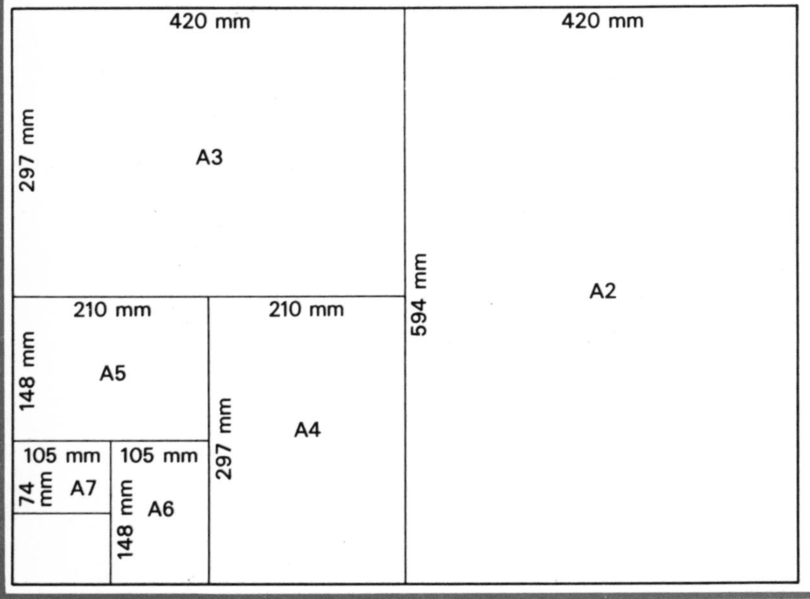

25 mm = 1″

Sizes

Size	mm	inches
A2	420 × 594 mm	
A3	420 × 297 mm	
A4	210 × 297 mm	$8\frac{1}{4}'' \times 11\frac{3}{4}''$ (approx)
A5	210 × 148 mm (landscape)	$8\frac{1}{4}'' \times 5\frac{7}{8}''$ (approx)
A5	148 × 210 mm (portrait)	$5\frac{7}{8}'' \times 8\frac{1}{4}''$ (approx)
A6	148 × 105 mm	$5\frac{7}{8}'' \times 4\frac{1}{8}''$ (approx)

VERTICAL LINE-SPACING

6 single vertical lines = 25 mm (1″)

Number of single-spaced lines in the full length of A4 and A5:

70 single-spaced lines on A4 paper
35 single-spaced lines on A5 landscape paper
50 single-spaced lines on A5 portrait paper

HORIZONTAL SPACING

The 3 most usual typefaces are

12 characters = 25 mm (1″)—known as 12 pitch (elite)
10 characters = 25 mm (1″)—known as 10 pitch (pica)
15 characters = 25 mm (1″)—known as 15 pitch

Number of horizontal characters in full width of A4 and A5 paper:

	12 pitch (elite)	10 pitch (pica)	15 pitch
A4	100 (centre point 50)	82 (centre point 41)	124 (centre point 62)
A5 (landscape)	100 (centre point 50)	82 (centre point 41)	124 (centre point 62)
A5 (portrait)	70 (centre point 35)	59 (centre point 29)	88 (centre point 44)

Typist - words in heavy print to be underscored

The telephonist (1) ← caps

As she is often the first person in the firm to whom an enquirer speaks, the switchboard operator or telephonist is an important link between the business and the outside world.

1. In a large company Some firms have such large switchboards that several telephonists are fully employed attending to incoming and outgoing calls.

2. In a small company In firms with smaller switchboards, the telephonist may work alone or act as receptionist as well, and even do some clerical work or typing.

3. Switchboard operators A private switchboard operator's many duties may include:

Block the paras under first letter of text

3.1 Putting all incoming calls thru to the appropriate person.

3.2 Linking up outgoing calls, or making a line available so th an outgoing call may be dialled direct.

3.3 Helping callers who are not sure to whom they need to speak.

3.4 Locating staff for making receiving calls.

v.c. 3.5 tracing numbers wanted by staff.

3.6 Obtaining information, such as times of trains.

Reference sources

Whatever the size of company, the telephonist's reference sources are important and must be fully adequate and kept constantly up to date.

1. Personal index The telephonist should maintain her own index of frequently used numbers. She should amend this record immediately a change of number is notified to her.

Typist - leave 2" (51 mm) clear

Amendments can be made quickly and easily if a strip index is used.

LINE-SPACE SELECTOR

The line-space selector is a lever situated at the left- or right-hand end of the paper table. Most machines can be adjusted for single and double spacing and may also have the facility for $1\frac{1}{2}$, $2\frac{1}{2}$ and treble spacing. The selector controls the distance between the lines of typing. In previous exercises you have been typing in "single" spacing—the line-space selector has been set on "1". You can also type in double (one clear space between each line of typing) or treble spacing (2 clear spaces between each line of typing).

		Single spacing (type on every line)	*Double spacing* (type on every second line)	*Treble spacing* (type on every third line)
	↑	I am	I am	I am
		going	(space)	(space)
6 single-line spaces equal 25 mm (1 inch)	25 mm	to	going	(space)
		the	(space)	going
		market	to	(space)
	↓	today	(space)	(space)

FORMAT FOR BLOCKED PARAGRAPHS

Paragraphs are used to break up the writing into short passages to facilitate reading and understanding. There are 3 different styles of paragraph, but for the time being, we will deal with the BLOCKED paragraph where all lines start at the left margin.

When typing BLOCKED paragraphs in SINGLE SPACING, turn up 2 SINGLE spaces between each paragraph, ie, leave one blank space between each paragraph.

Practise typing blocked paragraphs in single spacing

1 Type the following paragraphs on A5 landscape paper. (a) Margins: elite 22–82, pica 12–72. (b) Leave 25 mm (one inch) clear at the top of the page, ie, turn up 7 single spaces—for explanation of alignment guide, see page 3, No 8. (c) Single spacing. (d) Correct one word error.

It is generally thought that there will be a greater need
for basic keyboarding skills in the future.

It will be necesary to have the ability to transfer these
skills to a variety of machines and keyboards.

When typing BLOCKED paragraphs in DOUBLE SPACING, turn up 2 DOUBLE SPACES between each paragraph, ie, leave 3 blank spaces between each paragraph.

Practise typing blocked paragraphs in double spacing

2 Type the following paragraphs on A5 portrait paper. (a) Margins: elite 13–63, pica 6–56. (b) Leave 25 mm (one inch) clear at the top of the page, ie, turn up 7 single spaces. (c) Double spacing.

As you have already learnt, in blocked paragraphs

all lines start at the same scale point.

When typing blocked paragraphs in <u>double spacing,</u>

you must turn up 2 double spaces between each

paragraph.

Task 31 continued

He was evidentally a happy person because a friend said of him

Typist - insert no. 1 from previous page.

first/ Scott/ became famous f his poem THE LAY OF THE LAST MINSTREL fr wh the following is quoted

Typist - insert no. 2 from previous page

~~The~~ This poem illustrated the customs + manners of the people of the Borders of Scotland & England.

Scott's next poem was THE LADY OF THE LAKE fr wh the following verse is taken

Typist - insert no. 3 fr previous page

In this poem Scott took his readers into the delightful scenery of The Trossachs v.c./ + life in the Highlands. The scene was set in the area around Loch Katrine in Perthshire. It was said th his third poem, MARMION, was composed while he rode round the country on horseback! TROSSACHS

For a time Scott was out of favour but soon Edinburgh people were ~~all~~ talking abt WAVERLEY + wondering who cd be the author. Over the years some 27 WAVERLEY NOVELS were written.

---

* He was made a baronet in 1820.

I The word "lave" means "others".

BACKSPACE KEY

Locate the backspace key on your machine. This is situated on either the top left or right of the keyboard. When the backspace key is depressed, the carriage/carrier will move back one space at a time. On most electric machines the carriage/carrier will continue to move for as long as the backspace key is depressed.

FORMAT FOR HORIZONTAL CENTRING—BLOCKED STYLE

When centring a piece of display in the full width of the paper, take the following steps:

(a) See that the left edge of the paper is at 0 on the carriage position scale.
(b) Move margin stops to extreme left and right.
(c) Divide by 2 the total number of spaces between 0 and the scale point reached by the right-hand edge of paper; this gives the centre point of paper.
(d) Bring carriage/carrier to the centre point.
(e) Locate the backspace key and backspace once for every 2 characters and spaces in the longest line. Ignore any odd letter left over.
(f) Set the left margin at the point reached.
(g) All lines in the exercise start at the left margin.

Practise horizontal centring

1 Type the following exercise on A5 landscape paper. (a) Leave one inch (25 mm) clear at the top of the page. (b) Double spacing. (c) Centre the longest line. (d) Set left margin at point reached. (e) Start all other lines at this point.

```
For Sale

12 Months Interest Free Credit    ←This is longest line

Dining Room Suite

Ready-made Velvet Curtains

Persian Carpets

Pine Dresser

Divan Set
```

2 Type the following exercise on A5 portrait paper. (a) Leave one inch (25 mm) clear at the top of the page. (b) Double spacing. (c) Centre the longest line. (d) Set left margin at point reached. (e) Start all other lines at this point.

```
Examinations

will be taken in

Shorthand Transcription

Typewriting

Audio-typewriting

and

Data Processing
```

A4 paper Double spacing unless where otherwise instructed
Indented paragraphs

(1) "Eh me, sic an endless fund o' humour and drollery as he had wi' him! Never 10 yards but we were either laughing or roaring and singing; whenever we stopped how brawlie he suited himsel' to everybody! He aye did as the lave* did - never made himsel' the great man, or took ony airs in the company."

To be typed in single spacing and blocked style para.

(2) *Single spacing and centred with blocked style para*

"Ten squires, ten yeomen, mail-clad men,
Waited the beck of the warders ten;
Thirty steeds, both fleet and wight,
Stood saddled in stable day and night,
Barb's with frontlet of steel, I trow,
And with Jedwood-axe at saddlebow;
A hundred more fed free in stall:
Such was the custom of Branksome Hall."

(3) *Single spacing and centred with blocked style para*

"The stag at eve had drunk his fill
Where danced the moon on Monan's rill,
And deep his midnight lair had made
In lone Glenartney's hazel shade;
But, when the sun his beacon red
Had kindled on Benvoirlich's head,
The deep-mouth'd bloodhound's heavy bay
Resounded up the rocky way,
And faint, from farther distance borne,
Were heard the clanging hoof and horn."

TYPIST Please start here

* SIR WALTER SCOTT - 1771- 1832

A Scottish writer of poetry, ballads and historical novels who was born in Edinburgh. As a child he was frail [+ slightly lame,] + his parents thought him too delicate to attend school + sent him to live w his grandparents who resided near Kelso, Roxburghshire. N.P. [When he did attend school, he was thought to be a stupid boy +, in later years, he himself said th he was the dunce of the school. However, he was gd at Latin [+ modern languages,] + later attended Edinburgh University.

V.C. As a young man he used to visit the border country so as to get to know the characters + life of the local people whom he described so well in his writings. His greatest pleasure was to sit by the silvery Tweed reading ballads, poetry or a story book. It was said by friends th. if a ballad were repeated to him only once, he wd never forget it.

FORMAT FOR VERTICAL CENTRING

To centre matter vertically on a sheet of paper take the following steps:

(a) Find the number of vertical single spaces on the paper.
(b) Count the number of lines and blank spaces between the lines in the exercise to be typed.
(c) Deduct (b) from (a).
(d) Divide answer in (c) by 2 to equalise top and bottom margins (ignore fractions).
(e) Insert paper with left edge at 0 on paper scale. See that the top edge of the paper is level with the alignment scale.
(f) Turn up the number of spaces arrived at in (d) PLUS ONE EXTRA SPACE.

Practise vertical and horizontal centring

3 Display the following notice on A5 landscape paper. (a) Centre the notice vertically. The vertical spacing at the side of the notice and the calculation below are given as a guide. (b) Centre the longest line horizontally. (c) Set the left margin and start all lines at this point.

			Turn up
1	Line 1	BRITISH TELECOM SERVICES	
2	Space		3 spaces
3	Space		
4	Line 2	Bedtime Stories	
5	Space		2 spaces
6	Line 3	Weather	
7	Space		2 spaces
8	Line 4	The Speaking Clock	
9	Space		2 spaces
10	Line 5	Dial-a-Disc	
11	Space		2 spaces
12	Line 6	Motoring Information	

The calculations for the vertical centring in the above exercise are as follows:

(a) Number of lines on A5 landscape paper =35
(b) Number of lines and spaces in exercise =12
(c) Deduct (b) from (a) 35−12=23
(d) Divide answer in (c) by 2 for top and bottom margins (ignore fractions) 23÷2=11
(e) Turn up 12 single spaces and type the first line of the notice. As you wish to leave 11 clear spaces, it is necessary to turn up the extra space as you will type on the 12th line, so leaving 11 clear spaces.

4 Display the following notice on A5 landscape paper. (a) Centre the notice vertically. (b) Centre the longest line horizontally. (c) Set the left margin and start all lines at this point. (d) Correct one word error.

CHEQUE BOOK CALCULATOR

Makes Cheque Book Calculations Easy

Three Seperate Memories for

Cheque Book and
Credit Card Balances

Designed with your budget in mind

See Typing Target Practice, page 1, for further exercises on

Task 30 continued

[N.P. Of] The season is not limited to just June, July + Aug. In fact, trans-atlantic (u.c.) air fares are ~~substan~~ substantially cheaper in winter, + the weather is often better. (Typist—please insert this para before the heading "Cruise No. ONE")

A Caribbean cruise is an unbeatable combination of

1 Sun ~~fear~~ all the year round
2 the world's clearest waters
3 the world's most beautiful beaches

4 unlimited dining, entertainment +
5 duty-free bar prices
6 a variety of exotic islands
marvellous shopping.

On your cruise liner there are hundreds of activities, ample sun decks + lounging chairs (no charge!) Swimming pools and bars. Deck Sports include clay pigeon shooting, shuffle-board, table tennis, jogging, volleyball + keep fit classes.

ST THOMAS – VIRGIN ISLANDS
This is everyone's idea of the perfect Caribbean island. A delightful mixture of Danish, American, English and, some say, pirate influences. It has one of the world's 10 best beaches + fantastic duty-free shopping.

DINING

NASSAU – BAHAMAS
Late evening arrival gives you ~~time~~ a full night to enjoy the Bahamas' best night-life before breakfast sailing. Do NOT miss the revere + Casino at Paradise Island. REVUE

After your cruise, why not extend yr stay at one of our hotels in Miami Beach, Key Biscayne or Nassau?

FORMAT FOR EFFECTIVE DISPLAY

Important lines can be given prominence by using:

(a) Spaced capitals, ie, leave one space between letters and 3 spaces between words. To centre words that have to be typed in

S P A C E D   C A P I T A L S

say the letters and spaces in pairs, backspacing once for each complete pair, including the extra 2 spaces between words; eg, Sspace Pspace Aspace Cspace Espace Dspace space-space Cspace Aspace, etc. DO NOT backspace for the last letter in the final word.

(b) Closed capitals—leave NO space between letters and ONE space between words.

(c) Capitals and small letters.

(d) Underscoring.

Practise making your display effective

Notice the use of spaced capitals, closed capitals and the underscore to stress important lines in the exercise below.

5 Display the following notice on A5 portrait paper. (a) Centre the whole notice vertically. (b) Centre the longest line horizontally.

MEDWAY SECRETARIAL COLLEGE

offers Courses for

Leave 2 clear spaces here, ie, turn up 3 single spaces

Secretarial Linguists and

Executive Secretaries

also

S H O R T   C O U R S E S

for

Word Processor Operators

6 Display the following notice on A5 landscape paper. (a) Centre the whole notice vertically. (b) Centre the longest line horizontally.

P E N S O N ' S   R A D I O   C A R S

2 clear spaces here

24-hour Service

All cars radio-controlled

ANYWHERE/ANYTIME

Charged from point of pick-up

2 clear spaces here

Long Distance
Weddings
Airports

Type last 3 lines in single spacing

See Typing Target Practice, page 2 for further exercises on
Effective Display

A CARIBBEAN CRUISE – 27th Sept. – 6 Oct 1985

← It is no secret that ~~America~~ the U.S.A has become one of the most popular & reasonibly-priced holiday destiniations of the 1980s. [Where is the best place to go in a country three times the size of Europe? For an idea, look at the Americans themselves. You wl discover th the swing is to cruises in a big way. It is said th more people are cruising the Caribbean than anywhere else in the world.

Please correct 3 word errors

← CRUISE NUMBER ONE

DAY/DATE	PLACE	ARRIVE	DEPART
Friday 27 Sept	London Heathrow.	–	1025
	Miami Airport	1430	–
Saturday 28 Sept	Miami	–	1700
Sunday/ ~~29 Sept~~ Monday 29–30 Sept	At Sea	–	–
Tues 1 Oct	St. Thomas (Virgin Islands)	0700	1700
Wed 2 Oct	At Sea	–	–
Thurs/Fri 3–4 Oct	Nassau (Bahamas)	1800	0700
Friday 4 Oct	Out Island (Bahamas)	1100	1800
Sat 5 Oct	Miami	0800	–
	Miami Airport	–	1845
Sun 6 Oct	London Heathrow	0755	–

Continued/

Main headings
The main heading, the title of a passage, is blocked at the left margin when using blocked paragraphs. Unless otherwise instructed, always turn up 7 single spaces 25 mm (one inch) from the top edge of the paper before starting the main heading. It may be typed in:

(a) Closed capitals—leave one space between each word. The heading may or may not be underscored.
(b) Spaced capitals—leave one space between each letter and 3 spaces between each word. This heading may or may not be uncerscored.
(c) Lower case with initial capitals. This heading MUST be underscored.
(d) The underscore must not extend beyond the typing.

Practise typing an exercise with a main heading

1 Read through the exercise. (a) Type it on A5 landscape paper. (b) Single spacing. (c) Margins: elite 22–82, pica 12–72. (d) Follow layout and instructions given in the exercise.

↓ Turn up 7 single spaces

MAIN HEADING

↓ Turn up 2 single spaces

You must turn up 7 single spaces from the top edge of the paper before typing the main heading and, if the first paragraph is in single spacing, the paragraph starts on the second single space after the heading.

↓ Turn up 2 single spaces

Notice that in this exercise the heading is in closed capitals and is not underscored.

Subheadings
The main heading may be followed by a subheading which further clarifies the contents of the passage. Turn up 2 single spaces after typing the main heading and then type the subheading.

Practise typing an exercise with a subheading

2 Read through the following exercise. (a) Type it on A5 landscape paper. (b) Single spacing. (c) Margins: elite 22–82, pica 12–72. (d) Follow the layout and instructions given in the exercise.

↓ Turn up 7 single spaces

MAIN HEADING

↓ Turn up 2 single spaces

Subheadings

↓ Turn up 2 single spaces

The subheading is also typed at the left margin when the paragraphs are in blocked style. It may be typed in CLOSED CAPITALS or in lower case with initial capitals. All headings in lower case must be underscored.

You should turn up 2 single spaces after the subheading (when the text is in single spacing) before starting the first paragraph.

See Typing Target Practice, page 3, for further exercises on

Typist: "% change" column – there is no space btwn the minus sign + the figure th follows. Please retain abbreviations

VEHICLE PRODUCTION - 000s

Country	Passenger cars		Total vehicles*		% Change
	1981	1982	1981	1982	
Belgium	216	246	248	278	1~~2~~1
France	2,612	2,777	3,019	3,149	4
Italy	1,257	1,280	1,434	1,432	0
UK	995	885	1,184	1,154	-3
West Germany	3,578	3,762	3,897	4,063	4
TOTAL EEC	8,~~696~~ 736	9,037	9,~~873~~ 872	10,176	3
Netherlands	78	87	90	100	10
Spain	855	910	987	1,045	6
Sweden	258	295	314	345	~~1~~ 9
Others	247	260	282	295	5
TOTAL	10,096	10,502	11455	11861	5
USA	6253	5073	7933	6984	-12
Canada	784	787	1,280	1,235	-4
Latin America	1119	1125	1549	1482	-4
Eastern Bloc	2,005	1,960	3,000	3,067	-2
Others	835	788	966	1,005	4
WORLD TOTAL	~~27,978~~ 28,019	27,172	37,430	36,30~~8~~4	-3

Please put in alpha order

* Includes commercial vehicles

Japan 6974 6890 11,180 10,737 -4

Paragraph headings
Apart from the main heading and the subheading at the beginning of a passage, paragraph headings are used to indicate subdivisions in the body of the text. In blocked style the paragraph heading starts at the left margin as in exercise 3 below.

Practise typing paragraph headings

3 Read through the following exercise. (a) Type it on A5 portrait paper. (b) Single spacing. (c) Margins: elite 13–63, pica 6–56. (d) Follow the layout and instructions given in the exercise.

Turn up 7 single spaces

G U I D E   T O   T Y P I S T S

Turn up 2 single spaces

Paragraph Headings

Turn up 2 single spaces

PARAGRAPH HEADINGS These may be typed in capitals with or without the underscore. Two spaces have been left, in this paragraph, between the paragraph heading and the first word of the text which follows.

Paragraph headings may run on without extra spaces after the last word (as in this paragraph) and, if typed in lower case, MUST be underscored.

Blocked exercises typed in double spacing

(a) If the text is typed in double spacing, turn up 2 double spaces after the main heading before typing the first paragraph.

(b) If, in addition to the main heading, there is a subheading, turn up one double between the main and subheading and 2 doubles after the subheading before typing the first paragraph.

Practise typing a blocked exercise in double spacing

4 Read through the following exercise. (a) Type it on A5 portrait paper. (b) Double spacing. (c) Margins: elite 13–63, pica 6–56. (d) Follow the layout and instructions given.

Turn up 7 single spaces

TYPING EXERCISES IN DOUBLE SPACING

Turn up 1 double space

Blocked Style

Turn up 2 double spaces

Two double spaces are turned up after the main heading or subheading - if there is one - before typing the first paragraph in double spacing.

Turn up 2 double spaces

Two double spaces are turned up between blocked paragraphs typed in double spacing.

See Typing Target Practice, pages 4 and 5, for further exercises on

Paragraph Headings
Typing in Double Spacing

Display on a card measuring 4″ × 6″ (shorter edge at top)

HOME-MADE SOUP ← closed caps

Side one

Avgolemoni: a popular Cypriot soup made from chicken, rice, eggs and lemon.

Psarosoupa: home-made fish + vegetable soup w. fresh fish, carrots, celery + spring onions. Extremely popular w. the Greek Islanders

Vegetable: home-made spring vegetable soup

~~Vothinosoupa: beef + onion soup~~ ℐ

DIPS ← spaced caps

Houmus: dip served w pitta PITTA

Gasiki: yogurt-based dip served w pitta

Tahini: a delicious dip w very strong garlic flavour served w. pitta

SPECIALITIES ← closed caps

Side 2

Mousaka: layers of potatoes, savoury mince, aubergines and marrows. Topped with cheese sauce.

Dolmas: vine leaves stuffed w savoury mince + rice. Served w. sliced potatoes + salad.

Stifado-beef: beef stuffed w onions + cooked in wine, vinegar + spices.

l.c. Vothino Psito: Traditional village Sunday dinner. Beef cooked in the oven w. local herbs + spices. Served w. wine + mushroom sauce, roast potatoes + salad.

ℐ v.c. Afelia: pork cooked in wine, ~~cariander~~ CORIANDER seeds + spices. ~~served w. wine, rice + salad.~~ Served w. rice + salad.

Shoulder headings
When this form of heading is used, it is typed at the left margin and may be in closed capitals. If it is typed in lower case with initial capitals, it must be underscored. It is preceded and followed by one blank line as in the exercises below.

Practise typing shoulder headings

5 Type a copy of the following on A5 landscape paper. (a) Blocked paragraphs. (b) Single spacing. (c) Margins. elite 22–82, pica 12–72. (d) Locate and correct 2 word errors.

FIRST AID

Turn up 2 single spaces

MINOR WOUNDS

Turn up 2 single spaces

All wounds and scratches must receive attention immediately. Delay increases the risk of infection. Cover the wound as soon as possible.

Turn up 2 single spaces

BLEEDING

Stop the bleeding at once and send promply for a doctor or an ambulance.

FRACTURES

Do not attempt to move a casuality with broken bones until the injured parts have been secured with triangular bandages or other suitable pieces of material, so that they cannot move.

6 Type a copy of the following on A5 portrait paper. (a) Blocked paragraphs. (b) Single spacing. (c) Margins: elite 13–63, pica 6–56. (d) Locate and correct one word error.

THE MANOR HOUSE

Great Hall

A carved stone chimney piece dominates the Hall. The central window on the courtyard side displays the family coat of arms.

Dining Room

The furniture in this room is made of oak and probably dates back to the 17th century.

Drawing Room

The portraits in the Drawing Room were all painted by the last Lord of the Manor. Concealed high up on the East wall is a hiding place, which is only accessable from the floor above.

See Typing Target Practice, page 6, for further exercises on
Shoulder Headings

CONSOLIDATION

Progress check

Task 27 ▶ *Format*
A4 paper

Output Target—20 minutes

<u>COMPUTER LANGUAGE</u>

Typist - please display w. side headings

KEYBOARD	Typewriter keyboard used for input & output of information.
FLOPPY DISK	Magnetic disk wh is inserted into the disk drive & stores large amts of information
HARDWARE	The machinery used in the system.
PRINTER	Machine wh produces permanent copies on paper.
SOFTWARE →	Instructions & programs tho make the computer work.
PROGRAMS →	The instructions needed to tell the computer what to do.
BASIC	Stands for: Basic All-purpose u.c. / instruction code. ← most commonly used personal computer language
CURSOR	The movable dot, hyphen or arrow wh indicates the typing point at wh the next typed character wl appear.
INPUT	Information entered in a data processing system.
OUTPUT	Information moved fr storage to an external source.
<u>Shared Logic</u> caps	Where a no. of keyboard terminals use the memory & processing ability of a single central processing unit.
TERMINAL	A ~~distant~~ remote device wh communicates w a central computer.
FORMAT	Arrangement & style of document.

<u>DISTRIBUTION</u>

Michael Craine
David Fletcher
Marie King
June Russell

Typist - please put side headings in alphabetical order.

Arrangement of items in columns
You may be required to arrange items in column form in such a way that they are horizontally centred on the page, with equal spaces between the columns and with equal margins. This can easily be done by means of the backspacing method you have already used in display work.

Tabulator key
All typewriters have 3 tabulator controls which you should locate on your machine as their positions vary on the different makes.

(a) A tab set key to fix the tab stops.
(b) A tab clear key to clear the tab stops.
(c) A tab bar or key to move the carriage/carrier to wherever a tab stop is set.

Horizontal centring
(a) Move margin stops to extreme left and right.
(b) Clear all previous tab stops that may be already set. On most machines this can be done by pressing the clear key while returning the carriage/carrier. On other machines there are special devices for this purpose.
(c) Make certain that the left edge of the paper is at 0 on the carriage position scale.
(d) Backspace once for every 2 characters and spaces in the longest item of each column saying them to yourself in pairs. If there is an odd letter left over in any column, carry this on to the next column.
(e) Add together the total number of spaces to be left between all the columns plus any odd character (if there is one) left from the last column and divide by 2—backspace this number (ignore fractions).
(f) Set left margin stop at the point thus reached.
(g) Starting from the left margin, tap space bar once for each character and space in the longest line of the first column and once for each blank space between first and second column. Set first tab stop at this point for the start of the second column and make a note of this figure.
(h) Starting from this first tab stop, again tap space bar once for each character and space in the longest item of the second column and for each blank space between second and third columns.
(i) Set second tab stop at this point for the start of the third column and make a note of this figure.
(j) Continue in the same way for any additional columns.
(k) Return carriage/carrier and test tab stop settings.

Vertical centring
The correct vertical arrangement of columns will add greatly to the effectiveness of your display. Use the same method of vertical centring as explained on page 34.

Typing the table
(a) Insert the paper and turn up the appropriate number of vertical line spaces.
(b) Type the main heading at the left margin.
(c) Turn up 2 single (one double) spaces.
(d) At left margin type first item in first column.
(e) Tabulate to second column and type first item; then tabulate to each of the remaining columns and complete the first line.
(f) Continue in the same way with the rest of the table.

Note: It is essential that you complete each horizontal line before starting the next.

FORMAT FOR ROUTING/CIRCULATION SLIP

Sometimes an instruction sheet, or a special bulletin, has to be seen by a number of persons. If there is no advantage in duplicating the message so that each individual may have a personal copy, a routing slip is attached so that each person concerned receives the original copy in turn. The routing slip will have a heading such as PLEASE READ, INITIAL AND DATE, AND PASS QUICKLY. Then the names of the persons who should read the material are typed below. C6 paper is used for a routine slip. When the person named has read the information, he crosses his name off the list and passes it along to the next person on the list.

FORMAT FOR DISTRIBUTION LIST

When a document has to be distributed to a number of people and the author wishes all of them to know that each has had a copy, a DISTRIBUTION LIST is typed at the foot of the document. Each person's name is then ticked or underlined on separate copies. An example of a distribution list is given at the end of the next exercise.

7 Type the following exercise on a sheet of A4 plain paper. Correct word errors.

FROM The Chairman TO The Managing Director

REF 129/AR/C/OD DATE 26 June 1985

At the end of May, after 4 years, it was found necessary to close the generous early retirement scheme which has helped to reduce our man-
C/ power by nearly 25% without/redundancy. /enforced
Run on

We take pride in this achievement, and are seeing its benefits in the shape of a high level of co-operation in seeking even greater
N.P./ efficiencies. Insert A Recruitment has been severely restricted in the last 3 years, but we continue to work closely w the Manpower Services Commission in the provision of training ~~and work experience courses~~
~~under the Government's new training~~ initiative. We are sponsoring an Industrial Training Workshop to serve the West Midlands area.
The directors are keenly aware of the necessity of ensuring that employers hv an adequate income Insert B. Accordingly, a pension scheme is now operated by the Company to provide retirement pensions with a maximum, after 40 years' contributory service, of two-thirds of final pensionible earnings; there are also lump sum dedath-in-service benefits and pensions for surviving spouses. ←

I hope th the currant yr wl bring some improvement and opportunities/: it wl certainly pose problems wh, I am confident, w our hard-working and resourceful employees, we wl solve.

'A' The objectives achieved wd hv bn costly indeed in human terms if they hd bn won at the expense of the livelihoods of persons who hv served the company loyaly.

'B' , not only when working f the co, but also when they retire.

The scheme was subject to a satisfactory actuarial valuation as at April 1985.

DISTRIBUTION

Company Secretary
Chief Accountant
Production Manager
Purchasing Manager
Marketing Manager

Routing/Circulation Slip

See Typing Target Practice, page 86, for a further exercise on

Distribution List

Practise typing column display

1 Carrying out the instructions given on page 39, type the following table on A5 landscape paper. (a) Centre the table vertically and horizontally. (b) Leave 3 spaces between columns. (c) Double spacing.

Left margin: 33(24)

1st tab stop: 47(38)
2nd tab stop: 58(49)

COMMONLY MISSPELLED WORDS

conscious	separate	medicine
regrettable	aerial	feasible
audio	eighth	withhold
woollen	schedule	privilege
rhythm	seize	tendency

The calculations for the vertical centring in the above exercise are as follows:

(a) Number of vertical line spaces on A5 landscape paper =35
(b) Number of vertical lines and spaces in table =11
(c) Difference to be divided between top and bottom margins 35 − 11 = 24
(d) Divide by 2 (ignore fractions) =12
(e) Begin typing heading on 13th line, so leaving 12 clear.

2 Type the following table on A5 landscape paper. (a) Centre vertically and horizontally. (b) Leave 3 spaces between columns. (c) Double spacing. (d) Correct the word error.

PRESTEL SERVICES

National News	Career Data	General Interest
Food prices	Racing Information	Weather Forcast
Zodiac	Stock Exchange	Good Food Guide

3 Type the following table on A5 portrait paper. (a) Centre vertically and horizontally. (b) Leave 3 spaces between columns. (c) Double spacing.

TELECOMMUNICATION SERVICE

Telephone Area Offices

Sales	Freefone 2461
General	Freefone 7402
Radio Paging	021-242 3061
Prestel Enquiries	Freefone 2692
Confravision Bookings	021-242 3641

See Typing Target Practice, page 7, for further exercises on

6 Type a copy of the following curriculum vitae on a sheet of A4 paper.

Katrina Maxwell de Barnes
7 Penzance Way
Madron
PENZANCE
Cornwall
TR20 8SW

DATE OF BIRTH	1 June 1967 (corrected to 6)
EDUCATION	Penzance High School - 1979-1985 (corrected to 1978-1984) 'O' Levels - 7 subjects including English & maths 'A' Levels - 3 subjects - English, French & maths
SECRETARIAL TRAINING	1984-1985
l.c.	PENZANCE COLLEGE OF FE (in full) Subjects included - communication, computer studies, structure of business, sec. duties, s'hand, typewriting, audio-typing Word processor - hands-on experience The classroom typewriters were electronic
EXAMINATIONS PASSED	S'hand Typists' Cert - 80 wpm " (typed transcript) 100 wpm Typewriting - Stage III Computers in Data Processing - Stage II Information Processing - Stage II Audio-Typing - Stage III
l.c. SPECIAL INTERESTS	Youth Club Activities, Swimming, Horse Riding, Skating
REFEREE	Mrs J Jackson, Hd of Sec. Dept Penzance College of FE Truro Road, Penzance, Cornwall. TR21 2RJ Telephone No. 0736 3553 (transposed to 3535)
AVAILABLE ~~FROM~~ FOR EMPLOYMENT	15 July 1985

24 June 1985

SECTION 54

See Typing Target Practice, page 85, for a further exercise on

Curriculum Vitae

FORMAT FOR COLUMN HEADINGS—BLOCKED STYLE

In addition to the main heading of a table, each column may have a heading. The length of the column heading must be taken into account when deciding which is the longest line in each column. When there are headings above columns, proceed as follows:

(a) Find longest line in each column. It could be the heading or a column item.
(b) Backspace as usual to find left margin, remembering to take into account the spacing between columns, and set left margin and tab stops. Column headings and column items start at the left margin and at the tab stops set for the longest line of each column/heading.
(c) Turn up 2 single (one double) after the main heading.
(d) Turn up 2 single (one double) after the column headings.

Practise typing column work with blocked headings

4 Following the above instructions, type this exercise on A5 landscape paper. (a) Centre the whole table vertically and horizontally. (b) Leave 3 spaces between columns. (c) Double spacing.

SALE BARGAINS

<u>All reduced</u>

<u>Ladies' Fashions</u>	<u>Furniture</u>	<u>Children's Wear</u>
Three-quarter length coats	Divan set	Nappies
Shoes	Brass light fitting	Track suits
Rainwear	Pine dresser	Pinafore dresses
Embroidered blouses	Corner cabinet	Dungarees

5 Type the following exercise on A5 portrait paper. (a) Centre the table vertically and horizontally. (b) Leave 3 spaces between columns. (c) Double spacing.

PRODUCTION

<u>Major subdivisions</u>

INDUSTRY	DIRECT SERVICES	COMMERCE
Farming	Judiciary	Banking
Fishing	Accountancy	Transport
Mining	Police	Insurance
Oil Drilling	Education	Warehousing

6 Type the following exercise on A5 landscape paper. (a) Centre the table vertically and horizontally. (b) Leave 3 spaces between columns. (c) Double spacing.

REFERENCE BOOKS

<u>General</u>	<u>English</u>	<u>Forms of Address</u>
Pear's Cyclopaedia	Modern English Usage	Titles and Forms of Address
Timetables	Roget's Thesaurus	Debrett's Correct Form
Whitaker's Almanack	Oxford Dictionary	Whitaker's Almanack

See Typing Target Practice, page 8, for further exercises on

(b) Using the original prepared on page 155, insert the following information:

Our Ref FE/your initials Today's date
Addressee Mr F L Wilkes 24–28 High Street Brierley Hill West Midlands DY3 1DE
Order dated insert sutable date and numbered S.2906 Delivery 4 weeks

(c) Using a carbon copy prepared in (a) on page 155, insert the following information:

Our Ref FE/your initials Today's date
Addressee Mrs S Franklyn 20 Market Street Barnsley South Yorkshire S4 8EZ
Order dated insert suitable date and numbered P.3347 Delivery 2 weeks

(d) Using the remaining carbon copy, insert the following information:

Our Ref FE/your initials Today's date
Addressee Mr L Yates 73 Lionel Street Burton-on-Trent Staffs DE13 1NF
Order dated insert suitable date and numbered A.6834 Delivery 3 weeks

FORMAT FOR CURRICULUM VITAE

5 Type the following exercise on A4 paper in double spacing and with blocked paragraphs.

CURRICULUM VITAE - A BRIEF ACCOAUNT OF ONE'S CAREER   Correct word errors

When you apply for a job, yr prospective employer wl require a summary of yr education & training. He wl want to know what academic qualifications y hv; what specialist qualifications you hv; what yr main interests are; what recreational activities and hobies y hv, etc. Sometimes this information is referred to as a personal data sheet or curriculum vitae.

lc/ No 2 people and no 2 personal data Sheets shd be exactly the same. It is possible th y wl arrange your record of yr career in a different (somewhat) way when applying f different jobs: y wl always wish to emphasise the qualities & qualifications th wd make y valuable in the particular job f wh y are applying. NP/ [If you hv worked in the - for a salary or as a volunteer - y shd mention this. Yr work need not be closely related to the work f wh y are applying, but it may indicate to yr prospective employer a measure of yr intelligent thinking, dependability, resourcefullness, etc. Always list part-time work. [It is usual to include the name and address of one referee. See th y give the person's name - correctly spelled - title (Mr, Mrs, Miss, Ms) & correct address & tel no. NEVER, in any circumstances, give as a reference a person whose permission y hv not asked in advance.

Yr curriculum vitae/personal data sheet must be perfectly typed & clearly displayed w main, sub, & side/shoulder headings. The following points shd be covered: lc Yr name & address; date of birth; work experience (if any); special interests; name & address of a referee; date on wh y are available f employment.

SECTION 54

Curriculum Vitae

See Typing Target Practice, page 84, for a further exercise on

Form Letters

FORMAT FOR MEASUREMENTS

When typing measurements note the following:

(a) the letter "x" (lower case) is used for the word "by",
eg, 210 × 297 mm (space before and after the "x").

(b) ONE space is left after the numbers and before the unit of measurement,
eg, 210 (space) mm; 2 (space) ft 6 (space) in.

(c) Groups of figures should not be separated at line ends.

(d) Abbreviations do not take an "s" in the plural, eg, 6 in; 2 yd; 6 lb; 2 mm; 4 kg.

(e) When using OPEN PUNCTUATION there is no full stop after any abbreviation, unless at the end of a sentence.

Practise typing measurements

1 Type each of the following lines 3 times on A5 landscape paper. (a) Margins: elite 22–82, pica 12–72. (b) Pay particular attention to spacing in measurements.

```
Height: 2 ft 6½ in (775 mm); Length: 1 ft 8 in (505 mm); 12 ft
1 lb 4 oz or 567 g.  50 kg or 7 lb 12 oz.  6 miles or 9.656 km
14 ft × 12 ft (4.26 × 3.65 m).  10 yd × 11 yd (9.14 × 10.05 m)
```

FORMAT FOR DECIMALS

(a) Always use full stop for decimal point. This is usually typed in the normal position of the full stop.

(b) Leave NO space before or after decimal point.

(c) No punctuation required at the end of figures except at the end of a sentence.

(d) Always insert the number of decimal places required by using zero.
Examples: 2 decimal places: type
86.40 NOT 86.4
3 decimal places: type
95.010 NOT 95.01.

Practise typing decimals

2 Type the following sentences 3 times. (a) Margins: elite 22–82, pica 12–72.

```
Add up 12.54, 13.02, 24.60, 6.75 and 0.20 and you get 57.11.
The sheet measures 1.200 × 5.810 × 2.540 m; the gross weight
is approximately 50.802 kg and the net weight is 38.102 kg.
```

FORMAT FOR SUMS OF MONEY IN CONTEXT

(a) If the sum comprises only pounds, type as follows: £5, £10 OR £5.00, £10.00.

(b) If only pence, type: 10p, 97p.
Note: No space between figures and letter p, and no full stop after p (unless, of course, it ends a sentence).

(c) With mixed amounts, ie, sums comprising pounds and pence, the decimal point and the £ symbol should always be used, but NOT the abbreviation p.
Example: £7.05.

(d) If the sum contains a decimal point but no whole pounds, a nought should be typed after the £ symbol and before the point.
Example: £0.97.

(e) The halfpenny is expressed by a fraction.
Example: 3½p or £0.03½.

Practise typing sums of money in context

3 Type the following exercise in double spacing. (a) Margins: elite 22–82, pica 12–72. (b) Locate and correct one word error.

```
We thank you for your check for £20.10, and we enclose our

credit note for £0.50, which, together with our previous

credit note for £1.90, makes up the total amount of our last

invoice for £22.50.  Our present discount for cash monthly

is 2½%.
```

See Typing Target Practice, pages 9 and 10, for further exercises on

FORMAT FOR FILLING IN FORM LETTERS

The following steps should be taken when you fill in a form letter:

(a) Insert the form letter into the machine so that the first line of the body of the letter is just above the alignment scale.

(b) By means of the paper release, adjust the paper so that the base of the entire line is in alignment with the top of the alignment scale (this position may vary with certain makes of machines) and so that an "i" or "l" aligns up exactly with one of the guides on the alignment scale.

(c) Set margin stops and paper guide. The margin stops should be set to correspond to the margins already used in the duplicated letter.

(d) Turn the cylinder back 2 single spaces (4 notches for machines with half-spacing) and, if not already typed, insert salutation at the left margin.

(e) Turn the cylinder back a sufficient number of spaces and type the reference.

(f) Turn up 2 single spaces and type the date.

(g) Turn up 2 single spaces and type the name and address of addressee.

(h) Insert any details required in the body of the letter. Remember to leave one clear space after the last character before starting to type the "fill in".

(i) Check carefully.

Note: DELETIONS. It is often necessary to delete letters or words in a form, form letter or a circular letter. For instance, in exercise 4(b) on page 156 you are writing to a man and, therefore, it will be necessary to delete /Madam in the salutation. To delete previously typed characters, use a small x aligned precisely with the characters previously typed.

2 Following the instructions given above, and using the original of the form letter prepared in exercise 1 on page 154, insert the following details:
Your Ref. MAP/RES   Our Ref. LDA/your initials   Today's date
Addressee: J. Ellis (Hardware) Ltd., 62 Ipswich Road, STOWMARKET, Suffolk. IP14 1AA
Invoice No. 5490   Dated (suitable date)   for £260.50

3 On the carbon copy of the form letter prepared in exercise 1 on page 154, insert the following details:
Your Ref. SW/SP   Our Ref. LDA/your initials   Today's date
Addressee: Messrs. Barrett & Obrien, 17 Hanover Road, STRANRAER, Wigtonshire. DG9 7SA
Invoice No. 3572   Dated (suitable date)   for £945.74

4 (a) Prepare the following skeleton letter, taking 2 carbon copies. Use A5 portrait paper and margins of elite 12–62, pica 5–55. A skeleton of the following letter is given in the *Teaching Notes and Solutions* and may be copied.

J A RANKIN & CO LTD
Trinity Road
LUTON Bedfordshire LU4 5TJ
(Turn up 2 single spaces)

Our Ref

(Turn up 10 single spaces)

Dear Sir/Madam

We thank you for your order dated (leave blank)
and numbered (8 blanks). We have pleasure in advis-
ing you that delivery will be made in (3 blanks) weeks.

Yours faithfully
J A RANKIN & CO LTD

Continued overleaf

FORMAT FOR ENUMERATED ITEMS

Paragraphs and items are sometimes numbered or lettered as follows. The numbers or letters may stand on their own or be enclosed in brackets. Two spaces follow the last figure, letter or bracket,

eg, 1 Surname	(1) Surname	A Surname	(a) Surname
2 Christian name	(2) Christian name	B Christian name	(b) Christian name

Practise typing numbered items

4 Type the following on A5 landscape paper. (a) Use single spacing if an item goes on to more than one line, but double spacing between each item. (b) Margins: elite 22–82, pica 12–72. (c) Leave 2 spaces after the item number.

ORGANISATION OF A MEETING

On the day of the meeting the secretary should:

1 Check that the room is prepared.

2 See that clear directions have been given at reception for the venue of the meeting.

3 Ensure that all attending sign the Attendance Register.

4 Take notes of the main points under discussion, including verbatim notes of motions.

5 Make a note of any actions which her boss is asked to undertake.

5 Type the following on A5 portrait paper. (a) Use single spacing with double between each item. (b) Margins: elite 13–63, pica 6–56. (c) Leave 2 clear spaces after the bracketed letters. (d) Correct the word error.

AUDIO-TYPING

Some Dictating Conventions

The following points should be noted before commencing your audio-typing course.

(a) New paragraphs will be indicated.

(b) All punctuation marks (with the exception of the comma and apostrophe) will be dictated.

(c) The spelling of unusual words will be given after the word has been dictated. The Post Office phonetic alphabet will be used only when dictating single letters which need identification.

(d) If a word is to be underscored the instruction "underscore" will be given after the word has been dictated.

(e) Any specific instructions for headings will preceed the words of the heading.

precede.

See Typing Target Practice, page 11, for further exercises on

FORMAT FOR FORM LETTERS

Many firms use duplicated letters, printed forms, or postcards to send to customers. Details for each customer have to be filled in. Such letters or forms are known as "Form Letters". If details have to be filled in on ruled lines, or over dotted lines, it is essential that you type slightly above these lines.

Preparation of a form letter

1 Prepare the skeleton letter below, taking one carbon copy. To do this take the following steps:

(a) Use A5 portrait paper.
(b) Centre and type the name and address of the sender, starting on the fourth single space from top edge of paper.
(c) Set margins at scale-points elite 12–62, pica 5–55.
(d) After last line of sender's address, turn up 2 single spaces and type Your Ref.
(e) Turn up one single space and type Our Ref.
(f) To allow for date, name and address of addressee and for one clear space after last line of address, turn up 10 single spaces. Care should be taken to see that there is a clear space between last line of address and the salutation. If necessary, put more than one item of address on a line.
(g) Type Dear Sirs,.
(h) Turn up 2 single spaces and type remainder of letter, leaving clear spaces as indicated to accommodate the details given in exercises 2 and 3 on page 155.

NEWTOWN WHOLESALE STORES LTD.
New Street, Sheffield. S5 8UP
(Turn up 2 single spaces)

Your Ref.
Our Ref.

Note: A skeleton copy of this letter is given in the *Teaching Notes and Solutions* and may be copied.

(Turn up 10 single spaces)

Dear Sirs,

Please send us a copy of your invoice No. (leave blank)
dated (leave 16 spaces) for (leave 9 spaces) the receipt
of which we cannot trace. Your prompt attention
will be appreciated.

Yours faithfully,
NEWTON WHOLESALE STORES LTD.

Secretary

EXPRESSING WORDS AND FIGURES

(a) Use words instead of figures for number one on its own and for numbers at the beginning of a sentence. But if number one is part of a list of figures it should be typed as a figure, eg, "Follow the instructions 1, 2 and 3."
(b) Use figures in all other cases.

TYPING FROM MANUSCRIPT COPY

You may have to type letters or documents from handwritten drafts. Take particular care to produce a correct copy. Before typing, first read the document through to see that you understand it. Some words or letters, not very clear in one part, may be repeated in another part more clearly. Check the completed exercise and circle any error before removing the paper from the typewriter.

Practise typing from manuscript copy

1 Type the following on A5 landscape paper. (a) Read the whole passage through before you start to type. (b) From the top edge of the paper turn up 7 single spaces. (c) Margins: elite 22–82, pica 12–72. (d) Double spacing. (e) Keep to the lines as in the copy.

HIGH SPEED SHORTHAND WRITING

If you wish to write at over 120 words per minute it is
imperative that you practise writing shorthand regularly.
The more effort you put into your practice, and the more
frequently you take dictation, at least one or 2 periods of
one hour a day, the faster you will write. You MUST perse-
vere. You will feel a great sense of achievement when you
are able to take dictation at high speeds — over 140 words
per minute.

2 Type the following on A5 portrait paper. (a) Read the paragraphs through carefully before you start to type. (b) From the top edge of the paper turn up 7 single spaces. (c) Margins: elite 13–63, pica 6–56. (d) Double spacing. (e) Keep to the lines as in the copy.

SEAT BELTS
Seat belts must be in proper working order to comply with the law. If your belts are damaged, they
may not function correctly and may, therefore, be
dangerous as well as illegal. Look out for any
sign of damage that may weaken the belts, particularly if they have been caught in doors or under
seats.
As from 31 January 1983, a law was enforced which
states that seat belts must be worn by all travelling in the front seats of a car.

See Typing Target Practice, page 12, for further exercises on
Typing from Manuscript

Details of any decisions or resolutions, or business discussed at a meeting, are recorded and preserved. These are known as minutes. Each minute is usually numbered as this facilitates indexing. The order in which the minutes are typed always follows the order in which the items appeared on the agenda.

1. Description of meeting, including time, date and place.
2. Names of those present—chairman's name appearing first, followed by the names of the officers/members.
3. Apologies received.
4. Reading of minutes of last meeting.
5. Matters arising.
6. Correspondence.
7. Reports of officers.
8. General business discussed—with details of any resolutions taken.
9. Any other business.
10. Place, date and time of next meeting.
11. Place for chairman's signature.
12. Date on which minutes were signed.

5 Type the following minutes with side headings and open punctuation on A4 paper. Set tab stop for the side headings at elite 13, pica 11, and at elite 21, pica 19. Set left margin at elite 42, pica 40. Leave 3 spaces between columns and follow the layout.

Minutes of a committee meeting of the Gardeners' Club held at the George Hotel, Scarborough, on 24 May 1985.

PRESENT

Ms Hilda Baker (Chairperson)
Mrs Reneé Long
Mr Seamus Cassidy
Rev Francis de Munck
Miss Harriett Humphrey
Mr Callum MacKay
Mr Kevin Brady
John Bryden (Secretary)

Please type in alphabetical order

182.1	APOLOGIES	Apologies were received from Ms Fiona Vanderbilt and Ms Matilda Brookside.
182.2	MINUTES	The Secretary read the minutes of the committee meeting held on 6 March. These were signed by the Chair~~man~~ person as being a correct record.
182.3	MATTERS ARISING	The Chair~~man~~ person was asked if the subcommittee had reported on the complaint about the jud~~i~~gi~~n~~ng at the Spring Show in April. She said that the subcommittee hoped to report this week.
182.4	CORRESPONDENCE	There was no correspondence.
182.5	FLOWER SHOW JUDGES	It was unanimously agreed that the same people as last year be asked to act as judges.
182.6	NEXT MEETING	It was agreed th the next meeting wd be held at the George Hotel on 5 July 1985 at 1900 hours.
1~~9~~82.7	CLOSE OF MEETING	The Chair~~man~~person thanked the committee members for attending.

CHAIR~~MAN~~PERSON ....

DATE ....

See Typing Target Practice, page 83, for a further exercise on

SECURING A SATISFACTORY RIGHT MARGIN

Up to this stage in the book you have always returned the carriage/carrier at the same point as in the exercise from which you have been copying. This is not usually possible, of course, and in a great many exercises you will have to decide your own line-endings to secure a satisfactory right margin. To warn you that you are nearing the right margin a bell will ring.

MARGIN BELL

Before you can practise making your own right margin, it is necessary to become accustomed to listening for the margin bell. On your own typewriter find out how many spaces there are after the margin bell has rung before reaching the set right margin.

Practise listening for the margin bell

1 Type the following on A5 landscape paper and note the instructions. (a) Use single spacing. (b) Margins: elite 22–82, pica 12–72. (c) Listen for the margin bell but follow the copy line for line. (d) Locate and correct one word error.

```
MARGIN BELL

Five to 10 spaces from the right margin a bell on your type-
writer will ring to warn you that you are almost at the end
of the writing line.  It is necessary to train yourself to
listen for this warning bell, and to react as follows:

(a)  if the bell rings at the begining of a new word of more
than 5-10 letters, divide the word at the first available
point;

(b)  if the bell rings at the end of a word, do not type a
new word on that line unless it is a word of less than
5-10 letters (or 2 words such as 'for it' or 'I am', etc) or
unless the new word can be divided at an appropriate point.

The object of dividing a word at the end of a line is to
avoid an uneven right margin.
```

MARGIN RELEASE

If you have to complete a word which cannot be divided, the margin can be unlocked by pressing the margin release key (usually found at the top right- or left-hand side of the keyboard). The word can then be completed. Use the margin release key only when absolutely necessary—a good typist rarely uses it. The margin release key will release the left margin as well as the right.

Practise using the margin release

2 Type each of the following sentences exactly as they appear, using the margin release key where necessary. (a) Use A5 landscape paper. (b) Double spacing. (c) Margins: elite 22–82, pica 12–72.

This is a luxury hotel in the heart of the Peak National Park.

All you have to do is book in advance – at least by 1600 hours.

The truth about cavity walls is that they should prevent dampness.

4 Type the following Notice of Annual General Meeting and Agenda of a Public Limited Company on A4 paper. Margins: elite 20–85, pica 11–76. Use open punctuation and follow the layout given in the exercise.

VIDEX OFFICE SUPPLIES plc

NOTICE OF THE ANNUAL GENERAL MEETING

Notice is heeby given that the Thirty-first Annual General Meeting of the Company will be held at the Grand Hotel, Leamington Spa, on Wednesday, 3 April, 1985, at 11.30 am for the following purposes:

1 To receive the Directors' Report and Accounts for the year ended 31 December, 1984, + to declare a final dividend.

2 To re-elect Mr S D Parker as a Director of the Company in accordance with Article 108.

3 To reappoint the Auditors, Watergate and Bright, and to authorize the Directors to fix their remuneration.

4 Special Business

To consider and if thought fit pass the RESOLUTIONS set out in The Notice of Special Business, enclosed w these accounts.

BY ORDER OF THE BOARD

FRASER SCOTT

SECRETARY

Hemming Road
LEAMINGTON SPA
Warwickshire CV32 4LY

A Member of the Company entitled to attend and vote at this meeting may appoint one or more persons as his proxy to attend and vote in his stead. A proxy need not be a Member of the Company.

Proxy cards must be lodged at the office of the Company's Registrars not less than 48 hours before the time appointed, for the mtg.

In accordance with the Companies Act 1967, and the requirements of The Stock Exchange, there are available for inspection at the Registered Office of the Company during usual business hours

(a) a register in which details of all transactions in the equity share capital of the Company in respect of all Directors, including family interests, are recorded;

(b) a copy of every service contract w the Company or any of its subsidiaries, or a memorandum ~~which~~ where applicable, for each and every Director of the Company.

NP The documents wl be available for inspection at the place of the Annual General Meeting for at least 15 minutes before + during the mtg.

See Typing Target Practice, pages 80, 81 and 82, for further exercises on

GUIDE FOR DIVIDING WORDS AT LINE-ENDS

It may be necessary to divide some words in order to keep the right margin as even as possible. Always type the hyphen at the end of the line before typing the remaining part of the word on the next line.

Divide words:

(a) According to syllables
per-fect, under-stand.
(b) After a prefix, or before a suffix
com-bine, wait-ing.
(c) When a consonant is doubled divide between the 2 consonants
excel-lent, neces-sary.
(d) Compound words and words already hyphenated must be divided at the hyphen
pre-eminent, self-taught.
(e) The pronunciation of a word must not be changed
prop-erty, not pro-perty.

Do not divide:

(a) Words of one syllable or their plurals
niece, nieces, case, cases.
(b) At a point which would bring 2 letters only to the second line
waited not wait-ed.
(c) After an initial one letter syllable
again not a-gain.
(d) Proper names
Johnson, Cambridge.
(e) Numbers or courtesy titles from the words to which they refer
10 years, Mr Jones.
(f) On more than 2 consecutive lines.
(g) The last word of a paragraph or page.
(h) Sums of money or figures.

Practise line-end division of words

3 Copy each of the following lines once for practice and then once for accuracy. (a) Use A5 landscape paper. (b) Margins: elite 22–82, pica 12–72. (c) Single spacing. (d) Note where the word is divided and where division is not possible.

```
sten-cil, pad-lock, mur-mur, pen-cil, prac-tise, elec-trical
com-ply, con-sent, dis-agree, sec-tion, trust-ing, pay-ments
cab-bage, stut-ter, neces-sity, suf-fix, sup-pose, sup-plied
self-support, re-entrance, dinner-time, chil-dren, prob-lems
case, cases, box, boxes, dose, doses; quickly, wrecked, into
unit, await, adore, Gladstone, Mrs Singh, London, £1,000,000
```

4 Type the following paragraph, making correct line-end division where necessary. (a) Use A5 landscape paper. (b) Margins: elite 22–82, pica 12–72. (c) Double spacing.
Note: The words to be divided are: banking, personal, customer, payment.

```
Today an American bank launched what it calls the home banking and

information system.  The customer needs a small personal computer, a

television set and a telephone line.  For a charge of about £5 a month

the bank will provide the customer with the full range of banking

services: direct payment of bills, checking account balances, trans-

fer of funds from one account to another, etc.
```

2 Type the following Notice of Meeting and Agenda on A4 paper. (a) Margins: elite 20–85, pica 15–75. (b) Single spacing for the Notice and double, NOT SINGLE, between the numbered items in the Agenda. (c) Use indented paragraphs and centred style. (d) Correct the word error.

centre on paper l.c./

THE GARDENERS' CLUB
20 Manor Road, SCARBOROUGH
NORTH Yorkshire YO11 7RY

3 May 1985

l.c./ A meeting of the Committee of the Gardeners' Club will be held in the Regency Room of the George Hotel, Station Street, Scarborough, on Friday, 24 May, at 1900 hours.

A G E N D A ← centre on typing line

Centre longest item on typing line

1 Apologies
2 Secretary to read the Minutes of last meeting /l.c.
3 Matters arising from the Minutes /l.c.
4 Correspondance
5 Judges for the September flower show
6 Any other business
7 Date and time of next meeting ← turn up 5 single spaces

John Bryden
SECRETARY

3 Type the following Chairman's Agenda on A4 paper in single spacing with double between the numbered items. (a) Margins: elite 13–90, pica 11–77. (b) Type the arabic numbers for the NOTES column at elite 54, pica 45, and centre the word NOTES between this point and the right margin. (c) Use the heading, date and first paragraph from the above exercise.

Double spacing between items

	AGENDA	NOTES
		(54, 45)
1	Ask the Secretary, Mr Bryden, to read the apologies	1
2	Ask Mr Bryden to read the Minutes /l.c. of the last committee Meeting /l.c.	2
3	Matters arising: result of the enquiry into the complaint about the judging ~~last Sept~~ at the Spring Show in April	3
4	No correspondence	4
5	Judges for the September Flower show /u.c.	5
6	Date and time of next meeting. Suggest 5 July	~~7~~ 6
7	Chairman to declare the meeting closed	7

Practise making your own line-endings

5 Type the following exercise on A5 portrait paper. (a) Make your own line-endings. (b) Margins: elite 12–60, pica 6–54. (c) Double spacing. (d) Locate and correct one word error.

DATA COMMUNICATIONS

Local Area Networks, Viewdata, Packet Switching - these are just some of the rapid and very exciting developements taking place in the field of Data Communications. As there is such a large demand for information on this very complex subject, we are arranging a special Seminar for Managers who are likely to be involved in computer or office machine communications.

The Seminar will be held on Monday, 17 September 1984, at our main offices in London.

6 Type the following exercise on A5 landscape paper. (a) Make your own line-endings. (b) Margins: elite 20–85, pica 11–76. (c) Single spacing. (d) Locate and correct one word error.

THE ELECTRONIC MEMORY TYPEWRITER

The electronic memory typewriter has a memory which is very versatile and provides maximum productivity to users.

The versatility of the electronic typewriter allows you, the operator, to fulfill most tasks with speed and ease. Special features, such as automatic carrier return, centring, error correction and paragraph indentation, all contribute to very high productivity.

7 Type the following exercise on A5 portrait paper. (a) Make your own line-endings. (b) Margins: elite 12–60, pica 6–54. (d) Single spacing. (e) Locate and correct one word error.

TELEPHONE CONFERENCING SYSTEM

A new telephone conferencing system which allows up to 10 people to hold a meeting over the phone is now undergoing trials by British Telecom.

The participants will be able to join the conference from the nearest phone, even from a public kiosk.

The conference will be set up by booking a date, time and duration through a London centre. A London telephone number will then be allocated for the conference. Particpants ring the number at the stated time, and will then be connected to the conference which can be arranged at any time between 8 am and 6 pm Monday to Friday, except public holidays.

See Typing Target Practice, page 13, for further exercises on

1 Type the following information about notices of meetings and agendas. Use A4 paper and suitable margins.

NOTICES OF MEETINGS & AGENDAS

Block

← For formal meetings such as Annual General Meetings, General Meetings, Extraordinary General Meetings, Committee Meetings, etc, written notices are sent to those entitled to attend. [The notice, wh is prepared by the secretary, shld contain details of date, place & time of mtg. The salutation & complimentary close may be omitted. The notice may be typed in centred or blocked style w open or full punctuation.

NP/

When the notice of a mtg is sent out, it is normal practice to include the agenda wh is a list of items to be discussed at a mtg, these being listed in a certain order & numbered for easy ref as follows:

1. Apologies.
2. Minutes of last mtg.
3. Matters arising out of minutes..
4.5 Reports.
5.4 Correspondence. 6. Any special points for discussion.
7. Any other business. 8. Date of next mtg.

NP/ [The agenda may be typed on a stencil, or one original prepared & then photocopied, or it may be printed if a great many copies are req'd. Whatever method is used, there shld be sufficient copies to send one to each person entitled to attend, & additional copies f those members who forget to bring one to the meeting.

CAPS/ The word agenda is blocked at the left margin or centred on the writing line, usually in spaced caps. The nos may be blocked, or, if indented fr the left margin, the longest line may end at the right margin or end the same no of spaces from the right margin.

lc/ Notices & Agendas f a public limited company are usually blocked w open punctuation. The wording is very formal & contain information (where applicable) is given abt: voting rights, proxy votes & forms, Directors' Service Contracts, Directors' Share & Debenture Interests, etc.

CHAIRMAN'S AGENDA The chairman's agenda may contain more information than the agenda for others attending the mtg. The right side of the chairman's agenda may be left blank so th he can write in the decisions reached on various points.

CAPS/ The word notes is typed (either centred or blocked) on the right side & the items are renumbered at approx the centre of the typing line. Open or full punctuation may be used.

VARIABLE LINE SPACER

The variable line spacer is found on the left or right cylinder knob. By pressing this in, the cylinder can be moved to any position desired. Its purpose is to ensure that you have proper alignment of the details to be typed on dotted lines, ruled lines, or when inserting details in a form letter or a memo.

FORMAT FOR INTER-OFFICE MEMORANDA

A message from one person to another in the same firm, or from the Head Office to a Branch Office, or to an agent, is often in the form of a memorandum—usually referred to as a "memo". Inter-office memoranda may be typed on any of the usual sizes of paper. The layout of headings may vary from organisation to organisation.

Important points to remember when typing memos on headed forms:

(a) Margins: elite 13–90, pica 11–75. These margins may vary depending on the size of the form and the length of the message to be typed.
(b) After the words in the printed headings leave 2 clear character spaces before typing the insertions and use the variable line spacer to ensure their alignment.
(c) Date: correct order—day, month, year. The month should not be typed in figures.
(d) Some memos have a subject heading which gives the reader information about the contents of the memo. The heading is typed 2 single spaces below the last line of the printed headings, ie, turn up 2 single spaces.
(e) If there is no subject heading, start the body of the memo 2 single spaces after the last line of the printed headings.
(f) The body of the memo is usually typed in single spacing with double between paragraphs.
(g) After the last line of the body, turn up 2 single spaces and type the reference. This is usually the dictator's and typist's initials which identify the department or person dictating the memo.
(h) If an enclosure is mentioned in the body of the memo, this must be indicated by typing Enc (or Encs if more than one enclosure) at the left margin. After the reference turn up at least 2 single spaces before typing Enc or Encs.

Note: A memo with printed heading is given in the *Teaching Notes and Solutions* and may be copied and duplicated.

Practise typing memos

1 Type the following memo on a printed A5 memo form or prepare your own form. (a) Follow the instructions given above. (b) Margins: elite 13–90, pica 11–75. (c) Make your own line-endings.

M E M O R A N D U M

From Managing Director

To Company Secretary

Date 4 October 1984

↓ Turn up 2 single spaces

ANNUAL GENERAL MEETING

↓ Turn up 2 single spaces

You will remember that last year Members suggested that the Imperial Hotel was not a convenient place for the Annual General Meeting to be held. Please let me know as soon as possible what other arrangements you have been able to make.

I am returning the Directors' Annual Report which is now ready for printing.

↓ Turn up 2 single spaces

AMB/ESA

↓ Turn up 2 single spaces

Enc

3 Type the following report on a sheet of A4 paper. Use side headings as in copy.

REPORT OF THE YOUTH DEVELOPMENT COMMITTEE ON THE FOUNDING OF A YOUTH CLUB AT EASTFIELDS, NOTOWN*

Terms of reference — The Committee was instructed by the Youth Facilities Board at the Meeting on 18th April, 19... to investigate whether a need existed for a youth club at Eastfields and possible steps for its establishment.

Proceedings — At a Meeting on 25th April, the Committee compiled a questionnaire, inviting young people to comment on present facilities, to state whether they would welcome and support a youth club in the area and, if so, to indicate what type of activity they would wish to see promoted.

By kind permission of the Headmaster of Eastfields School, the questionnaire was circulated to all pupils between the ages of 14 and 18.

Opinions were also obtained by means of random street interview [w] and visits to a cross-section of houses in the neighbourhood.

The results were studied at meetings of the Committee held on 1st and 8th June.

Findings — (a) Approx 80% of young people between 14-18 considered present facilities inadequate

(a) [b] Seventy-two per cent of those between 14 and 16, and 55 per cent of those between 16 and 18 would like a club and would join one, if established.

(b) [c] Forty per cent of all age groups hoped that sporting activities could be arranged, and that some coaching could be provided. Among the 14 to 16 age group, outside visits would be particularly popular, and miscellaneous indoor activities (discussions, record sessions, etc) were favoured by most of those between 16 and 18.

Conclusions — The committee considers that a need undoubtedly exists for a youth club and that, provided accommodation could be found, a suitable range of indoor activities would not be difficult to organize. To provide sufficient facilities for the type of sports indicated on questionnaires would be much more difficult and costly. /uc

Recommendations — (a) That the board should investigate suitable bldgs in the Eastfields area, w a view to the renting of accommodation on weekday evenings.

(a) [b] That the Notown Council be appraoched to see if there were any possibility of making public sports facilities available to a club at agreed times. /trs

(b) [c] That a public meeting of young residents between 14 and 18 be called meanwhile and a committee formed, if the meeting so desired.

11th June, 1985 — Robert White
Chairman

---

* From the book MODERN SECRETARIAL PROCEDURE (Second Edition) by Kathleen M. Trotman. Published by McGraw-Hill Book Company (UK) Limited TROTMAN

See Typing Target Practice, page 79, for a further exercise on
Reports

2 Type the following memo on a printed A5 memo form or on your own prepared form. (a) Follow the instructions given on page 48. (b) Margins: elite 13–90, pica 11–75. (c) Make your own line-endings.

MEMORANDUM

From Fraser Scott

To Christine Ford

Date 5 October 1984

ANNUAL GENERAL MEETING

At last year's Annual General Meeting, Members said that the Imperial Hotel was difficult to reach by public transport and that suitable parking facilities were about a quarter of a mile away. Therefore, Mr Blance has asked me to find a more central place. You mentioned a hotel in Broad Street which has a spacious parking area. Please telephone me and let me know the name of the hotel and also the Manager's name.

FS/EJ

3 Type the following memo on a printed A5 memo form or on your own prepared form. (a) Follow the instructions given on page 48. (b) Margins: elite 13–90, pica 11–75. (c) Make your own line-endings. (d) Locate and correct one word error.

MEMORANDUM

From Fraser Scott, Company Secretary

To Mr Andrew M Blance, Managing Director

Date 9 October 1984

ANNUAL GENERAL MEETING

In reply to your memo dated 4 October, I have booked the Annual General Meeting at the Ambassador Hotel in Broad Street. Our Cheif Accountant, Christine Ford, recommends this hotel very highly.

I enclose a number of buffet menus which the Manager of the Ambassador has sent to me.

FS/EJ

Enc

4 Type the following memo on a printed A5 memo form or on your own prepared form. (a) Follow the instructions given on page 48. (b) Margins: elite 13–90, pica 11–75. (c) Make your own line-endings.

FROM Canteen Manager TO Purchasing Officer
DATE 15 October 1984
I see that J Sadler & Sons are advertising a high-quality folding table, and sizes include rectangular tops from 2 ft 6 in × 5 ft (0.76 × 1.52 m) up to 3 ft × 9 ft (0.91 × 2.74 m) and round tops 4 ft and 5 ft (1.21 & 1.52 m) in diameter.

Please ask them to let us have prices.

CCM/GT

SECTION 32

See Typing Target Practice, page 14, for further exercises on

Inter-office Memoranda

Headings

Most formal business reports contain headings th introduce ea main division or subdivision. Insert 'A'

Style

Consistency in style is also essential. For example, if at the beginning of a report business titles are typed in capitals, then they shd not be typed in lower case later on. Or, if a term is abbreviated, it shd be abbreviated throughout.

The style y follow wl be determined by yr employer's preference. l.c./ Many Business Firms provide typists u.c./ w a typing manual + the instructions contained therein must be followed closely. Number every page of a report uniformly. Spacing

left/ If y are typing a DRAFT, type this word at the top margin of the first page + use double or treble spacing w. wide margins – $1\frac{1}{2}$" × 1". Run on ∂/ The final typing wh shd be single shd be single spacing w. appropriate spacing btwn headings, paras, etc.

Quotations

When preparing a business report, an executive may wish to quote excerpts fr other sources. Brief quotations run in w. text matter th introduces them. Run on/ These are enclosed in quotation marks. Longer quotations, say more than four lines, shd be started on a new line + preferably indented fr the left margin (or both margins). Quotation marks are put at the beginning of ea. para + at the end of the last para. Permission to use a quotation shd be requested fr the copyright owner.

'A' When such headings are used, be consistent throughout the report.

The most competent typist makes an error occasionally, but that error does not appear in the letter or document placed on the employer's desk for signature. Why? Because the typist has carefully proofread the work before it has been taken from the machine; the error has been detected and it has been corrected.

While proofreading has always been an integral part of the typist's training, it is now doubly important because if you wish to operate a word processing machine, your ability to check quickly and correct errors in typing, spelling, grammar, etc, is even more meaningful. Documents prepared on a word processing machine are often used over and over again, and you can well imagine the disastrous results if you typed the wrong figures, were careless in checking your finished work, and your original error is then repeated hundreds of times.

5 Type the following memo on a printed A5 memo form or on your own prepared form. (a) Margins: elite 13–90, pica 11–75. (b) Make your own line-endings. (c) Before removing from the machine check carefully and circle any errors.

M E M O R A N D U M

From Typing Pool Supervisor

To All Typists

Date 12 October 1984

It is imperative that you check your typing and if there is an error, correct it while the paper is still in the machine. You will find it much more difficult to make a neat correction if you have to put the paper back into the machine to make the correction.

When proofreading, bear in mind the following types of errors:

1 Spelling, punctuation and grammar.
2 Wrong, or inconsistent, spacing.
3 Typographical errors - you struck the wrong key.
4 Word substitution - FROM for FORM, YOU for YOUR, IS for IT, etc.
5 Figures not typed in correct sequence - check with original.
6 Inconsistencies: in use of capitals; in spelling.

One way to prevent errors is to read through the work to be copied and make any amendments in pencil before you start to type.

CAS/ANN

6 **Spot the errors**

In the exercise below, the sentences in COLUMN ONE have been repeated in COLUMN TWO. Those in COLUMN ONE are correct, but in each sentence in COLUMN TWO there is a typing error. Compare the sentences and see how quickly you can spot the errors. Then type the sentences correctly, looking at COLUMN TWO and keeping COLUMN ONE covered while you do so.

COLUMN ONE	COLUMN TWO
1 Thank you for your letter.	1 Thank you for your letter.
2 Please book the accommodation.	2 Please book the accomodation.
3 Our cheque for £221.00 is here.	3 Our cheque for £212.00 is here.
4 Ask to see that painting.	4 Ask to see the painting.
5 The book is on your desk.	5 The book is on your Desk.
6 His name is Mr B Edwardes.	6 His name is Mr B Edwards.
7 Call in to see me on 12 May.	7 Call in to see me on 12 May
8 He took 3 years to write the book.	8 He took three years to write the book.
9 Send me £20.00.	9 Send me £20.00p.

See page 180 of this book and pages 15 and 16 in Typing Target Practice for further exercises on Proofreading

2 Type the following on A4 paper with suitable margins and use double spacing.

BUSINESS REPORTS

A business report may be a simple inter-office memorandum abt the background of a would-be customer, or it may run into hundreds of pages and be as formal as a comparison of the relative merits of several proposed sites for a new factory, complete with facts presented in tabular form. The formal report may be drafted and rewritten several times.

+ figures at (handwritten)

l.c. While an Executive wd prepare a report, it is usual f the typist to be responsible f the layout of the report & f the details of style.

In his book THERE'S A LOT OF LANGUAGE ABOUT /published by McGraw-Hill Book Company (UK) Limited/ Mike Daniels writes:

(Typist - words in heavy type shd be typed in caps. Watch for words in italics.)

(Rather in the way you might set out notes of your own use.)

"A report on something you have been asked to *find out* about is often set out using **headings** and **subheadings** to show clearly the various sections covered. Where there is a lot of information to be given, this method has the advantage that the reader can pick out a particular section to concentrate on without having to read through the whole report, just as you would be able to find and check a particular point in your notes. An investigation report should be **presented in sections**, each with its appropriate heading, usually in the order shown in the following example.

"TITLE/TOPIC COVERED IN THE REPORT

l.c.

1. *Terms of reference*
   Simple statement of what you were asked to find out about.
3 2. *Findings*
   The results of your investigation. trs
2 3. *Procedure*
   How you went about finding out.
4. *Conclusions*
   What main points for consideration are to be drawn from your findings.
5. *Recommendations*
   You may or may not be asked to give your own recommendations. Often your report will be studied by the person who requested it, who will then make his own recommendations."

Typist - see next page

From now on, if you make an error in your Production Work, it must be corrected. Correct the error as soon as you know you have made a mistake and read through the whole exercise when you have finished typing it and while the paper is still in the machine, in case there is an error you had not noticed before.

There are various methods which may be used to correct errors:

Rubber

(a) Turn up the paper so that the error is on top of the cylinder or paper table.
(b) Press the paper tightly against the cylinder or paper table to prevent slipping.
(c) Erase the error by rubbing gently up and down, blowing away rubber dust as you do so. (Too much pressure may cause a hole.)
(d) If you are using a new or heavily inked ribbon, erase first with a soft rubber, and then with a typewriter eraser.
(e) Turn paper back to writing line and insert correct letter or letters.
(f) Always use a clean rubber.

Note: If the typewriter has a carriage, move it to the extreme right or left to prevent rubber dust from falling into the mechanism of the machine.

Correction paper

This specially-coated strip of paper is placed in front of the printing point over the error and the incorrect letter is typed again through the correction paper. The letter will then be covered with a film of powder and the correct letter may be typed on top.

Correction fluid

This correction fluid is produced in various shades to match the typing paper and is applied with a small brush. The incorrect letter is obliterated and when the fluid is dry, the correct letter may be typed over the top. The liquid may be spirit- or water-based. If the spirit-based liquid is used, it is necessary to add thinner to the bottle as, after a time, the original liquid tends to thicken. Spirit-based liquid dries more quickly than water-based.

Correction ribbons

Some electric typewriters and most electronic typewriters are fitted with a correction ribbon. When making a correction using a correction ribbon, it is necessary to (i) backspace to the error; (ii) press the correction key—the error is then removed; (iii) type in the correct letter(s). The electronic typewriters are also equipped with a memory, so that they can perform automatic corrections, from a few characters to 10 or more lines. (The electronic typewriters are usually fitted with a relocate key which, when depressed, returns immediately to the last character typed before the correction was made.)

7 Type the following exercise on A4 paper. (a) Margins: elite 22–82, pica 12–72. (b) Double spacing. (c) Check carefully and correct any typing errors.

THE FINISHED PRODUCT

When we look at a typewritten document, we notice immediately if it is well or badly displayed. We do not know, and do not care, about the speed at which it was typed. When we read it, any errors in typing are immediately noticed. Therefore, good display and accuracy are of first importance. But your employer, unlike the reader, is concerned about the time you take to produce a document.

Inserting the paper, deciding line-spacing and margins, accurate division of words at line-ends, are all essential typing techniques that require constant practice to ensure speed and accuracy.

In addition to the methods of enumeration already introduced, it is modern practice to use the decimal point, followed by a figure, for the subdivisions. For example, 4 (a) and 4 (b) would become 4.1 and 4.2, and 4 (a) i and 4 (a) ii would become 4.1.1 and 4.1.2. When using open punctuation, the decimal point for decimalised enumeration must be inserted. Leave 2 clear character spaces after the final figure.

1 Type the following exercise on A4 paper. Margins of elite 22–82, pica 12–72.

COMMERCE: STRUCTURE AND PRACTICE*

by T A C SHAFTO MA BSc(Econ) PhD

The following is an excerpt from page 68 of the above book:

"1 MOVEMENT OF GOODS

passenger/ In contrast to the situation for travel, intercountry goods transport still uses the sea. There are many reasons for this:

"1.1 Sea carriage is much cheaper for most types of heavy industrial goods. Air Carriage, however, becomes worthwhile when goods are of high value in relation to their weight, eg, for jewellery and some high-priced consumer goods. /l.c.

"1.2 Speed of travel, which is the main advantage of air transport, is not often important for industrial goods. For these the <u>certainty</u> that they will . . . needed for machine repairs. Then the extra cost of air movement is worthwhile.

been/ "1.3 Modern ships have adapted well to the demands of overland carriage before and after the sea voyage. Two developments have been especially important.

"1.3.1 *Containers.* The modern container is a reinforced box in a standard size developed for speedy transfer between road vehicle, train and ship. It can be quickly locked in place . . . by large cranes.

"Containers can contain goods belonging to several firms. Goods transported from, say, the industrial Midlands of England . . . containers. There are air containers but these are less easy to handle than those used in surface transport.

"1.3.2 *Roll-on, roll-off.* This is the term used to describe the carriage by sea of entire road vehicles; or sometimes the trailer unit only. Roll-on, roll-off has replaced container transpoert for the 'short-haul' traffic around Europe . . . Asia and Australia."

---

* Published by the McGraw-Hill Book Company (UK) Limited

See Typing Target Practice, page 78, for a further exercise on Decimalised Enumeration

Progress check

Note: In the consolidation exercises you must carry out any instructions given. Where there are no instructions, you should follow the layout indicated and apply the theory points covered in previous units. Before typing, you MUST read through each exercise carefully to make sure that the words are spelt correctly and that you understand the exercise and what has to be done. What is important is that the final typing will look good and that there are no typing errors—you will have corrected them before taking the paper from the machine.

Margins: If the exact margins are not given, use the following as a guide:

	Left margin		*Right margin*	
	elite	pica	elite	pica
A4/A5 landscape	13	11 (1″—25 mm clear)	95	78 (½″—13 mm clear)
A4/A5 landscape	19	16 (1½″—38 mm clear)	89	73 (1″—25 mm clear)
A5 portrait	13	11 (1″—25 mm clear)	65	54 (½″—13 mm clear)

NB: Left and right margins may be equal but the right margin is NEVER wider than the left margin.

Task 1 ▶ *Format* Output Target—7 minutes
A5 portrait paper Blocked display

NEW POCKET COMPUTER
Measures 1" × 6½" × 3"

<u>Programs in Easy-to-learn Basic</u>
or
<u>Cosmic's Ready-to-run Software</u>

↓ Leave 2 clear spaces

24-CHARACTER ALPHANUMERIC READOUT
15 ARITHMETIC FEATURES

C O M P L E T E   W I T H

Batteries
Comprehensive Manual
Quick-reference Card

Check your work and correct any errors before removing the paper from the machine

Task 2 ▶ *Format* Output Target—10 minutes
A5 landscape paper Single spacing (double between items)
3 spaces between columns Blocked display Centred vertically and horizontally

LOCAL RADIO STATIONS

Station	Wavelength	Area Covered
Beacon Radio (Wolverhampton)	303 MW/97.2 VHF	South Staffordshire, Walsall, etc
BRMB Radio (Birmingham)	261 MW/94.8 VHF	West Midlands, South Staffordshire, etc
BBC Radio (Oxford)	202 MW/95.2 VHF	Banbury and District
Severn Sound (Gloucester)	388 MW/95.0 VHF	Gloucestershire, etc

FORMAT FOR TRAVEL ITINERARY

A travel itinerary usually implies travelling some distance by one or 2 types of transport and may or may not include certain appointments. Here again, headings may be blocked or centred and 3 spaces are left between columns.

4 Type the following travel itinerary on A4 paper. Follow display given. Use margins of elite 20–85, pica 11–76.

I T I N E R A R Y

MR PATRICK HAWKINS' VISIT TO SCOTLAND AND SHETLAND

27-31 MAY 1985

← 2 clear

correct 2 word errors
The word "airport" shd hv a capital 'A'

MONDAY 27 MAY

```
0645   check in   Birmingham airport
0730   depart     Birmingham airport, Flight BA 5662
0825   arrive     Edinburgh airport to be met by Trevor Fountain
                  Accommodation booked at the Argyle Hotel,
                    Groom Street, Edinburgh
                    Telephone number: 465 7863
                  Trevor Fountain has arranged visits to customers
                    in Kirkcaldy, Dunfermline and Grangemouth
```

TUESDAY *28 May*

```
0730   check in   Edinburgh airport
0815   depart     "         "     , Flight TR 234
0905   arrive     Aberdeen airport to be met by Alasdair Millar
                  Accommodation booked at the Crest Hotel,
                    Commercial Street, Aberdeen
                  Visits to customers in Peterhead and Fraserburgh
                  Dinner with Jim Hudson and his wife Morag
                    (Alasdair Millar has made the arrangements)
```

Telephone No 617751 →

WEDNESDAY 29 MAY

```
0845   check in   Aberdeen airport
0935   depart     Aberdeen airport, Flight BA 5748 9
1040   arrive     Sumburgh airport to be met by Peter Leask
                  Accomodation booked at the Lerwick Hotel
                    Telephone number: 4455 6
                  Visits to customers in Lerwick, Scalloway and
                    Sandwick
```

THURSDAY 30 MAY

1030 check in Sumburgh Airport
1110 depart " " , Flight BA 5749
1330 arrive Glasgow " to be met by Alex Chisholm
u.c. / Accommodation booked at the bridge hotel,
Upper Bridge Str., Glasgow
Tel. No. 342 4826
(Mr J Jefferies) ⅃ Visit a customer in Motherwell
Alex Chisholm has arranged for y to hv diner w a few customers

FRIDAY 31 MAY
0800 check in Glasgow Airport
0840 depart " , Flight BA 5651
0935 arrive B'ham " to be met by Eileen Evans

See Typing Target Practice, page 77, for a further exercise on Travel Itineraries

Task 3 ▶ *Format* Output Target—5 minutes

A5 landscape paper   Leave one inch (25 mm) clear at top of page
Single spacing   Margins: elite 22–82, pica 12–72

WINTER BREAKS

Heart of England

REGENCY HOTEL (2 clear spaces) This 3-star hotel is near Warwick and is an ideal touring base for those of you who like to get out and about.

IMPERIAL HOTEL (2 clear) Successfully combines the old with the new. From here you can tour the Severn Valley and explore the beautiful Welsh border country. If you like country towns, try Bridgnorth and Ludlow.

Task 4 ▶ *Format* Output Target—10 minutes

A4 paper   Margins: 1½" (38 mm), 1" (25 mm)

TELEVISION/VIDEO TAPES

Video has a number of advantages over conventional television. You can:

(a) erase and re-record your own tapes over and over again;

(b) play recordings made on a friend's machine;

(c) record while watching the same programme;

(d) record while watching another programme;

(e) play the tapes as and when convenient;

(f) play the same tapes over and over again;

(g) play pre-recorded programmes.

Further, in order to decide what to record, you become more discerning.

On Tuesday, 2 November, 1982, Channel 4 ~~appeared~~ appeared on our screens. The slogan says, "Channel 4 means more". More recording on video tapes?

FORMAT FOR JUSTIFIED RIGHT MARGIN

The right margin in typewriting cannot be completely regular as in printing, but for purposes of display it may be made regular by adopting the printer's method. This is known as "justifying", ie, the space between words is increased (where necessary) so that the last character in each line is typed at the same scale point.

Before you can justify the right margin you must first type a draft of the passage, making certain that no line extends beyond the point at which the right margin is set. On the draft copy additional spaces are indicated so that when the passage is retyped, and the additional spaces inserted, the lines will end at the same scale point.

Note: It would be wrong to try and justify "short" lines.

Electronic typewriters and word processing machines usually have function keys which will justify the right margin.

1 Use margins of elite 20–85, pica 11–75. Type a draft copy, taking care not to type outside the right margin. On draft copy insert extra spaces. Type with justified right margin.

```
Our doors are beautiful to look at and they are also safe
because they are made from thick tempered safety glass which
is 4 to 5 times stronger than ordinary glass and will with-
stand hard impacts.  Additionally, because they are made of
glass, you can see who is at the other side.
```

2 Go back to page 47 and type exercises 5 and 7 with justified right margins.

FORMAT FOR ITALICS

Words to be printed in italics (or already printed in italics) must be underscored in the typescript.

FORMAT FOR APPOINTMENTS ITINERARY

If your employer has appointments outside the office, an appointments itinerary may have to be prepared for him which will enable him to know exactly where he should be at any given time. This schedule of a day's appointments should be typed on a convenient size of paper or, preferably, on a card which he can carry about with him. There are many ways of setting out an appointments itinerary, but the one given below is in common use. The headings may be blocked or centred, and 3 spaces are left between columns.

3 Type the following appointments itinerary on a card measuring (6" × 4"). Use margins of elite 12–62, pica 6–56. Leave 3 spaces between the 2 columns and set a tab stop for the second column at elite 25, pica 19. The words in italic type must be underscored.

I T I N E R A R Y

Mrs B Chambers' schedule for 17 May 1985

1000 hours	Blandford Computers PLC, Park Street
	Buyer – *Miss Brenda Taylor*
1115 "	Exhibition – Electronic Typewriters and Computers
	At the Royal Hotel, Broad Street
	Videx Stand—Ask for *Mr F Langstone*
1430 "	Brown & Gilbert, Solicitors, Victoria Street
	See *Ms V Gilbert*
1600 "	Appointment with Chairman in his office

See Typing Target Practice, page 76, for a further exercise on Justifying Right Margin

Task 5 ▶ *Format*
A4 paper Leave one inch (25 mm) clear at top of page
Double spacing Margins: elite 20–85, pica 11–76
Correct one word error

Output Target—9 minutes

BOOKS OF REFERENCE

Finding Information

The efficient typist carries in her head only essential information that she uses frequently. She knows immediately where to check or find unusual or important information. She makes good use of reference books.

The preface of a book will tell you about the purpose and content of that book. Always read the preface to see what the author(s) has to say. One good example of this is an English Dictionery where you will probably be unable to recognize the abbreviations, accents, etc, used in the main part unless you have read the preface.

Check your work and correct any errors before removing the paper from the machine

The index is an alphabetical list of the contents of a book.

Task 6 ▶ *Format*
A5 landscape paper Blocked display Centred vertically

Output Target—3 minutes

REMEMBER

Saturday 8 September

J U M B L E S A L E
↓ Leave 2 clear spaces
in

JARDINE CRESCENT HALL

Commencing 1400 hours
↓ Leave 2 clear spaces
TEAM MANAGER - Michael Lander
TEAM SECRETARY - Malcolm Parkinson

4 Type the following exercise on A4 paper in single spacing. Make all the necessary corrections and rule the boxes as indicated.

BRITISH BIRDS ← sp. caps

JAY

The jay is more often heard than seen as it is a wary bird. It can sometimes be observed hopping along the ground picking up seeds or acorns fr under trees. In flight it has a distinctive, jerky beat of its rounded wings. The jay sometimes steals nestlings & eggs of other birds.

MAGPIE

The magpie has a long, glossy tail, & a wing plumage wh shines purple, red, blue & green. It normally lays a clutch of 5 to 8 bluish-green eggs once a year fr April onwards. The young ones - fed by both parents - fledge after 3 to 4 weeks.

← 2½" (64 mm) →

2" (51 mm) (Space for photographs)

TYPIST

Make all the boxes the same size.

GREY WAGTAIL

An adult male in breeding plumage is identified by grey upper parts, yellow under parts (UNDER) & black throat. A constant bobbing of the long tail is another characteristic. An adult female is duller than the male & lacks the black throat. It often catches insects in flight, particularly over water.

GREEN WOODPECKER

The largest of Britain's woodpeckers has an attractive, loud laughing call wh sounds like a rapidly repeated 'kew-kew-kew...' The adult bird's green, black & red crown is distinctive. The male also has a red moustache. It lays 5 to 7 eggs, feeding the young for 18 to 21 days.

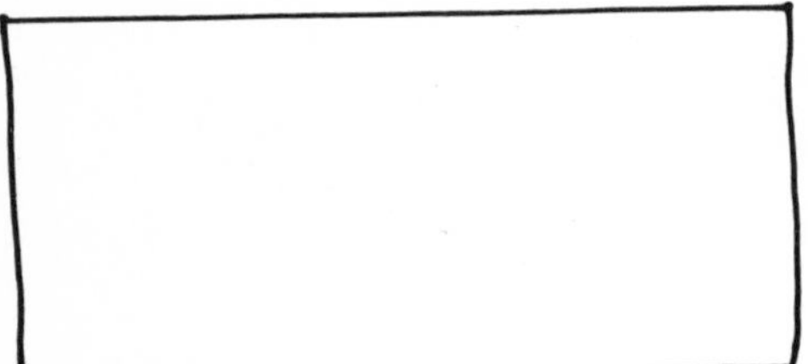

See Typing Target Practice, page 75, for a further exercise on

Diagrams

Task 7 ▶ *Format*
A4 paper Margins $1\frac{1}{2}$" (38 mm), 1" (25 mm)
Correct one word error

Output Target—10 minutes

Cosmic & Co Ltd offer you the following at very low prices.

GENERAL COVERAGE RECEIVER

You can tune in to world news, sports and music. An easy-to-operate receiver which offers exciting global listening.

PROGRAMMABLE SCANNER

A 50-channel scanner with a digital keyboard on which you can enter up to 50 frequencies for monitoring, storing and efploring. Search button helps you find new channels.

PORTABLE SCANNER

Automatically scans up to 6 channels. Channel lockouts bypass unwanted channels. Built-in speaker, earphone jack, etc.

ELECTRONIC CLOCK RADIO

Wake on time to radio or buzzer alarm. Display has bright/dim swich. Radio has 3" (76 mm) lighted dial, ceramic filter and earphone jack.

Task 8 ▶ *Format*
A5 memo form

Output Target—6 minutes

Check your work before removing from machine and correct any errors

To Office Manager

From Chief Accountant

Date 19 October 1984

G R PLESSEY & CO

I am sorry to have been so long in replying to your request for clarification about the amount of discount to allow the above-named company. At a meeting with our Sales Director this morning, it was decided that up to £9,999.99 the discount will be 2½% for settlement within 7 days; orders valued £10,000 to £20,000, 3% for settlement within 7 days; orders from £20,000.01 and over, 3½% within 7 days. If the amount is not settled within 7 days, net monthly account will apply.

AM/ES

2/

N.P. ["Teaching," said Elgar, "was like turning a grindstone with a dislocated shoulder." As he taught he also composed & never lost sight of his aim of earning a living as a composer.

It was not until 1902 that Elgar's greatness fully as a composer was acknowledged, & shortly v.c. | afterwards a spectacular 3-day Elgar festival was held at Covent Garden attended by the King & Queen. Never before had an English composer bn honoured on this scale w. a festival devoted exclusively to his own music. Elgar was acclaimed & knighted.

Among his many compositions were the following:

Leave 3 spaces here

1892 The Black Knight, cantata for chorus and orchestra

1903 The Apostles, oratorio

1899 Enigma Variations

1898 Caractacus, cantata

1900 The Dream of Gerontius, oratorio

1901 Pomp and Circumstance No 1 and No 2, military marches

1904 In the South, concert overture

1902 Coronation Ode, for soloists, chorus and orchestra

In date order, please

Sir Edward Elgar died on 23 February 1934, & is buried in his beloved Malvern.

v.c. | when "The Dream of Gerontius" was performed at Düsseldorf,

FORMAT FOR BUSINESS LETTERS—OPEN PUNCTUATION—FULLY-BLOCKED

Letters are ambassadors and advertisements for the firm who sends them. You must therefore ensure that your letters are well-displayed and faultlessly typed. Each firm has its own method of display, but the examples which follow are in fully-blocked style (sometimes known as blocked) where every line begins at the left margin.

VIDEX OFFICE SUPPLIES plc — Registered No 12345 (England)
Office Equipment Manufacturers and Suppliers
Registered Office
Hemming Road, LEAMINGTON SPA, Warwickshire, CV32 4LY
Telephone: 0926 23432 or Freefone 32594 — 24-hour Answering Service
Telex 848484 — Telephone: 0926 28134

Turn up 2 single spaces

1 Reference — Our Ref FL/SY

Turn up 2 single spaces

2 Date — 31 October 1984

Turn up 2 single spaces

3 Attention of — FOR THE ATTENTION OF MRS T EGGAR

Turn up 2 single spaces

4 Addressee — A J Quinney & Sons Ltd
104 Northern Avenue
PURLEY
Surrey
CR2 4TJ

Turn up 2 single spaces

5 Salutation — Dear Sirs

Turn up 2 single spaces

6 Subject heading — 1984 OFFICE EQUIPMENT BROCHURE

Turn up 2 single spaces

7 Body — Thank you for your letter of 23 October in which you state that you require information about dedicated word processors.

Turn up 2 single spaces

We are enclosing our latest Office Equipment Brochure which gives details of word processors supplied by us. We would be very pleased to make arrangements for you to visit our showrooms so that we could demonstrate any machines in which you may be interested.

Turn up 2 single spaces

8 Complimentary close — Yours faithfully

Turn up 1 single space

9 Name of firm — VIDEX OFFICE SUPPLIES plc

Turn up 5 single spaces

10 Name of signatory — F LANGSTONE

Turn up 1 single space

11 Designation — Marketing Director

Turn up minimum of 2 single spaces

12 Enclosure — Enc

OPEN PUNCTUATION

(a) You will see from the business letter set out above that no punctuation is inserted in the reference, date, name and address of addressee, or salutation.
(b) In the body of the letter, the points mentioned on page 27 apply.
(c) There is no punctuation in the complimentary close or in any of the wording which follows it.

PRINTED LETTERHEAD

When using paper with a printed heading, turn up 2 single spaces before typing the reference—unless the reference is already printed—and then type it in the space provided and turn up 2 single spaces before typing the date.

You may be asked to leave blank spaces for the insertion of photographs, etc, or you may have to draw geometrical figures. The diagram or blank space left must be the exact size indicated. For instance, if you were asked to leave a BLANK space of 2" (51 mm), you should turn up 13 (thirteen) single line spaces. However, if you have to insert lines and use the underscore for the horizontals, you would turn up the exact number of lines. For example, if you have to draw a square 2" (51 mm) deep and you were using the underscore for the horizontal lines, type the first horizontal line, turn up 12 (twelve) and type the second horizontal line.

Horizontal and vertical lines may be drawn in ink or by means of the underscore. Alternatively, the horizontal lines may be typed by the underscore and the vertical lines drawn in ink, provided the ink is the same colour as the lines typed by the underscore.

When typing from complicated copy, it is a good plan to type a draft quickly to see how much space the typing, drawing, etc, is likely to take up. It is essential, when a diagram has typing before and after it, that there is a blank space before the first line and after the last line. The same spacing would apply if you were leaving a given space for a photograph or picture—there should be a clear space above and below.

3 Type the following exercise on A4 paper in double spacing. Make all the necessary corrections and leave the spaces indicated. Margins: elite 20–85, pica 11–76.

caps

Sir Edward Elgar Bart OM GCVO

2 June 1857 – 23 February 1934

Leave a 2" (51 mm) square here for Sir Edward's photograph

Sir Edward Elgar was born on 2/6/87 (5) near the Malvern Hills, in the village of Broadheath. His father was a piano tuner + 2 yrs after Sir Edward's birth moved to Worcester to expand the family music business. Elgar had no formal music training, + taught himself to play half a dozen musical instruments. He assisted his father as organist at the Catholic Church of St. George, + eventually took the job over. Elgar married one of his pupils, Caroline uc/alice Roberts, a general's daughter. They had one child, Carice, born on 14 August 1890. CARICE also gave violin lessons, + in 1889

1 Reference—Our Ref, Your Ref
  (a) Type at the left margin or in the space provided on the headed paper.
  (b) In their simplest forms they consist of the dictator's and typist's initials, eg, AMD/ACM.

2 Date
  (a) Correct order is day, month, year, eg, 3 May 1984. Do not type the month in figures.
  (b) Turn up 2 single spaces after reference and type date at left margin. (c) No punctuation.

3 For the attention of
  (a) Some companies adopt the rule that all correspondence should be addressed to the company and not to individual persons by name. The sender of a letter may wish it to reach or be dealt with by a particular person or department. This is indicated by typing the words FOR THE ATTENTION OF . . . at the left margin and 2 single spaces below the date. (b) No punctuation.
  (c) The modern tendency is to type in capitals without the underscore.

4 Addressee (Inside address)
  (a) Turn up 2 single spaces after FOR THE ATTENTION OF and type name and address of addressee at left margin. (If there is no FOR THE ATTENTION OF line, then turn up 2 single spaces after the date before typing the name of the addressee.)
  (b) No punctuation. (c) Single spacing. (d) Each item on a separate line.
  (e) Name of post town in capitals.

5 Salutation
  (a) Turn up 2 single spaces after the last line of the address and type the salutation at left margin. (b) No punctuation.

6 Subject heading
  (a) Turn up 2 single spaces after the salutation and type at the left margin.
  (b) Usually typed in capitals when it need not be underscored. (c) No punctuation.

7 Body of letter
  (a) Turn up 2 single spaces after salutation and type the paragraphs—each line starts at the left margin.
  (b) Type in single spacing with double between paragraphs.
  (c) Short letters may be typed in double spacing.

8 Complimentary close
  (a) Turn up 2 single spaces after the last line of last paragraph and type at left margin.
  (b) No punctuation.

9 Name of firm sending the letter
  (a) Some companies type the name of their firm immediately after the complimentary close.
  (b) Turn up one single space after complimentary close and type name of firm.
  (c) Type at left margin. (d) No punctuation.

10 Name of signatory
  (a) Turn up 5 single spaces after the complimentary close (or name of firm if there is one) before typing the name of the person who will sign the letter.
  (b) Type at left margin. (c) No punctuation. (d) A lady may wish to insert a title (Mrs/Miss/Ms) either before her name or in brackets after her name.

11 Designation
  (a) After the name of the person signing the letter, turn up one single space and type the designation (official position of the person signing the letter).
  (b) Type at left margin. (c) No punctuation.

12 Enclosure
  (a) The inclusion of papers or documents in a letter is indicated by typing the abbreviation Enc (or Encs if more than one) at the left margin.
  (b) Turn up a minimum of 2 single spaces after the designation. (c) No punctuation.

FORMAT FOR POETRY

The following points are a guide to the typing of poems.

(1) *Positioning* The longest line of the verse should be centred on the page horizontally with uniform margins all round.

(2) *Spacing* Single spacing, double between verses.

(3) (a) If alternate lines rhyme, these usually begin at the same scale point (unless they are of irregular length, when they are centred). The first line and all lines rhyming with it are written at the margin, while the second and all lines rhyming with it are indented 2 spaces from the start of the first, third, etc, lines. (Short lines may be indented more than 2 spaces).

(b) In blank verse (ie, where no lines rhyme), all lines start at the margin.

(c) When lines are of approximately equal length and when successive lines rhyme, these start at the margin, ie, there is no indentation.

(d) If all lines rhyme, these also all start at the left margin.

(4) Each line starts with a capital letter.

1 Read and study the above explanation and then type the following extract from a poem by John Keats.

TO AUTUMN

Season of mists and mellow fruitfulness!
  Close bosom friend of the maturing sun;
Conspiring with him how to load and bless
  With fruit the vines that round the thatch eaves run;

TYPIST: The last letter of the author's surname ends underneath the last letter of the longest line.

JOHN KEATS

2 Type the following personal letter. Insert today's date. Take one carbon copy.

42 Forest Road
Quinton
BIRMINGHAM B32 2SL

Dear Anne

As promised, I am sending the verses you once wrote for the School Magazine, published in 1980.

COOL THOUGHTS

The mistress in the form room said 'Amo, amas, amat',
But I couldn't think of Latin, nor anything like that.
The heat was so oppressive, my brain it seemed to sear,
And I dreamt of children paddling in a stream so cool and clear.

I wished that I were with them, paddling in the brook,
Or eating ice cream sundaes in a small and shady nook.
I saw the snow capped mountains, tall, serene and proud,
And floating high above them, a mass of fleecy cloud.

My thoughts were slowly drifting, when suddenly rang out,
The bell to end the lesson, and put my dreams to rout.

ANNE ELGAR

I thoroughly enjoyed the Dinner on Sat evening — the food was delicious, & it was delightful to see so many old pupils again.

Very best wishes

Miss Anne Elgar
62 Tranter Ave RYDE IOW PO33 2DS

Practise typing fully-blocked letter with open punctuation

1 Type the following letter on A5 portrait paper. (a) If you are not using headed paper turn up 7 single spaces before typing Our Ref. (b) Margins: elite 13–63, pica 6–56. (c) Keep to the spacing and layout indicated. ***Note:*** A letterhead for this and other letters is given in the *Teaching Notes and Solutions.*

	DAVID JESSOP (Insurance Brokers) LTD	
	Hanbury House 20 St Mary's Street BRIGHTON BN4 2EQ	Registered No 24689 (England)
	Telephone 0273 426205	Telex 974211
		Turn up 2 single spaces
1 Reference	Our Ref JWDD/ACM	
		Turn up 2 single spaces
2 Date	6 November 1984	
		Turn up 2 single spaces
4 Name and address of addressee	Betta Selection Services 26 Piccadilly Arcade West Street EDINBURGH EH3 9HS	
5 Salutation	Dear Sirs	
		Turn up 2 single spaces
7 Body of letter	Thank you for your enquiry about car insurance. Car insurance is available to all members of the Society holding 3 or more shares, or a life assurance policy.	
		Turn up 2 single spaces
	Members receive a discount of 15 per cent, thus securing cover at a very competitive premium.	
		Turn up 2 single spaces
	If you require any further information, please do not hesitate to contact me again.	
		Turn up 2 single spaces
8 Complimentary close	Yours faithfully	Turn up 5 single spaces
10 Signatory	J W DOSSETT-DAVIES	Turn up 1 single space
11 Designation	General Secretary	
	Registered Office as above	

2 Type the following letter on A5 portrait paper. (a) If you are not using headed paper turn up 7 single spaces before typing Our Ref. (b) Margins: elite 13–63, pica 6–56. (c) The details as far as the salutation are exactly as those in the letter above. (d) After typing the salutation, turn up 2 single spaces and then type the following paragraphs. (e) Correct the word error. (f) The complimentary close, etc, is the same as in the letter above.

Further to your telephone call received this morning, I wish to inform you that your premium would be calculated from the information given on your Proposal Form.

Please forward this Form to the above address, and then more definate information can be given to you.

See Typing Target Practice, page 17, for further exercises on

10 Ellipsis - (omission of words) Words are sometimes deliberately omitted at the beginning, end, or in the middle of a sentence. Such omission is indicated by the use of 3 spaced full stops, with a space either side, as follows: . . .

11 Elision This is the omission of a letter (usually a vowel) when pronouncing a word, eg, wouldn't, can't, don't. This form of abbreviation must not be used in typescript unless you are quoting direct speech, ie, using quotation marks.

---

* If the continuation sheet is typed on the reverse of the paper, the margins are also reversed, eg, in this exercise the margins for the reverse side would be 13-82 elite, 6-72 pica.

4 Type the following extract from a chapter of a story in double spacing. Make all the corrections indicated, and also correct any word errors.

2ins

CHAPTER IV ← centre & u/sc

MEDLOC D/S NEW YEAR'S EVE ← centre Use a dropped head

The 'Medloc' * train chugged & rumbled through the mountain villages of northern Italy. As it shuddered to a temporary stop the laughter of the holiday makers & the bright lights of the hotels woke a young soldier who was dozing in a corner of the compartment labelled "Prisoner & Escort." Looking out over the Alpine scene w a sleepy eye he noticed th a church clock said 10 to 12." Hey, wake up, you chaps — nearly New Year's Day", he sd, kicking the other inert occuppants to life. "Hasn't anyone anything to celebrate with?" "Yes, George has," replied a l/c Sapper who bore a strange resemblance to Bob Hope. NP [After many threats & extortions George unearthed a bottle of cognac wh was gratefully rec'd . . .

ITALY LABELLED

Later the train clicked over the points into the trs| station, & the occupants of the "Escort & Prisoner" carriage were rudely awakened by the voice of the 316 Transit Camp announcer booming, "Attention, all ranks. De-train now."

"what a way to start a new year," said uc| the sapper (who looked like Bob Hope) as he lugged his kit bag through the snow. "Could be worse," replied the young soldier reflect- ively. "~~Please~~ Perhaps it will be." REFLECTIVELY

---

* An army train wh ran from Italy to the Hook of Holland, for some yrs after the Second World War.

See Typing Target Practice, page 73, for a further exercise on

Practise typing letters with attention line and enclosure

3 Type the following letter on A4 paper. (a) If you are not using headed paper, turn up 7 single spaces before typing Our Ref. (b) Use margins of elite 25–80, pica 15–70. (c) Keep to the spacing and layout indicated. (d) Correct the word error.

BETTA SELECTION SERVICES
Registered Office
26 Piccadilly Arcade
West Street
EDINBURGH
EH3 9HS

Telephone: 031 246 8321
Telex: 264081

Registered No 54387 (Scotland)

Turn up 2 single spaces

Our Ref PQ/EDH   Your Ref JWDD/ACM

Turn up 2 single spaces

14 November 1984

Turn up 2 single spaces

3 Attention of   FOR THE ATTENTION OF MR J W DOSSETT-DAVIES

Turn up 2 single spaces

David Jessop (Insurance Brokers) Ltd
Hanbury House
20 St Mary's Street
BRIGHTON
BN4 2EQ

Turn up 2 single spaces

Dear Sirs

Turn up 2 single spaces

We enclose the Proposal Form for car insurance to cover 3 of our staff. You will note that we require 3rd party cover, and that the car will be used for the purpose of business only.

Would you please let us know, as soon as possible, the exact amount of the premium, as it is imperitive that we have the use of the car by the end of this month.

Yours faithfully

PETRA QUINNEY
Secretary

Turn up minimum of 2 single spaces

12 Enclosure   Enc

4 Type the following letter on A4 paper. (a) Margins: elite 25–80, pica 15–70. (b) The details as far as the salutation are the same as the letter above except for the date which is 21 November 1984. (c) After typing the salutation, turn up 2 spaces and then type the following paragraphs. (d) Correct the word error.

Further to our letter of 14 November, we have not received any information from you with regard to the amount of the premium on our car insurance policy.

As we explained in our previous letter to you, we are most anxious to settle this matter as it is imperative that the car is available for use on 30 November.

I am enclosing a medicle (medical) form for Miss A J Smith-Brook, who is a diabetic.

See Typing Target Practice, page 18, for further exercises on

FORMAT FOR REPORTS, THESES, BOOKS, ETC—see exercise below

3 Type a corrected copy of the following exercise in double spacing. Use margins of elite 19–88, pica 11–76.

REPORTS, THESES, BOOKS, ETC

For the typing of work such as reports, short stories, books, theses, etc, the following will be a guide:

1 Size of paper A4 - normally only one side is used.*

2 Spacing Single or double according to instructions or house rules.

3 Margins Left - never less than 1" (25 mm) clear, ie, elite 13, pica 11. However, if you hv to leave a binding or stitching margin then the left margin would need to be 1½" (38 mm), ie, elite 19, pica 16. Right - ½" to 1" (13 mm to 25 mm) depending on width of the left margin. Top and bottom margins shld be equal - first line of matter starting 25 mm fr the top and the last line ending 25 mm fr the bottom. To ensure equal top and bottom margins on each sheet, adopt one of the following methods:

(a) Put a light pencil mark 25 mm fr top & bottom edge of paper before it is inserted in the machine.

(b) Rule a heavy line on backing sheet (wh is usually wider than the typing paper) across the complete width of sheet 25 mm fr the top and at a point 25 mm fr the bottom.

4 Pagination - the numbering of pages. The first page is not usually numbered, second and subsequent pages are numbered 13 mm (turn up 4 line spaces) fr the top edge of the paper in arabic figures. The number may be blocked at the left or right margin or centred on the typing line. Some business houses prefer to hv the pages numbered at the bottom.

5 Chapter headings and numbers The first page of a chapter may be in the form of a "Dropped Head", ie, the chapter no. is typed 2" (51 mm) to 3" (76 mm) from the top edge of the paper in roman numerals or arabic numbers. The heading is typed in capital letters 2 single spaces below the chapter no. The chapter number & heading may be centred on the typing line or blocked at the left margin. It wld seem sensible to block when blocked paragraphs are used and to centre when indented paragraphs are being used.

6 Catchwords When a continuation sheet is necessary, the first word or 2 appearing on the continuation sheet are sometimes typed at the foot of the preceding page below the last line & aligned with the right margin - this is known as a "catchword". CONTINUED or PTO may be used in place of the catchword, but not the number of the next page.

7 Correction of errors The typist is expected to correct errors in spelling, grammar, or punctuation, should these occur in the original draft. Where a word can be spelt in 2 ways, the same spelling must be adopted throughout.

8 Words that have been printed in italics, must be underscored in typewritten matter.

9 Throughout the whole work, the layout for chapter headings, use of capitals, numbering, etc, must be consistent.

/Continued

Practise typing letters with subject heading

5 Type the following letter on A4 paper. (a) Margins: elite 22–82, pica 12–72. (b) Correct the 2 word errors.

Our Ref FL/SY

31 October 1984

FOR THE ATTENTION OF MRS T EGGAR

A J Quinney & Sons Ltd
104 Northern Avenue
PURLEY
Surrey
CR2 4TJ

Dear Sirs

Turn up 2 single spaces

6 Subject heading — 1984 OFFICE EQUIPMENT BROCHURE

Turn up 2 single spaces

Thank you for your letter of 23 October in which you state that you require information about dedicated word processers.

We are enclosing our latest Office Equipment Brochure which gives details of word processors supplied by us. We would be very pleased to make arrangments for you to visit our showrooms so that we could demonstrate any machines in which you may be interested.

Turn up 1 single space

Yours faithfully
9 Name of company — VIDEX OFFICE SUPPLIES plc

F LANGSTONE
Marketing Director

Enc

> ***Note:*** This exercise contains all the parts of a business letter. Keep your copy and refer to it when necessary.

See Typing Target Practice, page 19, for further exercises on

2 Type the following exercise on A4 paper in double spacing. Margins: elite 20–85, pica 11–76. Correct any word errors.

Education in India (1) ← centre in caps

Double

Education usually starts at the age of 6 & consists of elementary or primary shool classes 1 to 5. Similar subjects are taught to those of a British school, in the mother tongue. (2) Education is compulsery to the age of 11, but there are exceptions to this rule in most states.

There are three types of secondary school w pupils starting at the age of 11yrs, but going on to different levels.

(a) Middle schools consisting of Classes 6 to 8.

uc/ c (b) Higher secondary schools consisting of classes 6 to 11.

Trs/ b (c) High schools consisting of Classes 6 to 10.

Additionally a new type of school has recently bn introduced – the basic school, which consists of Classes 1 to 8, covering the curricula of both Elementary & middle schools. [University education consists of 3 or 4 yrs of study for a general or honours BA/BSc degree. (3) English is the normal medium of tuition in all universities & the Dept of Education & Science recognizes an Indian MA degree as the equivalent of a British BA degree.

l.c./ NP/ stet/ equal

Single

(1) Education in Pakistan is not substantialy different from th of India; Both English & Urdu being the medium of instruction.

URDU l.c./ HINDI

(2) Sometimes the official language, Hindi, is also taught.

(3) MA degrees are obtained by examination after a further 2 yrs' study.

See Typing Target Practice, page 72, for a further exercise on

Footnotes

6 Type the following letter on A5 portrait paper. (a) Margins: elite 13–63, pica 6–56. (b) It will be necessary for you to listen for the margin bell and make your own right margin in the body of the letter.

> ***Note:*** After "Our ref" turn up 2 single spaces and type "Your ref KFC/TW", then turn up 2 single spaces and type the date.

Our ref EFY/RA/AN/4

Your ref KFC/TW

28 November 1984

FOR THE ATTENTION OF MR K F CHEUNG

W H Leon & Co Ltd
12-15 Hardon Road
YORK
YO1 6EB

Dear Sirs

RING BINDERS

We are now able to offer you A4 Ring Binders of excellent quality, with the standard 2-ring mechanism, at 38p per binder, plus carriage and VAT.

We also enclose leaflets giving details of our other products. These items all represent very good value for money at the prices quoted.

Yours faithfully

> ***Note:*** As there is no name or designation, turn up 8 single spaces before typing Encs, so that there is sufficient space for the signature.

Encs

7 Type the following letter on A5 portrait paper. (a) Margins: elite 13–63, pica 6–56. (b) It will be necessary for you to display the letter according to the instructions given on page 57 and to make your own right margin. (c) Correct the word error.

Our Ref TP/FRC

1 December 1984

FOR THE ATTENTION OF MRS A CHOUDHURY

Cleeton International PLC 15 Church Place LICHFIELD Staffordshire WS14 9DX

Dear Sirs

NEW COURSES FROM XENIDES MACHINARY LTD

We are pleased to introduce to you a new and extended programme of customer training courses. As you will see from the enclosed Information Pack, we will be providing a wide range of courses covering all areas of office automation. These courses provide a cost-effective means for your staff to get the best out of all up-to-date technology, equipment and software.

Yours faithfully MS F SMITH-BROOKES Marketing Manager Enc

See Typing Target Practice, page 20, for further exercises on

1 Type the following exercise on A4 paper in single spacing with double between the enumerated items. Follow the instructions contained in the exercise when typing the footnotes. Margins: elite 20–86, pica 11–77.

F O O T N O T E S

1 Footnotes are used:

(a) To identify a reference or person quoted in the body of a report.

Trs/ (c) To give the source of a quotation cited in a report.

(b) For explanations that may help or interest a reader.

2 Each footnote is:
TYPIST: Change small roman numerals to letters, as above, please.

lc/ (i) Preceded by the Reference Mark wh corresponds to the reference in the text.

(ii) Typed in single spacing.

The reference mark in the text must be a superscript.* In the foot-note, it is typed either on the same line or as a super script. In the text NO space is left between the reference mark and the previous character. In the footnote ONE SPACE is left between the reference mark and the first word. The reference mark may be a number, asterisk, dagger or double dagger. (See page 93)

In ordinary typewritten work, the footnote is usually placed on the page on wh the corresponding reference appears in the body, & typed in SINGLE spacing.‡ Care must be taken to leave enough space at the bottom of the page for the footnote, and, if a continuation page is needed, a clear space of 25 mm must be left after the footnote at the bottom of the page. The footnote is separated fr the main text by a horizontal line fr margin to margin. The horizontal line is typed by the under-score and the footnote is typed on the second single space below the horizontal line. If there is more than one footnote, turn up 2 single spaces between each.

Trs/ If the typewriter has an asterisk key, it will automatically be raised half a space when it is typed, but if a small x and the hyphen key hv

stet/ to be used then it will be necessary to use the half ~~space~~ spacing mechanism on the typewriter, or the interliner, to raise it above the line of typing. All the footnote signs must be superscripts if the asterisk key on the typewriter is used.

---

* Also known as a superior character.

‡ If the main text is in double spacing, the footnote is still typed in single spacing.

one single space after the last line of the text,

FORMAT FOR ENVELOPES

There are numerous sizes of envelopes, but the size will be used that best fits the letter and enclosures. The 3 most commonly used sizes are:

C5—229 × 162 mm (9″ × $6\frac{3}{8}$″) takes A5 paper unfolded and A4 folded once.
C6—162 × 114 mm ($6\frac{3}{8}$″ × $4\frac{1}{2}$″) takes A4 folded twice and A5 folded once.
DL—220 × 110 mm ($8\frac{5}{8}$″ × $4\frac{1}{4}$″) takes A4 equally folded into 3 and A5 folded once.

1 Type the following exercise on A4 paper. (a) Leave 25 mm (one inch) clear at the top of the page. (b) Margins: elite 20–85, pica 11–76. (c) Single spacing with double between each numbered item. (d) Locate and correct one word error.

GUIDE FOR TYPING ENVELOPES

1 Always type the envelope for each letter immediately after typing the letter.

2 The name and address should always be parallel to the longer side of the envelope.

3 On most envelopes the address should be started about one-third in from the left edge.

4 The first line must be approximately half-way down the envelope.

5 Each line of the address must occupy a separate line.

6 Single spacing is preferable on smaller envelopes - double spacing on larger envelops.

7 The post town must be typed in CLOSED CAPITALS.

8 The postcode is the last line in the address and should have a line to itself. The code is always typed in BLOCK CAPITALS. Do not use full stops or any punctuation marks between or after the characters in the code. Leave one clear space between the 2 halves of the code.

9 Special instructions such as PERSONAL, CONFIDENTIAL, PRIVATE or FOR THE ATTENTION OF should be typed 2 spaces above the name of the addressee.

FORMAT FOR FORMS OF ADDRESS—OPEN PUNCTUATION

Degrees and qualifications
Do not use punctuation. No spaces between the letters representing a degree or qualification, but one clear space between each group of letters,

eg, Mr (space) F (space) Eastwood (space) MA (space) BSc   Mr F Eastwood MA BSc.

Courtesy titles
(a) Must always be used with a person's name,
eg, Miss M K Green   J Bishop Esq   Mr W P Stevens   Mrs G Hill   Ms S G Matthews.
(b) Use either Mr or Esq when addressing a man, never both.
(c) Rev replaces Mr or Esq, eg, Rev R S Smith.
(d) Partnerships—the word Messrs is used before the name of a partnership,
eg, Messrs Martin & Sons   Messrs Johnson & Co   Messrs Bowron & Jones.
(e) Courtesy titles are not used in the following cases:
(i) Before the name of a limited company,
eg, P Yates & Co Ltd   W Robertson & Sons Ltd   Carter & Bailey PLC.
(ii) With impersonal names, eg, The British Non-ferrous Metal Co.
(iii) When a title is included in a name, eg, Sir John Brown & Co   Sir Arthur Hamilton-Grey.

Page 2

centre - spaced caps & u/s → C O L O U R

↓ 2 clear

DEVELOPING AND PRINTING ← centre

1½" clear to left ←
12 exposures £2.09
24 exposures £3.10
36 exposures £4.10
→ 1½" clear to right

SAME DAY SERVICE

↓ 2 clear

HAND ENLARGEMENTS ← centre

1½" clear
7" x 5" £2.00
10" x 8" £3.50
16" x 12" - - - - £5.00
20 x 16 - - - - £6.12
1½" clear

↓ 2 clear

DEVEØLOP AND CONTACT ← centre

1½" clear
Develop only £1.50
Contact only - - - £1.50
1½" clear

SAME DAY SERVICE

↓ 2 clear

UNLESS OTHERWISE STATED
WORK USUALLY TAKES 3 to 7 DAYS] centre

Page 3 / centre-spaced caps & u/s → BLACK AND WHITE

↓ 2 clear

1½" clear
Develop only £1.50
Develop and contatc ... £2.50
Reprints - - - £0.25
1½" clear trs

↓ 2 clear

Centre → SELECTIVE HAND ENLARGEMENTS

7" x 5" - - - - £1.00
10" x 8" - - - £2.00
16 x 12 - - - £3.00
20 x 16 - - - - £4.00

↓ 2 clear

Centre → ENLARGEMENTS

7" x 5" - - - - £2.00
10 x 8 - - £3.50

↓ 2 clear

A SELECTION OF FRAMES AND FOLDERS
IS ALWAYS AVAILABLE] centre

Proofreading: please turn to page 180 and complete exercise 5

Approximately one-third in from left edge ↓

First line half way down ⟶ Mr F Eastwood MA BSc
12 The Grove
Post town in capitals ⟶ OTTERY ST MARY
Devon
One space between 2 halves of code ⟶ EX11 1AD

Each item on a separate line

C6 envelope—162 × 114 mm ($6\frac{3}{8}'' \times 4\frac{1}{2}''$)

FOR THE ATTENTION OF MS S G MATTHEWS

P Yates & Co Ltd
17 New Street
DUDLEY
West Midlands
DY1 FG6

Practise typing envelopes

2 Type the following addresses on paper cut to represent C6 envelopes. Mark the first envelope PRIVATE and the second FOR THE ATTENTION OF MR J KENNEDY.

A W F Tegetmeir Esq 26 Coningsby Avenue Willerby HULL HU10 6EW

C T Bristow plc 3 Main Street Sandford CREDITON Devon EX17 4NG

Mr Liam O'Grady 5 Hope Street Ballinamore Bridge BALLINASLOW Co Galway IRISH REPUBLIC

Rev W Walcott The Rectory Bridle Road BOOTLE Merseyside L20 OAA

Miss D Chudasama Moorend 26 Forest Road HARROGATE North Yorkshire HG2 9DG

The Ferris Carpet Manufacturing Co The Parade Coryton CARDIFF CF4 7YR

Ms I Fabrizio 12 Kingsbridge Road DERBY DE1 8ZL

J R Cleeton & Co Ltd 87 Detheridge Drive BIRMINGHAM B3 2PP

See Typing Target Practice, page 21, for further exercises on

In business or in an examination, you may have to type on 3 or 4 pages of a folded leaflet. The contents of the pages may be centred vertically (each page as a whole) and each line centred horizontally, or the longest line on a page centred horizontally to give the starting point for all lines. In a folded programme you may have a column aligned at the left margin and a column aligned at the right margin with the lines in the middle centred. Whatever the layout, follow the instructions very carefully.

The paper may be folded and then fed into the machine, but this will crease it unless you are very careful. Provided the carriage is long enough, insert the paper lengthwise but, before doing so, mark the pages clearly. The following diagram will help:

FRONT SIDE OF PAPER (UNFOLDED)

Front page—right-hand side | Back page—left-hand side

Fold

Back page left-hand	Front page right-hand

It is advisable to mark these 2 pages on your paper before inserting it.

REVERSE SIDE OF PAPER (UNFOLDED)

Page 2—left-hand side of fold | Page 3—right-hand side of fold

Page 2 left-hand	Page 3 right-hand

3 Type the following folded leaflet which has typing on the front page and on pages 2 and 3. On each page centre the whole vertically.

FRONT PAGE

BARN STUDIOS ← spaced caps
29 Oulton Boulevard
LIVERPOOL L6 2AP

Telephone: 051-422 2985

(2 clear)

spaced caps and u/score → PRICE LIST

for

DEVELOPING AND PRINTING

(centre each line horizontally)

(2 clear)

Centre longest line to give starting point for all lines:

HAND ENLARGEMENTS
SLIDE COPYING
REPRINTS
PRINTS FROM PRINTS
CONTACT SHEETS, ETC

Pages 2 & 3 on next page

FORMAT FOR CARBON COPIES

All business firms keep an exact copy of letters, invoices, and other documents they send out. For this purpose the typist uses *carbon paper.* To take a carbon copy:

(a) Place face downwards on flat surface the sheet on which typing is to be done.
(b) On top of this, with coated (shiny) surface *upwards*, place a sheet of carbon paper.
(c) Place on top of these the sheet of paper on which carbon copy is to be made. If additional copies are required, repeat steps (b) and (c).
(d) Pick up all sheets together and insert into machine with coated surface of carbon paper facing cylinder.
(e) Make sure that feed rolls grip all sheets at the same time.

Carbon paper has a dull side and a glossy side. The glossy side does the work.

Glossy side of carbon is put against the paper on which the copy is to be made.

You always have one more sheet of typing paper than of carbon paper.

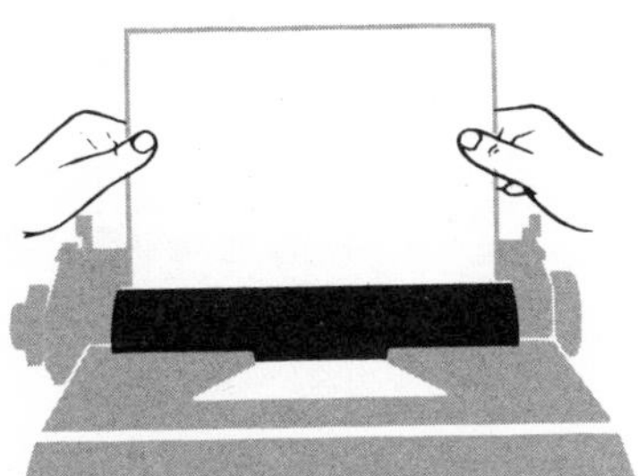

Straighten sides and top of pack carefully before inserting it in your machine.

Hold pack with left hand; turn cylinder smoothly with right hand.

Erasing errors on carbon copies

Correction paper
Before inserting the correction paper in front of the printing point for the top copy, insert the special correction paper prepared for carbon copies between the shiny side of your carbon paper and the carbon copy. Then place the correction paper for the top copy in front of the printing point and type the incorrect letter through all sheets. Remove the strips of paper and type the correct letter(s).

Correction fluid
Apply the appropriate fluid to the error on the carbon copy and the appropriate fluid to the error on the top copy. It is imperative that the fluid should be quite dry before any attempt is made to type in the correction.

Rubber
Before erasing, insert a strip of thickish paper between the shiny side of your carbon paper and the carbon copy. Then erase on the top copy. Remove the strip of paper and erase on the carbon copy. If you are taking more than one carbon copy, insert strips of paper behind the shiny surface of each sheet of carbon paper. Erase on top and all carbon copies. Remove the strips and then return the carriage/carrier to the typing point and type the correct letter(s).

Decide on margins. Set left margin and right margin. From right margin backspace one for one for the longest item in the money column and set a tab stop. Where an item runs on to 2 lines, it is usual to indent the second line 2 spaces.

2 Display the following profit and loss statement on a sheet of A4 paper. Use margins of elite 22–82, pica 12–72. Please insert leader dots.

VIDEX OFFICE SUPPLIES plc
PROFIT AND LOSS STATEMENT
FOR YEAR TO 31 OCTOBER 1984

	1984 £000's
Property and investment	23,725
Contracting, structural and specialist engineering	42,386
Shipping and magazines	6,827
	72,938
Interest	17,934
	55,004
Net profit before taxation	4,502
Profit attributable to minority interests	1,376
Net profit after taxation	49,126
Extraordinary items	22,039
Net profit after taxation and extraordinary items	71,165
Dividends	
On preference shares	80
On ordinary shares	14,945
	14,945
Dividend rate per ordinary share	6.20p
Earnings per ordinary share	20.04p

The figures for dividends and earnings per ordinary share have been adjusted to take account of the capitalisation issue in 1980.

See Typing Target Practice, pages 68 and 69, for further exercises on Financial Statements

Practise typing letters with a carbon copy

3 Type the following letter on A4 paper. (a) Margins: left $1\frac{1}{2}$", right 1". (b) Take a carbon copy. (c) Make your own line-endings. (d) Type a C6 envelope. (e) On completion read through carefully and correct any errors.

Ref GSP/ACM/RI

5 March 1985

Ms L O Fahey
112 Fleet Street
Storth
MILNTHORPE
Cumbria LA7 7HT

Dear Ms Fahey

FULL-TIME SECRETARIAL COURSE - SEC1FA

Thank you for your enquiry about the above Course which is to be held at this College from September 1985.

I am enclosing a pamphlet which gives brief details about this Course. If you are interested, I should be glad if you would complete and return the enclosed Application Form.

When I receive the completed Form I will write to you again and arrange a suitable date for an interview, when further details can be discussed.

Yours sincerely

MISS F A DETHERIDGE
Course Supervisor

Encs

4 Type the following letter on A4 paper. (a) Margins: left $1\frac{1}{2}$", right 1". (b) Take a carbon copy. (c) Make your own line-endings. (d) Type a C6 envelope. (e) Correct the word error. (f) On completion read through carefully and correct any errors.

Your ref GSP/ACM/RI   12 March 1985

Miss F A Detheridge Course Supervisor Marston Technical College
MILNTHORPE Cumbria LA7 7AA

Dear Miss Detheridge

FULL-TIME SECRETARIAL COURSE - SEC1FA

Thank you for your letter of 5 March and the details of the above Course.

I am enclosing the completed Application Form as I am very interested in this Course and would like to attend for an interview. Unfortunately I will be on holiday from 2 April to 16 April, but shall be available any time after that.

I look forward to hearing further from you.

Yours sincerely   Linda A Fahey   Enc

See Typing Target Practice, page 22, for further exercises on

FORMAT FOR ALIGNED RIGHT MARGIN

Programmes, display, financial statements, etc., sometimes have a right column and the last character of each line of this column may have to end at the same scale point. To do this:

Decide on the exact scale point at which you wish the last character to be typed and set a tab stop one space to the right of that point. From the tab stop backspace once for each character and space in the line to be aligned; from point reached, type the word(s)/figure(s).

FORMAT FOR TELEPHONE INDEX

It is usual to keep a list of names and addresses and telephone numbers which are frequently required. For this purpose use is made of the strip-indexing method, whereby each name and address and telphone number is typed on a separate strip. The strips are usually supplied in sheets, and the details are typed on the strips which are afterwards separated from the sheet. They are then inserted alphabetically in devices or frames specially made to take them. These strips can be moved up or down to allow additional strips to be inserted in their correct order or to remove strips containing obsolete names. The surname is usually typed first, in upper case letters, followed by the initial(s) and then the address, all on one line if possible. If 2 lines are needed, these must be in single spacing, as the strip is usually not more than 6 mm in depth. In order to carry the eye from the end of the address to the telephone number, continuous dots may be inserted, leaving one clear space before the first dot and one clear space after the last dot.

Note: In an index or alphabetical list, a comma is typed after the surname and after the initials. In the following example it will be seen that the right margin has been aligned.

Open punctuation

BROWN, A J, 46 Thomas Street, Leeds. LS2 9JT 0532 21375
FISHER, L, & Co Ltd, 20 Clitton Road, Northampton. NN1 5BQ 0604 6868

Full punctuation

BROWN, A. J., 46 Thomas Street, Leeds. LS2 9JT 0532 21375
FISHER, L., & Co. Ltd., 20 Clitton Road, Northampton. NN1 5BQ 0604 6868

1 Type the following names and addresses in alphabetical order according to the surname (if a personal name) or the first word of the name (if an impersonal name). Leave double spacing between each name. Margins: leave $\frac{1}{2}$" either side. Use A5 landscape paper.

Susan Brennan, 17 Broad Street, Basingstoke, Hants 0256 234567

William Craddock, 30 Bradford Road, Burnley, Lancs 0282 786655

Wilma Pugh, 49 High Holborn, London 01-472 2677

Harry Morgan, 23 St John's Way, Llanelli, Dyfed 0554 544366

R Cameron PLC, Kingseat, Dunfermline, Fife 0383 229175

U V Best & Co, 14 High Street, Leominster, Herefordshire 0568 678432

Charlotte Whelan, 12 Woodford Way, Edgware, Middx 01-654 3296

Sir Brian Winterford, Penrose, Wadebridge, Cornwall ... 020 881 54678

The Victoria Casting Co, 84 West Road, Lewes, East Sussex 079 16 2343

F McDonald, 17 Bridge Street, Stornoway, Isle of Lewis .. 0851 119732

See Typing Target Practice, page 67, for further exercises on

FORMAT FOR SIMPLE DISPLAY IN FULLY-BLOCKED LETTERS

Emphasis may be given to important facts in a letter by displaying these so that they catch the eye of the reader. Such displayed matter starts at the left margin, one clear space being left above and below, as in the specimen that follows.

Practise typing fully-blocked letter with displayed matter

5 Type the following letter on A4 paper. (a) Margins: elite 22–82, pica 12–72. (b) Take one carbon copy. (c) Type a C5 envelope. (d) Correct the word error. (e) On completion read through carefully and correct any errors.

Ref FL/JCM

14 December 1984

Miss A Syrota
General Manager
Graham Bond Engineering Ltd
24 Royal Square
Middleton in Teesdale
BARNARD CASTLE
Co Durham DL12 0QA

Dear Madam

PLAIN PAPER COPIERS

I understand that you wish to install a plain paper copier in your office for your own use. Despite the fact that you have a Reprographic Centre in your Company you will find a great saving in time and energy by having your own quiet, economical and reliable personal copier close to hand.

I give below the technicle information for which you asked.

Turn up 2 single spaces

Process - electrostatic direct copy
Dimensions - 39 × 35 × 16 cm

Turn up 2 single spaces

If you require any further information please contact me.

Yours faithfully
VIDEX OFFICE SUPPLIES plc

F LANGSTONE
Marketing Director

See Typing Target Practice, page 22, for a further exercise on

FORMAT FOR INVITATIONS

It is customary to use formal wording when sending out invitations to weddings, twenty-first birthday parties, etc. The invitations are written in the third person with a blank space left for the insertion of names of the guests in ink. The invitation begins with the name(s) of the writer(s) whose address is placed at the bottom left-hand margin. The date and R.S.V.P. are at the lower right-hand margin. Invitations are not signed.

6 On 2 cards type the following invitation from Mr & Mrs Ian Cruickshanks and the reply from the Santamaria family. Centre the whole vertically and each line horizontally on the card.

(a) Formal invitation

Mr and Mrs Ian Cruickshanks request the

pleasure of the company of

Mr + Mrs Peter Santamaria and José..........

at their daughter's twenty-first birthday party

on Saturday, 21st September, at ~~5~~ 8 pm

Glenavon
Kirkliston
West Lothian
EH29 4AB

2 September, 1985

RSVP

(b) Reply to a formal invitation

Mr + Mrs Peter Santamaria and José
have pleasure in accepting the kind invitation
of Mr + Mrs Ian Cruickshanks to their
daughter's twenty-first birthday party
on Saturday, 21 September, at 8 p.m.

27 Forth Road
Edinburgh
EH10 7BQ

10 September 1985

(c) On a card or suitable paper, type an invitation inviting a friend to your next birthday party.

When matter is to be displayed in columns, 3 spaces should be left between the longest line of one column and the start of the next. The first column starts at the left margin and tab stops are set for each of the other columns as explained on page 39 (g–k).

6 Type the following letter on A4 paper. (a) Margins: elite 22–82, pica 12–72. (b) Take one carbon copy. (c) Type a C5 envelope. (d) Make your own line-endings. (e) Correct the 2 word errors. (f) On completion read through carefully and correct any errors.

Ref JG/APT

Today's date

David Jessop (Insurance Brokers) Ltd
Hanbury House
20 St Mary's Street
BRIGHTON
BN4 2EQ

Dear Sirs

POLICY NO 44915

I wish to insure 3 items of jewelery under Policay No 44915 Section 4 - All Risks.

Item	Description	Price
1	One 9 ct Gold Fob	£39.50
2	One Lady's 15 ct Gold Bracelet	£265.00
3	One Silver Brooch with Gold Inlay	£36.50

As these items will obviously increase in value, is it possible to insure them for more than their purchase price?

I am enclosing the Valuation Certificates. I should be glad if you would return these Certificates to me with your reply.

Yours faithfully

MISS JANET GWYN

Encs

See Typing Target Practice, page 23, for a further exercise on

FORMAT FOR CARDS

The typist will have to type cards for a variety of purposes such as a mailing list, telephone index, credit sales index, etc.

When cards are to be filed in alphabetical order, then the filing "word" must start near the top edge of the card, say half an inch down. Other information on the card should be suitably displayed with at least half an inch margins all round, unless the contents are such that it is not possible to leave margins.

A fair amount of practice in typing cards is essential and a great deal of care is necessary in order to see that the card does not slip, or become out of alignment, when turned up/down; a backing sheet will help.

3 Type the following on a card measuring approximately 6" × 4" (152 × 102 mm). Read the instructions very carefully. Address the reverse side of the card to yourself.

Turn up 4 single spaces for top edge

Centre on page [
McGRAW-HILL BOOK COMPANY (UK) LIMITED
SHOPPENHANGERS ROAD MAIDENHEAD BERKSHIRE SL6 2QL

Turn up 2 single

Left margin of ½". Right not less than 2 spaces. [
Our Ref MT/BW

Turn up 2 single

YOUR ORDER NO 22 2 May, 1985

Thank you for the above order, dated 25 April, for 50 copies of APPLIED TYPING, fourth edition. These will be despatched tomorrow, 3 May.

4 Type the following index card which measures approximately 6" × 4" (152 × 102 mm). Find the left margin by centring the longest line. Leave one clear space after colon.

SURNAME: HEWSON FORENAME(S): Charles

ADDRESS: 91 Beach Avenue, Swansea, Glamorgan.

DATE OF BIRTH: 29 March 1950

QUALIFICATIONS: B.Com., Diploma in Management

EXPERIENCE: 3 years in computer programming

REFERENCES: Richard Fitzwarren,
Electronic Computing Co. Ltd.,
40 Bristol Road,
Swansea. SA7 9AN

Telephone: 0792 853741

5 Type the following information on a card measuring approximately 4" × 6" (102 × 152 mm), ie, the shorter edge at the top.

MICROWAVE RUNNING COSTS

Usually costs less to cook by micro-wave — sometimes much less. Some approximate comparisons with conventional cooking methods illus-trate this:

Roasting 3 lb topside Beef *lc.*
Conventional oven: 1¾ units
Microwave: under ½ unit

Steaming apple suet pudding
Boiling ring: just under ½ unit
Microwave: just " ¼ "

Grilling 2 herrings
Grill: just under ¼ unit
Microwave: just over ⅓ unit

Boiling cabbage
Boiling ring: just under ¼ unit
Microwave: " " ¼ "

See Typing Target Practice, page 66, for further exercises on

Cards

When alterations have to be made in typewritten or handwritten work of which a fair copy is to be typed, or in copy for printers, these are indicated in the original copy by proof-correction marks. To avoid confusion, the proof-correction mark is placed in the margin against the line in which the correction is to be made, with an oblique line placed after it, to show that it is the end of the particular correction. Study and learn the following proof-correction marks.

Sign in margin	*Meaning*	*Mark in text*	
l.c. or lc/	Lower case = small letter(s)	— /	under letter(s) to be altered or struck through letter(s)
u.c. or uc/ or Caps/	Upper case = capital letter(s) When a word(s) is underlined, Caps is written in the margin and this means type the word(s) in capitals; DO NOT underscore the word(s) unless specifically asked to do so, when the instruction would be Caps and u/s (underscore)	— /	under letter(s) to be altered or struck through letter(s)
ꝺ	Delete (take out)	—	through letter(s) or word(s)
NP or // N.P.	New paragraph	[	placed before first word of paragraph
Stet/	Let it stand, ie, type the word(s) that have been crossed out and have a dotted or broken line underneath	----	under word(s) struck out
Run on/	No new paragraph required. Carry straight on	⟶	
⅄	Caret—insert letter, word(s) omitted	⅄	placed where the omission occurs
⁀‿	Close up—less space	⁀‿	between letters or words
trs/	Transpose, ie, change order of words or letters as marked	⊓⊔	between letters or words, sometimes numbered
#	Insert space	⅄	
CLARKE	If a word is not clear in the text, it may have been written in the margin in capitals in a ruled box. The word should be typed in lower case or as indicated in the original script.		

Personal business letters
Used when writing to an unknown person or firm about a personal business matter. The layout is similar to that of a business letter. If your home address is not printed on your stationery, type it about 13 mm from the top and centre on page or in such a way that the last line ends flush with the right-hand margin. Date in usual place. Name and address of addressee may be typed in usual place or at bottom left-hand margin, 2 spaces below your name.

Formal personal letters
Used when writing to someone older than yourself or to whom you owe respect. Layout as for personal business letter. Salutation is formal, e.g., Dear Miss Brown, Dear Mrs. Taylor, Dear Dr Emery.

Personal letters
Used when writing to a personal friend. Your address and date as in a personal business letter. No name and address of addressee. Salutation is informal, e.g., Dear Mary, Dear Arthur, Dear Uncle George.

2 Type the following personal business letter on A4 paper. Use margins of elite 22–82, pica 12–72. Centre the sender's address on the page half an inch from the top. Type an envelope and take one carbon copy. Correct word error.

17 Londonderry Road
ARMAGH BT61 7AA

23rd April 1985

Messrs Aitken & Wright
27 Cork Street
COLERAINE
Co Londonderry

Dear Sirs

I have today received the set of 7 heavy gauge non-stick aluminimum pans which you advertised in last Saturday's HERALD and for wh I sent y a cheque for £36.70.

The lid of the casserole is twisted and does not fit. This lid is also meant to be used with the deep-fry pan but here again it does not fit properly.

The 4 egg poachers, which should have accompanied the omelette pan, are missing.

Please let me have a new lid for the casserole pan together w the 4 missing egg poachers.

Yours faithfully

Mrs Margaret Donovan

See Typing Target Practice, page 65, for further exercises on
Personal Letters

Practise typing from typescript with proof-correction marks

1 Type a copy of the following exercise on A4 paper. (a) Make all the necessary corrections. (b) Margins: elite 22–82, pica 12–72. (c) Double spacing.

INCOME BONDS ← *spaced caps*

u.c./ If you have £5,000 or more to invest, the national Savings
⁋/ Income Bonds will provide you with a ~~good~~ regular monthly income, leaving your capital untouched.

Interest Rates. The interest rate is varied from time to time, and the interest is earned on a day-to-day basis from
N.P. the date your payment is received. [The income can be paid
trs./l.c./ into your Bank Account directly, or sent to you by post.

Maximum Holding. Income Bonds can be purchased in multiples
stet/ of £1,000, with a ~~first~~ *minimum* purchase of £5,000, and a maximum of £200,000.

2 Type the following exercise on A5 portrait paper. (a) Make all the necessary corrections. (b) Margins: elite 13–63, pica 6–56. (c) Single spacing.

Induction Courses ← *caps + u/score*

⁋/ A new employee needs time to settle in to his ~~new~~ environment, to meet his new colleagues, and time to learn about the organ-
stet/ ization ~~who~~ *which* has employed him. An induction ~~course~~ *training* should, therefore, be given to every newcomer, no matter what his previous experience. The terms of employment should be explained to
N.P. him, together with any office rules, etc. [In small businesses, newcomers may undergo their induction training individually, and
trs./ insruction can be informal and personal.
Run on/ In larger organizations, it may be possible to form small groups
l.c./ to go through the Induction Course together. *(of the business)*

> ***Note:*** Certain words which have been inadvertently omitted from the original text may be inserted in the margin and encircled in a balloon. The words in the balloon must be typed where indicated by the caret sign.

See Typing Target Practice, page 24, for further exercises on

Proof-correction Marks

FORMAT FOR ALTERNATIVE PLACEMENT OF NAME AND ADDRESS OF ADDRESSEE

This may be typed in single spacing at the foot of the page at left margin. If the letter finishes with the complimentary close, turn up 9 single spaces before typing the name and address of the addressee. If the letter finishes with the name and designation of the signatory, turn up 2 single spaces before typing the name and address of the addressee. If you are using a continuation sheet and the name and address of addressee has not been typed before the salutation, then it may be typed at the bottom of the FIRST page, 2 single spaces after the last typed line and ending one inch (25 mm) from the bottom of the page. If you type the name and address of the addressee at the bottom of the page and the letter is marked for the attention of a particular person, the attention line is typed before the salutation. Similarly, any special directions must be typed in the usual place and not at the bottom of the page.

FORMAT FOR DITTO MARKS

When the same word is repeated in consecutive lines of display matter, quotation marks may be used under the repeated word. If there is more than one word repeated, the quotation marks must be typed under each word. The abbreviation "do" (without the full stop in open punctuation) may be used under a group of words. When used with blocked style, the ditto marks should be blocked at the beginning of each word; with centred style the ditto marks should be centred under the word(s).

1 Type the following letter on A4 paper with margins: elite 22–82, pica 12–72. Put the name and address of the addressee at the end and type an envelope.

GAS/BMM 1st May 1985 FOR THE ATTENTION OF MR. CYRIL BURGOYNE

Dear Sirs, ENQUIRY

We thank y for yr letter asking f details and prices of our shaped car covers for all makes of cars, & we encl. our catalogue of these covers.

We would point out that the prices below apply only to minimum orders of 20 covers in sizes of any assortment.

```
Length 366 cm for small cars .... £12.60 each
"      396 "  "   medium cars ... £13.75 "
"      427 "  "   large cars .... £14.15 "
```

Please let us know if you require further information.

Yours faithfully,
BRACKNELL AND PALMER LIMITED

G. A. SANDERS
MARKETING MANAGER

Stewart & Goodall Ltd.,
Norton Road,
IPSWICH.
IP4 2DF

Enc.

PS. Prices for smaller quantities will be quoted on request.

LONGHAND ABBREVIATIONS

In a rough draft certain longhand words may have been abbreviated, but these must be typed in full. Some of these abbreviations are given below.

Abbreviation	*Word in full*	*Abbreviation*	*Word in full*	*Abbreviation*	*Word in full*
bn	been	co	company	dept	department
f	for	fr	from	hv	have
recd	received	rect	receipt	ref	reference
sec	secretary	sh	shall	shd	should
th	that	togr	together	w	with
wd	would	wh	which	wl	will
yr	your	yr	year		

Note: & (ampersand), Co, Ltd, are only abbreviated in the names of companies; the & may also be abbreviated with figures.

Practise typing from abbreviated typescript

3 After studying the above abbreviations, read the following passage to see that you understand it and then type a copy on A4 paper. (a) All abbreviations to be typed in full. (b) Margins: elite 22–82, pica 12–72. (c) Double spacing.

CARDPHONES

It is now possible to make telephone calls without the use of coins, fr certain tel kiosks. Cardphones allow you to use cards, wh can be obtained fr Post Offices f £2 f a 40-unit card, or £10 f a 200-unit card.

The card is inserted into the slot th is provided on the tel. The digital display wl show the no of unused units as yr call is being made.

The card wl be ejected automatically when yr call is finished & the handset replaced.

4 Type the following exercise on A5 portrait paper. (a) Margins: elite 13–62, pica 6–56. (b) Single spacing. (c) Correct the word error.

THE TELEMESSAGE

Do you know th a Telemessage can be sent fr any tel or by telex? The standard 50-word charge pays f the message itself, & the address is free. Additional blocks of 50 words wl be charged at a reduced rate, & duplicate messages may be sent to any no of addresses.

The Telemessage is delivered in a bright yellow envelope w bold, blue printing. Shd y wish to send a telemessage f a special ocassion, there is a wide variety of attractively designed cards.

Format

A5 landscape paper   Double spacing except for headings

Output Target—10 minutes

FINANCIAL STATEMENT

Average Salaries According to Age Group ← centre

Group	Average Emoluments	Range		Recent Annual Percentage Increase
		Lowest	Highest	
	£	£	£	%
25-29	4,750	4,000	5,500	4
30-34	5,500	4,500	6,500	
3~~2~~5-39	6,300	5,000	7,600	5
40-44	7,500	6,000	9,000	

Task 26

Output Target—8 minutes

Display this menu on a sheet of A5 portrait paper. Centre the whole vertically & each line horizontally. Correct one ~~word error~~.

STRATHALLEN HOTEL

GAIRLOCH, ROSS-SHIRE

← 2 clear

M E N U ← spaced caps

← one clear

DINNER - 7 October 1985

← 2 clear

Hairst Bree Soup

Pâté Maison

Grapefruit Cocktail

← 2 clear

Haggis and mashed swede (lc)

Stake Diane, Brandy & Cream Sauce

Sirloin Steak & Red Wine Sauce

Fried Fillet of Plaice & Tartare Sauce

Chipped Potatoes, Boiled Potatoes, Peas

← 2 clear

Apple Pie

Sherry Trifle

Cheese Board

← 2 clear

Coffee

HAIRST BREE

Insert accents in ink

5 Type a copy of the following on A4 paper. (a) Make all the necessary corrections. (b) Margins: elite 22–82, pica 12–72. (c) Double spacing. (d) Take a carbon copy.

CAPS/ The Horn Dance

trs/ It is beleived th the Abbots Bromley horn dance was performed /uc
in 1226. originally

words/ The 12 dancers are, by tradition, always male. (6) men carry the
reindeer antlers, accompanied by Maid Marian, the Hobby Horse,
+ arrow/ the Juster, a boy carrying a bow, another a triangle, & a
stet/ muscian. The 6 horns together weigh well over ~~100~~ 200 lb, &
NP/ measure fr 29 to 39 inches across. [The original purpose of the
uc/ horn dance is no longer clear, but it is a tradition wh still
survives to this day.

6 Type a copy of the following on A4 paper. (a) Make all the necessary corrections. (b) Margins: elite 22–82, pica 12–72. (c) Single spacing with double between each numbered item.

SEAT BELTS

There are certain cases where you may be exempt fr wearing
run on/ a seat belt.
I give below one or 2 instances.

lc/ 1 If you hv a valid Medical exemption.

2 If yr seat belt has become faulty on yr journey, or previously, + you
trs/ hv arranged to hv the belt replaced or repaired.

5 ~~3~~ If you are the driver of a licensed taxi wh is being
used to carry a passenger f hire.

4 If you are driving a specially-constructed or adapted
local/ vehicle f the purpose of making deliveries or collections.

stet/ 3 ~~5~~ If you are reversing a ~~vehicle~~ car, or, if you are a
qualified driver, + if you are supervising a learner
who is reversing.

See Typing Target Practice, page 25, for further exercises on

FOOD PRICES COMPARED

DECEMBER 1982

Typist - I think one of the Totals is wrong - please check

Retain abbreviations

Commodity	Malta	Greece	Spain Costa del Sol	Spain Costa Blanca	U.K.	U.S.A.
	£	£	£	£	£	£
Bread	0.14	0.22	0.10	0.10	0.38	0.34
Butter(1)	0.19	0.40	1.09	0.85	0.44	0.40
Cheese(1)	0.22	0.35	1.09	0.85	0.44	0.40
Chicken(2)	1.10	0.96	0.73	0.70	1.30	1.17
Eggs(3)	0.51	0.52	0.60	0.57	0.68	0.45
Chops(2)	1.50	1.90	1.83	1.76	1.48	2.24
Fish(2)	1.80	3.07	2.09	1.91	2.60	2.70
Milk(4)	0.16	0.15	0.24	0.22	0.35	0.34
Margarine(1)	0.26	0.23	0.36	0.32	0.21	0.27
Oranges(2)	0.29	0.30	0.42	0.22	0.72	0.67
Potatoes(2)	0.35	0.23	0.17	0.19	0.12	0.56
Sugar(2)	0.55	0.39	0.29	0.28	0.40	0.45
Tomatoes(2)	0.96	0.48	0.52	0.31	1.60	0.78
Total	8.07	9.20	9.56	8.41	10.70	12.27

caps/

The amts purchased were as follows:

(1) 250 gm
(2) 1 kilo
(3) 1 dozen
(4) 1 litre

It shd be noted th the type of shop at wh the goods were bought can make a difference to the price. Obviously, certain items wl be cheaper when in season.

Use of roman numerals

(a) For numbering tables and paragraphs instead of using ordinary (arabic) figures, eg, Chapter IX, Table XIII.

(b) Sometimes to express the year, eg, 1985, MCMLXXXV.

(c) For designation of monarchs, forms and class numbers, eg, George VI, Form V, Class IX.

(d) Small roman numerals are used for numbering prefaces of books, sub-paragraphs or subsections.

Examples of roman numerals

Study the following table. Note the 7 symbols: I (one), V (five), X (ten), L (fifty), C (one hundred), D (five hundred) and M (one thousand). Note also that when a smaller numeral precedes a larger one, it is subtracted, eg, IX=9; but when a smaller numeral follows a larger one it is added to it, eg, XI=11.

Roman numerals may be typed in upper or lower case. It is important to remember to use a capital or small I (i) to represent the roman numeral one.

Arabic	*Capital Roman*	*Small Roman*	*Arabic*	*Capital Roman*	*Small Roman*
1	I	i	20	XX	xx
2	II	ii	30	XXX	xxx
3	III	iii	40	XL	xl
4	IV	iv	50	L	l
5	V	v	60	LX	lx
6	VI	vi	70	LXX	lxx
7	VII	vii	80	LXXX	lxxx
8	VIII	viii	90	XC	xc
9	IX	ix	100	C	c
10	X	x	500	D	d
			1000	M	m

Note: In the above example the roman numerals are blocked at the left.

Practise typing roman numerals

1 Type the following exercise on A5 landscape paper. (a) Margins: elite 22–82, pica 12–72. (b) Double spacing.

Refer to Section IX, Chapter II, Page 340, Paragraph 2(iii).

Read parts XVI, XVII, and XVIII, subsections iii, vi, and x.

The boys in Forms VI and IX will take Stages I, II, and III.

Charles II, Henry VIII, George IV, James VI, and Edward III.

Proofreading: please turn to page 180 and complete exercise 1

See Typing Target Practice, page 26, for further exercises on

Format
A4 paper Blocked paragraphs Full punctuation
Leave room for name and address of addressee

Output Target—15 minutes

Our Ref TID/MAR

18 April, 1985

Dear Sir/Madam

(Please take one carbon copy & on the carbon copy type in yr name & address, & delete the unnecessary word in the salutation.)

MICROWAVE COOKING AT HOME

The microwave cooker is not just another cooker – it is a new & easier way of ~~making~~ preparing food. It saves time & trouble because it can give y a hot meal in minutes, even straight fr the freezer. It is a boon in other ways:

i. It saves money by saving energy.
ii. It is cheaper to use than an ordinary cooker.
iii. It is simple & flexible to use & clean.
iv. It does not need any special installation – it just plugs in.

[Microwave cooking is essential to busy housewives; to professionals in a hurry; to shift workers & others who eat at irregular hrs; to retired people w. small cooking requirements; for the single & f the young. It fits a casual unpredictable life style as well as doing the family cooking.

[Microwave cooking has bn used by commercial caterers f yrs. Now designed f home use, it is working miracles in the domestic kitchen.

[Although it can perform most cooking operations fr scrambled eggs to a family dinner, it is not a complete substitute f the conventional cooker.
[Why not complete the tear-off portion below, send it to us & we wl let y hv complete details.

Please send me details of your MX 120 Microwave Cooker

SURNAME ______________ FORENAME(S) ______________

ADDRESS ______________________________

FORMAT FOR ENUMERATIONS—ROMAN NUMERALS

When roman numerals are used for enumerations they may be blocked at the left,

eg, (i)	Surname	Leave 4 spaces after right bracket.
(ii)	Christian Name	Leave 3 spaces after right bracket.
(iii)	Address	Always leave 2 spaces after right bracket, or last letter, in the longest number.

Practise typing numbered items

2 Type the following exercise on A4 paper. (a) Margins: elite 20–85, pica 10–75. (b) Single spacing.
Note: Arabic figures in colour indicate the number of spaces to be left after the roman numeral.

PERSONAL PENSIONS

Everyone who is self-employed or not covered by a company pension scheme ought to have a Personal Pension Fund investment.

I [4] SIZE OF INVESTMENT

The investment should provide a useful cash sum on retirement plus an income for life of 50 per cent of a person's average earnings.

II [3] AMOUNT OF INVESTMENT

At present, for people under 40, it is 17.5 per cent of "net relevant income", and for those between 41 and 65 it is 20 per cent.

III[2] FULL TAX RELIEF

Pension funds invest free of tax, enabling them to make very substantial gains over the years.

3 Type the following on A5 landscape paper. (a) Margins: 20–86, pica 11–76. (b) Double spacing. (c) Correct the word error.
Note: The first word after the enumerations must always start at the same point on the scale.

FISH PONDS

(i) [4] DO make sure the water temprature is similar to that in which the fish are delivered, before releasing them into the pond.

(ii) [3] DO top up the water level regularly in hot weather.

(iii)[2] DO supply shade so that the fish will not be subjected to direct sunlight.

(iv) [3] DO protect the pool from icing up in the winter.

(v) [4] DON'T handle the fish.

(vi) [3] DON'T overfeed.

(vii)[2] DON'T introduce predatory fish into a pool with gold-fish.

See Typing Target Practice, page 27,
for further exercises on

(c) Empty contents of bucket into clean water tank. Test for colour fastness on a hidden part of the carpet.

(d) Empty 150 ml of Fortuna De-Foamer into the bucket.

(e) Position cleaning head on carpet several feet away fr you.

(f) Do not clean the same area more than 3 times w'out first allowing it to dry thoroughly.

(b) Add 350 ml of Fortuna Carpet Cleaner

For the best results, heavily soiled or stained areas may need pre-treating. Our Fortuna pre-spotter has been specially formulated to treat most household stains gently and effectively.

J R Brockhurst and Son (at 17 High Street, East Grinstead, West Sussex, RH19 1AA) are our agents and they will be delighted to help you.

Yours sincerely

(e) Plug in m/c + switch on both switches to start vacuum pump motors.

Squeeze trigger to release spray of cleaning solution + move cleaning head HEAD steadily towards you. (This is part of (f))

Task 22 Output Target—6 minutes

Please send the following memo to Irina Sinclair from Terry MacKenzie. Date 3rd April 1985. Use subject heading: SALES FIGURES JAN-MARCH 1985

Our sales figures for the first 3 months of 1985 were as follows:

January £304,076
Feb £372,851
March £413,922

These figures wl be discussed at the Sales Meeting on 24th April.

The figures for 1984 were:

Jan £297,777
February £302,861
March £375,490

FORMAT FOR SUMS OF MONEY IN COLUMNS

Refer to the instructions given on page 42 with regard to the typing of decimals. Then note the following.

The £ sign is typed over the first figure in the £'s column.
Units, tens, hundreds, etc, fall under one another.

Example:

```
  £
110.05
 20.00
  0.10
 13.72
```

Practise typing sums of money in columns

1 Type the following on A5 portrait paper, taking care to type the decimal points, units, tens and hundreds figures under one another. (a) Centre the exercise vertically and horizontally. (b) Leave 3 spaces between the columns. (c) Single spacing.

```
£         £         £
146.57    358.25    216.90
200.06    347.12    325.89
 19.55     20.75     77.00
  4.56      7.89      7.49
```

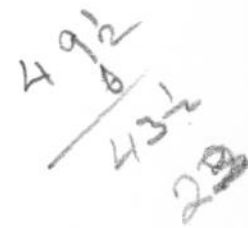

INTERLINER LEVER

The interliner lever may be found on the right or left side of the typewriter. Locate this on your machine. The interliner lever frees the platen from the ratchet control, so that the platen may be turned freely forward or backward as required. When the lever is returned to its normal position, your machine will automatically return to the original spacing.

FORMAT FOR DOUBLE UNDERSCORING OF TOTALS

If you have to type double lines underneath the totals, use the interliner. When typing totals proceed as follows:

(a) Type the underscore for the first lines above the totals. (Do not turn up before typing the first lines.) These lines extend from the first to the last figure of the longest item in each column.
(b) Turn up twice and type the totals.
(c) Turn up once and then type the lines below the totals.
(d) Turn the cylinder up slightly by using the interliner lever and type the second lines. Then return the interliner lever to its normal position.

FIGURES IN COLUMNS

Thousands and millions marked by commas or space, e.g., 42,000   42,000,000   42 000   42 000 000

Practise typing double lines under totals

2 Display the following exercise on A5 landscape paper. (a) Single spacing for the main part. (b) Leave 3 spaces between columns. (c) Follow the instructions for the total figures. (d) Decimal points must fall under one another.

```
£           £           £           £
  228.90       12.34      212.34      109.87
  404.75      566.78       33.44      654.57
  323.25       90.12      105.62    1 010.85
1 234.56       35.45    1 212.05      354.25
  789.00    1 237.95      343.18    1 213.65
  654.32      220.16      331.26      434.12   <—— Do not turn up
________    ________    ________    ________   <—— Turn up 2 spaces

3 634.78    2 162.80    2 237.89    3 777.31   <—— Turn up one space
========    ========    ========    ========   <—— Use interliner
```

See Typing Target Practice, page 28, for further exercises on
Sums of Money in Columns
Interliner Lever
Double Underscoring of Totals

A4 paper Semi-blocked style
Insert subject heading CARPET CLEANING MACHINE

Our Ref BAR/TWO

Typist - take 2 carbon copies - one for R L Brockhurst [BROCKHURST] and Son & one for file. Type 2 envelopes - one for Miss Neenan & one for R. L. Brockhurst and Son. Correct 2 word errors.

3 April 1985

Miss K W Neenan
14 Northcote Drive
EAST GRINSTEAD
West Sussex
RH19 1AA

Dear Miss Neenan

Thank you for your letter of enquiry dated 29 March.

u.c./ Our Fortuna Carpet cleaning machine lifts out the dirt from the carpet by forcing a jet of powerful but gentle carpet cleaning solution deep into the pile to clean the carpet fibres and free ground-in soil & dirt particals. You can actually see the ⁁ amt of dirt th the Fortuna machine has extracted fr yr carpet. (amazing ⁁ whole)

ANTI-STATIC AID

The very best carpet shampoo may leave a residue on yr carpet to attract dirt and cause rapid re-soiling. The fortuna system (completely overcomes this problem because) no residue is left behind in the pile. Also, The Fortuna Carpet Cleaner contains an anti-static ingredient wh helps prevent dirt fr gathering ⁁ on newly-cleaned carpets.

u.c./ l.c.

QUICK DRYING

Because most of the moisture is vacuumed up immediately, (probably in less than one hr) the pile hardly gets damp. Therefore, yr carpet dries quickly ⁁ and when used correctly there is no chance of soaking and shrinkage.

[handwritten margin: ☐/ cor]

EASY TO USE

The Fortuna machine is very light & as easy to use as a vacum cleaner.

[handwritten margin: please use hanging paras.]

2 1. It is fast because no vacuuming is needed after using the Fortuna system.

3 2. Fortuna is the system th you ~~operate~~ (stet) (use) yourself, so you not only clean w professional thoroughness, but save on the purchase of a machine & save on labour costs too.

1 3. It is excellent f fitted carpets as it gets right into corners & up to the skirting board.

The machine is easy to prepare. This is all y hv to do:

(a) Fill bucket to within 2" of top w warm water (30 °C). Do not use hot water as this may damage yr carpet.

QUOTATION FORM - MOTOR CAR

Surname: REID Mr/Mrs/Miss/Ms: Ms

Forenames: Charlotte Mary

Home Address: 14 Heath End Grove

Town: Coventry County: Warwickshire Postcode: CV17 2RT

Telephone Number: 0203 466223 Occupation: Co. Director

Age - Years: 30 Months: 2 Date of Birth: 01 06 1952

1 Make of car: Austin Model: Mark II

cc: 1800 Year: 1969 Letters and numbers: WOM 234J

2 How many years have you held a UK driving licence? 10

3 Will there be any drivers under the age of 25?* NO

4 How many years NO CLAIM DISCOUNT earned? 10

---

5 Will the car be used for business purposes?* YES

6 Have you been involved in any accidents in the last 3 years?* NO

7 Have you been convicted of any motoring offence (except parking) or is any offence pending?* NO

* Answer YES or NO

FORMS

Business organisations have a great variety of forms which have been printed or duplicated, with guide headings, boxes, columns, etc, and the typist has to type in additional information. When the insertion is typed on the same line as the printed heading, there are 2 clear spaces before the start of the insertion. Where the insertion comes below a printed heading, it is typed on the next line. However, if the column is deep and the information to be inserted is short, it will look better with a clear space between the printed heading and the inserted matter.

Information typed in opposite headings should be on the same line as the base of the printed heading and, therefore, it is important to know how close your typewriter prints to its aligning scale. Type a sentence and study exactly the space between the typing and the scale so that, when you insert a form and wish to align your typing with the bottom of the printed words, you will know how much to adjust the paper with the variable line spacer. When typing over ruled or dotted lines, no character should touch the ruled or dotted line. Therefore, with the variable line spacer adjust the typing line so that, when typed, the descending characters y, p, g, etc, are very slightly above the dotted line or underscore.

Practise typing information on a skeleton form

3 There is a skeleton of the above form in the *Teaching Notes and Solutions* and copies may be duplicated. Insert the form into your typewriter and then type in the handwritten words and figures.

See Typing Target Practice, page 29, for further exercises on Printed Forms

Task 20 ▶ *Format* A4 paper

Output Target—25 minutes

PROMOTION SUMMARY

Typist - type a skeleton form - omit handwriting - & take a carbon copy. On the original type in the handwritten details. Retain the carbon until a later date.

1. Recommended for: Bookshop Promotion .... ✓

Typist: insert "ticks" in ink

Library Promotion .... ✓

Direct Marketing .... ✓

2. Quarterly "New Books" Entry

Type of Entry (A, B, C): ....A.... Date ....3rd Quarter....

3. Other catalogue entries: General; International; Business Education; British Titles

....

4. Exhibitions and Conferences: BMC, EPC(3), Seminars (10)

....

....

5. Complimentary copies:

		Quantity			Quantity
(a)	Copyright	12	(e)	Research	-
(b)	Author	6	(f)	Reviews	50
(c)	Subsidiaries	10	(g)	Academics	500
(d)	Foreign Rights	10	(h)	Exhibitions	10

	COSTS	
	ESTIMATED	ACTUAL
6. Advertising (in detail on separate sheets) TES, NATFHE, TCom, CT	£900.00	£932.50
7. Mail Promotion (in detail on separate sheets) GMS, General Buyers	£3,000.00	£3,265.00
8. Other (in detail on separate sheets) Stands	£500.00	£402.60
	£4,400.00	£4,600.10

FORMAT FOR INVOICES

INVOICE NO 1543

THE BLACKBURN SUPPLY CO
West Addison Street
BLACKBURN
BB2 6AT

4 November 1984

Mrs B Granger
42 Witton Street
BLACKBURN
BB1 6JN

Note: After the second horizontal line, turn up 2 spaces and type the £ sign in the appropriate columns. Then turn up another 2 spaces before starting the items.

FIGURES—units must always be typed under units, tens under tens, etc. Follow the text carefully when typing the TOTAL column and, if necessary, refer to page 74.

Where possible, leave 2 clear spaces after the vertical lines before typing the items with the exception of the money columns where the decimal points must fall underneath one another.

QUANTITY	DESCRIPTION	PRICE	TOTAL
		£	£
1	Lounge Unit	64.95	64.95
2	Shelf Units	79.95	159.90
1	500 mm Chest Unit	59.95	59.95
			284.80
	Delivery charge		15.00
			£299.80
	Prices include VAT E & OE		

INVOICES

An invoice is the document sent by the seller to the purchaser and shows full details of the goods sold. The layout of invoices varies from firm to firm according to the information to be given. Invoices are always printed with the seller's name, address and other useful information.

Practise typing invoices

4 There is a skeleton invoice form in the *Teaching Notes and Solutions* and copies of this may be duplicated. If you do not have a suitable invoice form, place a sheet of A4 paper over the exercise above and lightly trace with a pencil the printed ruling. Insert the paper into your typewriter and set margin and tab stops for the beginning of each column. Then type the information exactly as it appears.

5 On another invoice form display the following:

Invoice No. 1723 Supplier: the same as above Date: 8 December 1984
Purchaser: P W BURNETT & CO 11 Brownhill Road BLACKBURN BB1 9BA

100	1 kg Bags Superfine Sugar	0.30	30.00
50	tins (large) Garden Peas	0.21	10.50
60	tins Best Quality Salmon	0.98	58.80
40	tins (medium) Tomato Soup	0.25	10.00
			109.30
	Container (returnable)		10.00
			£119.30
	Prices include VAT E & OE		

Task 19 ▶ *Format* Output Target—12 minutes

A4 paper (use one side only) Suitable margins
Shoulder headings instead of paragraph headings

ALL CHANGE

Up until 1st May 1983 I used my cheque card when I cashed a cheque abroad and this was an acceptable and handy way of acquiring currency in a foreign country.

Run on/ The cheque card is still valid in the United K. whether I am cashing cheques or purchasing goods, but abroad I need a different card.

EUROCHEQUE ENCASHMENT CARD I must now hv a v.c./ Eurocheque encashment card wh is solely f use abroad. I can cash a max. of 2 cheques a day, ea. up to the value of £50; however, they must be cashed at the same time + at a bank showing an EC symbol.

PASSPORTS In 1983 applications for British passports totalled over 3,000,000 + it is estimated th there are currently over 16 million valid British l.c./ Passports. N.P./ In the 18th century British passports were written in Latin + English + then until abt the middle of the 19th century they were in French.

The currant British passport has a gold-embossed hard cover + inside the cover I read:

"Her Britannic Majesty's Principal Secretary of State for Foreign and Commonwealth Affairs Requests ℓc and requires in the name of Her Majesty all those whom it may concern to allow the bearer to pass freely without let or hindrance and to afford the bearer such assistance and protection as may be necessary."

At some time fr. 1984 onwards this noble document wl pass into oblivion OBLIVION because members of the EEC hv decreed th I must use a laminated plastic card wh has Optical Character Recognition capabilities.

When I fly to the sun + land at Alicante airport, I wl show my new "passport" to an electronic scanner; the scanner wl convey the details to a central computer + if I am not on the "wanted" list a green light wl flash + I wl be free to sizzle in the sun. However, if a red light ~~shines~~ shows I may be in trouble.

(Typist - indented paras, please. Correct 2 word errors.)

A trader registered for VAT who supplies taxable goods to another taxable person must issue a VAT invoice giving the VAT registration number, tax point, type of supply, etc. (For details of VAT regulations as applied to invoices, please see *Practical Typing Exercises, Book One,* page 66).

Practise typing a VAT invoice

6 Type the following invoice on a suitable form. Please see *Teaching Notes and Solutions* for printed form. ***Note:*** In business, where space on a document may be limited, it is permissible to type the date in figures.

VIDEX OFFICE SUPPLIES plc OFFICE EQUIPMENT MANUFACTURERS AND SUPPLIERS
Hemming Road
LEAMINGTON SPA
Warwickshire
CV32 4LY

Telephone: 0926 23432
Telex: 848484
Freefone: 32594

Invoice Reference	
Number	*Tax point*
1834	09.01.84

Ventura Electrical Ltd
18 High Street
SHIPSTON-ON-STOUR
Warwickshire CV36 4AA

24-hour Answering Service
Telephone: 0926 28134

VAT REG NO 208 0341 07

Customer number	Order number	Order date	Delivery date	Invoice date
1782/69	VE/126/84	04.01.84	10.01.84	09.01.84

Type of supply	Description	Quan-tity	Amount	VAT Rate	VAT Amount
			£	%	£
Sale	80-column Screen Computer with data control, printer etc @ £3,000 each	3	9,000	15	1,350
	Total Goods		9,000		1,350
	Total VAT		1,350		
	E & OE				
	Amount due		£10,350		

DELIVER TO: Oxford Branch, 73 Banbury Road

See Typing Target Practice, page 30, for further exercises on

Invoices (VAT)

Sometimes a letter will have a tear-off portion at the foot, so that a customer can fill in certain details and return the tear-off portion to the sender.

The typing on the tear-off section should end about an inch (25 mm) from the bottom of the page and any space not required for the tear-off portion should be left after the complimentary close or the name of the signatory if this is given.

The minimum number of spaces to be left after the complimentary close or signatory is 4. In other words, turn up a minimum of 5 single spaces and then type, from EDGE TO EDGE of the paper CONTINUOUS HYPHENS or CONTINUOUS DOTS; then turn up 2 single spaces and type the information on the tear-off portion.

When blank spaces are left for details to be filled in, use CONTINUOUS DOTS or the UNDERSCORE and DOUBLE SPACING. Remember to leave one clear space after the last character typed before starting the dots or underscore and one clear space at the end of the dots or underscore before the the next typed character if there is one, eg,

space space space
Surname↓ . . . . ↓Christian names↓ . . . .

Practise typing letter with tear-off portion

6 Type the following letter on A4 paper in single spacing in blocked style. Margins: 1½" (38 mm) and 1" (25 mm). A name and address will not be inserted at a later date.

Our Ref PW/SM

Month and year only

Dear Sir

HIGH INCOME INVESTMENT

l.c/ In these days of inflation, a high yield from your Capital is not enough; it is essential also to protect the real value of your capital. Our new High Income Investment ~~schemem~~ Scheme has been designed to meet this requirement.

trs

High ⅄

By investging in specially selected ordinary shares, we aim not only /uc to provide an income which starts at a high level & wh wl go on growing over the years, but also to provide the growth needed to keep the value of your investment ~~in line with~~ ahead of inflation. This is the advantage th our High Income Investment has over other forms of investment wh are not designed to combat inflation or rising prices. [If you require any further information, complete the form below and return it to us, when our representative will make an appointment to ~~see you~~. suit your convenience

Yours faithfully
20TH CENTURY INVESTMENT CO LTD

(Typist: type line from edge to edge of paper.)

- -

Please send me full details of your High Income Investment Scheme.

SURNAME . . . . Christian Name (s) . . . .

ADDRESS . . . .

. . . .

See Typing Target Practice, page 63, for further exercises on

FORMAT FOR CREDIT NOTES

(a) Usually printed and typed in red.
(b) Used to cancel an incorrect invoice. (A new, correct invoice would then be issued.)
(c) Used for crediting goods or packing cases returned.
(d) A supplier who credits a customer for goods/services relating to taxable supplies must issue a VAT credit note which should give: VAT registration number, amount credited for each item, rate and amount of VAT credited, etc. (For details of VAT regulations as applied to credit notes, please see *Practical Typing Exercises, Book One,* page 66.)

Practise typing credit notes

7 Type the following credit note on a suitable form. Please see *Teaching Notes and Solutions* for a printed form.

VIDEX OFFICE SUPPLIES plc
Hemming Road
LEAMINGTON SPA
Warwickshire
CV32 4LY

Telephone: 0926 23432
Telex: 848484

CREDIT NOTE REFERENCE
Number: 15
Date: 16 January 1984
Account Number: 1782/69

Ventura Electrical Ltd
19 High Street
SHIPSTON-ON-STOUR
Warwickshire
CV36 4AA

24-hour Answering Service
Telephone: 0926 28134

VAT REG NO 208 0341 07

Reason for credit	Quality and description	Total credit excluding VAT	VAT credited	
			Rate	Amount
		£	%	£
2 ordered 3 sent	One 80-column Computer with data control, printer etc	3,000	15	450
	Total credit	3,000		
	Total VAT	450		
		3,450		
	Original tax invoice No 1834 dated 9 January 1984			

Proofreading: please turn to page 180 and complete exercise 2

See Typing Target Practice, page 31, for further exercises on Credit Notes

REARRANGEMENT OF TEXT The operator can alter the sequence of words, lines, paragraphs or whole pages by a simple one-key action. Existing text can be merged w new text or with stored data. The entire text can be scanned for a specific word or phrase & changes made instantly ea & every time it appears. SCANNED

u.c./ EMPLOYEES' random RECORDS The mistra 2000 wl classify alphabetically any information such as registration of personal data, including name, age, title, address, marital status, etc. on the disk

STANDARD ADDRESSES These may be stored & all the operator has to do is to key in the name required & the complete name & address wl be typed & merged w the letter to be typed (or already typed).

u.c./ I know th ~~Marcth~~ Marcus Allen, the purchasing officer, was anxious to know the dimensions & weight &, for his information, I give these below.

Visual Display Unit 610 x 381 x 483 mm (24" x 15" x 19")
Weight 40 kg (88 lb.)
Keyboard Unit 457 x 76 x 203 mm (18" x 3" x 8")
Weight 5 kg (11 lb.)
Printer 635 x 203 x 381 mm (25" x 8" x 15")
Weight 22 kg (49 lb.)

May I suggest th we order one of these m/cs & use it in the Contracts Department where the documents are of a somewhat standard form.

PS. I read an article in today's 'POST' which suggests there are over 120 models of screen-based word processors on the market. Needless to say, I have not tried them all!!

Proofreading: please turn to page 180 and complete exercise 4

See Typing Target Practice, page 61, for a further exercise on

Progress check

Task 9 ▶ *Format* — Output Target—5 minutes

A5 landscape paper   Centre the whole vertically
Centre horizontally in blocked style

HIGH-QUALITY ASIAN SWEET CENTRE

T A K E - A W A Y   P R I C E S

67 ← Leave 2 clear spaces

Cholay Bhatura   ~~66~~p plate

Chuppati   14 ~~12~~p each

Katlama   47 ~~46~~p each

85

Tandoori Chicken   ~~80~~p each

Veg Samosa   14 ~~15~~p each

← Leave 2 clear spaces

<u>Orders taken for WEDDINGS</u>

Task 10 ▶ *Format* — Output Target—6 minutes

A4 paper   Margins: elite 22–82, pica 12–72
Use shoulder headings

WINDSURFING (BOARDSAILING)

years

Windsurfing began in California some 15 ⁄ ago, but it is only in the
few ⁄ last ⁄ years that this sport has become popular.

MASTERING THE ART   DERIVE

You wl learn much more quickly + derive more pleasure fr windsurfing if y hv a few days' instruction fr a qualified instructor who wl probably use a land-based simulator. Once y know how ⁄ the simulator, ⁄ (to handle) the real thing wl be easy.

COST
new
A ⁄ board wl cost between £400 + £600, +, if y wish ⌒ to be very professional, a wet suit will ⌒ be about £100.
l.c. The Basic Training fee is approx £50.

FORMAT FOR TWO-PAGE MEMORANDUM

The way in which the heading is set out on a memorandum continuation sheet is the same as for the business letter, see page 109.

FORMAT FOR QUOTATION MARKS

Used when typing direct speech, eg, Mr Carmichael said, "I will leave on the 1330 plane to Turin." Quotation marks are usually placed after the comma, question mark and exclamation mark, eg, "Will I see you tomorrow?" The full stop is placed inside the final quotation mark unless the sentence ends with a title in quotation marks or a single word quotation. For example, "I will see you at the meeting." June brought me a copy of the "Times".

When 2 or more paragraphs are quoted, the quotation marks are placed at the BEGINNING OF EACH PARAGRAPH and at the END OF THE LAST PARAGRAPH.

5 Type the following 2-page memorandum in semi-blocked style with full punctuation. Use suitable margins and take 2 carbon copies: one for the Purchasing Officer and one for File. Correct 3 word errors.
Note: It is essential of course that (i) the top copy of the continuation sheet is plain BOND paper and that (ii) carbon copies are typed on plain BANK paper.

FROM Judy Garland **TO** ~~The~~ Managing Director

REF. JG/NewE/BS **DATE** 20 March 1985

WORD PROCESSING MACHINES

I have now had an opportunity of using a variety of word processing machines and have come to the conclusion that the Mistra 2000 would suit our requirements.

The manufacturers describe the ma/chine as follows:

"The Mistra 2000 is elegantly designed and has a wide variety of pre-programmed functional capabilities. The typist is guided through the various processes by messages displayed on the Visual Display Unit and there is abundant storage capacity and a high-speed printing capability together with a great number of program functions.

"It is possible to store up to 460 pages of text, or other data, on a double-sided, double-density disk. This obviously provides an enormous text prep/ration capacity as well as a document filing capability which will save both paper and space for filing purposes."

HIGH-SPEED PRINTING The daisy-wheel printer provides high-quality printing at a speed of 45 characters per second. A variety of fonts are available and the daisy wheel is easy to take out and put back. The printer is bidirectional and the distance to the nearest margin is checked automatically to determine which print direction provides the greatest speed. This minimizes printer wear as well as enhancing oöperational efficiency.

ELECTRONIC KEYBOARD The electronic keyboard is seperate and, therefore, allows the operator to adjust its position for maximum personal comfort.

VISUAL DISPLAY UNIT Twenty-four lines of 80 characters each which can be scrolled horizontally and vertically. The typist can also have a full page display to decide on layout but, in this case, the text ~~is~~ may be unreadable.

Rearrangement/

Task 11 ▶ *Format* Output Target—8 minutes

A4 paper Margins: 1½" (38 mm), 1" (25 mm)
Single spacing
2 spaces after right bracket in longest numbered item, ie, (iii)

METRIC MEASUREMENTS

When typing metric measurements, pay particular attention to the following:

(i) Never add an 's' to the symbol to form the plural - symbols are the same in the plural as they are in the singular, eg, 20 metres - 20 m.

(ii) Never put a full stop after a symbol unless it ocurs at the end of a sentence.

(iii) Always leave a space between the figure (s) & the symbol, eg, 20 (space) m.

(iv) Most symbols are small letters, but there are a few in l.c. Upper case, such as C and M which stand for Celsius and Mega. Certain keyboards (teleprinters for example) have upper case letters only, and in these cases the unit should be typed in full, eg, 15 MILLIMETRES.

u.c. (v) the symbol l (small L) shd nt be used for litre - type the word in full or insert a handwritten, looped ℓ.

Task 12 ▶ *Format* Output Target—15 minutes

A5 landscape paper Double spacing 3 spaces between columns
Centre horizontally and vertically

EXPORTS AND HOME SALES FOR THE PERIOD
JANUARY-JUNE 1984

MONTH	EXPORTS	HOME SALES	TOTAL
	£	£	£
January	175,063.84	140,873.22	315,937.06
February	87,021.75	99,673.46	186,695.21
March	38,465.80	102,654.78	141,120.58
April	40,339.21	109,444.20	149,783.41
May	42,211.95	223,869.64	266,081.59
June	90,267.44	367,461.34	457,728.78
	473,369.99	1,043,976.64	1,517,346.63

INCOME TAX RELIEF

u.c. Our savings plan is approved as a "qualifying" policy by the Inland Revenue. This means that your employees obtain tax releef of 15% (this may, of course, be changed at some future date by the Chancellor of the Exchequer) on the whole of their savings, ⊙

MEDICAL EXAMINATION

No medical examination is required unless an employee wishes to save more than £55 a month

u.c./ (£35 if double life cover is required).

Please point out the following to yr employees:

1. They can join at any age betwn 18 and 57.
2. They can backdate their savings by up to 3 months.
3. When they withdraw their savings they can take them in cash / ~~investment~~.
4. They can continue until their 60th (women) or 65th (men) birthday or finish earlier and withdraw the acumulated savings.

(margin: for in units as a continuing investment)

DOUBLE LIFE INSURANCE COVER

The following table shows gross monthly savings including u.c. 15% for double life cover, tax relief & net amt payable.

Gross Savings £	Tax Relief £	Net Payments £
12	1.80	10.20
18	2.70	15.30
24	3.60	20.40
30	4.50	25.50
48	7.20	40.80
60	9.00	51.00

Typist — please centre table.

GROWTH RATE

Indent →

We hv an annual growth rate of between 8% and 11%. Actual results hv in fact exceded 11%.

Please do not hesitate to contact me if any points require elucidation.

Yrs sincerely,

Typist — after yours sincerely, turn up 8 single spaces before typing the postscript.

PS. I look forward to your joining me for lunch on Tuesday next.

See Typing Target Practice, page 59, for a further exercise on

Task 13 ▶ *Format* Output Target—10 minutes

A4 paper Margins: elite 22–82, pica 12–72
Insert subject heading ENQUIRY NO 817/84

Our ref KFC/TW

FOR THE ATTENTION OF MR F LANGSTONE

Videx Office Supplies plc
Hemming Road
LEAMINGTON SPA
Warwickshire
CV32 4LY

Typist – take a carbon copy.
Insert today's date.

Dear Sirs

ed/ #/ caps We obtain yr address from the enclosed advertisement wh appeared in Office Supplies. [Wd you please quote /NP us f the following Unit Furniture:

UF 477	Sliding Door Unit	500 x 700 x 400 mm
UF 833	4-drawer Unit	500 x 500 x 400 mm
UF 983	Open Storage Unit	500 x 500 x 245 mm

stet In the first ~~case~~ instance we wd place an order for 3 of ea item, but, shd this type of furniture prove popular, we wd then order in larger quantities. Please let us know yr Trade and Cash Discount Terms.

Yrs faithfully

K F CURTIS
FORWARD PLANNING

Enc

Check work before removing paper from machine and correct any errors

Task 14 ▶ *Format* Output Target—8 minutes

C6 envelopes

Peter Hands A Hands & Sons Ltd 19 Victoria Street GRIMSBY South Humberside DN31 1AB

F O Madden PLC 5 Queen St MAIDSTONE Kent ME14 1AA

Patricia Milligan 84 Townhall Rd, ENNISKILLEN Co Fermanagh

Glenavon & Sons 14 Allan's Park STIRLING FK8 2LT

FORMAT FOR SEMI-BLOCKED LETTER WITH CONTINUATION SHEET

For an explanation of the heading to a continuation sheet see page 109.

FORMAT FOR POSTSCRIPTS

Sometimes a postscript has to be typed at the foot of a letter, either because the writer has omitted something he wished to say in the body of the letter, or because he wishes to draw special attention to a certain point. The postscript should start 2 single spaces below the last line of the complete letter and should be in single spacing. With full punctuation, the abbreviation, PS., has one full stop and that is after the S. With open punctuation, there is no full stop. In either case leave 2 character spaces before starting the text that follows.

4 Type the following 2-page letter in semi-blocked style. Use margins of elite 19–89, pica 11–77. Take an original and one carbon. Correct 4 word errors. Type an envelope. Use full punctuation.

Your Ref. FL/CoSec/SY 15th March, 1985

Our Ref. JWDD/ACM

Jasper Teesdale, Esq.,
Company Secretary,
Videx Office Supplies plc,
Hemming Road,
LEAMINGTON SPA,
Warwickshire.
CV32 4LY

Dear Mr. Teesdale,

STAFF PENSION SCHEME ← u/score

Further to our telephone conversation of this morning, I hope that the following information will be of help to your employees.

ENDOWMENT INSURANCE

Our Savings Plan is an endowment assurance but differs from conventional endowment policies in a number of ways. Perhaps the most outstanding difference is that, with our plan, your employees are in no way committed to saving for a specific period: they can terminate payments whenever they wish.

UNIT TRUSTS

A Unit Trust is simply a group of people joining together for cooperative invesment under the management of expert financial advisers: on joining, your employees become members of this group.

Members acquire units at less than average cost because, with regular monthly investment, their savings buy more units when prices are low.

trs./ The Turst was formed in 1959 and invests in the best of this country's commercial and industrial undertakings. A detailed portfolio of investments is available for inspecion. t

Continued/

Task 15 ▶ *Format* Output Target—10 minutes

A4 paper Margins: elite 22–82, pica 12–72

THE MAIL ROOM

Typist - take a carbon copy, + correct word error.

Opening and Distributing the Post

Each organisation has its own particular method of dealing with incoming mail, and you MUST follow exactly the system employed. The following points are those used in many offices when dealing with incoming mail.

1 Letters addressed to individuals or departments are not opened before being distributed. This, of course, includes letters marked PERSONAL and PRIVATE.

2 Open envelopes carefully with letter opener or with letter-opening machine.

4 ~~3~~ Stamp all documents w date and time of receipt.

(a) Clip letter and enclosure(s) together.
(b) Retain envelope.
(c) If an enclosure is missing, ~~ehcck~~ check th it is not in the envelope and make a note on the letter to say th it is missing.

3 ~~4~~ Take out documents and check to see th any enclosure(s) is there.

5 Sort documents into trays or other containers for ea. person or dept.

6. Registered letters shd be entered in a special register + a signature ~~be~~ obtained fr the person to whom they are delivered.

Task 16 ▶ *Format* Output Target—6 minutes

A5 memo paper Two spaces above printed heading, at left margin, type the word CONFIDENTIAL in capitals and underscore

Check work before removing paper from machine and correct any errors

FROM Purchasing Officer (Typist - take a carbon copy. Address an envelope to the Canteen Manager.)
TO Canteen Manager
DATE 8 January 1985

CANTEEN TABLES

Further to the correspondence we had last Oct abt the high-quality folding tables advertised by J Sadler & Sons, the Board of Directors has given permission for the following to be ordered:-

5 rectangular tables 3 ft × 8 ft (0.91 × 2.74 m) £65.34 each
5 round-topped tables 5 ft (1.52 m) in diameter £70.20 each

You may expect delivery in 10 days' time.

The usual method for displaying matter in semi-blocked letters is to arrange for the longest line of the matter to be centred in the typing line. To do this:

(a) Find the centre point of the body of the letter by adding together the points at which the left and right margins are set and divide by 2.
(b) Bring printing point to this scale point and backspace once for every 2 characters and spaces in the longest line of the displayed matter. This is the starting point for all items.
(c) ALWAYS leave one clear space above and below displayed matter.

Practise semi-blocked letter with displayed matter

3 Type the following letter on A4 paper in semi-blocked style. Use full punctuation, take a carbon copy and type a C6 envelope. Margins: elite 20–86, pica 11–77.

Our Ref. JT/SS 15th March 1985

FOR THE ATTENTION OF MRS. J. BEWICK

Messrs. C. R. Tomson & Sons,
16 Leicester Street,
Oundle,
PETERBOROUGH.
PE8 4EA

Dear Sirs,

ELECTRONIC TYPEWRITERS

Thank you for your enquiry dated 11th March. We supply 4 different makes of electronic typewriters and enclose information about these.

From what you say in your letter, we think that the Mistra 009 would suit your requirements. This machine incorporates every device that modern technology provides and its space-age design is the very essence of the typewriter of the future.

The following features will be of particular importance to your typists:

1. Cassette Ribbon - no soiled fingers.
2. One-line automatic corrections.
3. Automatic centring.
4. Automatic underlining.

We will be pleased to let you have 4 machines for a trial period of one week, and we look forward to hearing from you.

Yours faithfully,
VIDEX OFFICE SUPPLIES plc

Julian Turner
MARKETING DIVISION

Encs.

See Typing Target Practice, pages 57 and 58, for further exercises on

Task 17 ▶ *Format*

Output Target—3 minutes

Skeleton form as used in exercise on page 75
(See *Teaching Notes and Solutions* for blank)
Type in words and figures from manuscript below

QUOTATION FORM - MOTOR CAR

Surname: CRADDOCK Mr/Mrs/Miss/Ms: Mr
Forenames: William George
Home address: 30 Bradford Rd
Town: Burnley County: Lancs Postcode: B11 2DY
Telephone Number: 0282 299012 Occupation: Accountant
Age - Years: 42 Months: 3 Date of Birth: 19 02 43

1 Make of car: Ford Model: Escort
cc: 1300 Year: 1982 Letters and numbers: MAT 191X
2 How many years have you held a UK driving licence? 21
3 Will there be any drivers under the age of 25?* NO
4 How many years NO CLAIM DISCOUNT earned? 21

---

5 Will the car be used for business purposes?* YES
6 Have you been involved in any accidents in the last 3 years?* NO
7 Have you been convicted of any motoring offence
(except parking) or is any offence pending?* NO

* Answer YES or NO

Task 18 ▶ *Format*

Output Target—13 minutes

A4 paper Correct word error

BACKING SHEETS

To prevent damage to the cylinder of the typewriter, always use a backing sheet. Other uses of the backing sheet are:

I Typing on cards and memoranda

When typing on cards and memoranda, you may hv, of necessity, to type near the bottom. To ensure th yr typewriter grips the card (paper) & thus prevents the bottom line(s) fr "running off" the paper, always use a (backing) sheet. In fact, whenever you hv to type within one inch of the bottom, always use a backing sheet wh extends below the bottom of the page.

II Aid to centring

On yr backing sheet rule a vertical line down the centre & also a heavy horizontal line across the centre. This wl help you when centring material on a page.

III Top & bottom margins

With the underscore type a line on the seventh single space fr the top edge of the paper. This wl remind you th you always turn up 7 single spaces before you start to type. Likewise, one inch fr the bottom of the backing sheet draw a dark horizontal line to remind you th you are nearing the bottom of the page.

FORMAT FOR SUBJECT HEADING IN SEMI-BLOCKED LETTERS

In a semi-blocked letter turn up 2 spaces after salutation and centre the heading over the body of the letter. To do this:

(a) Add together the points at which the left and right margins are set and divide by 2.
(b) Bring the writing point to this scale point and backspace once for every 2 characters and spaces in the subject heading.
(c) Type heading.
(d) Turn up 2 single spaces before starting the body of the letter.

Note: th, st, rd, nd, etc, may be used, if desired, in fully-blocked or semi-blocked letters with open or full punctuation. There is NEVER a full stop after th, st, etc. Be consistent. When th, st, etc, are used in date above, then th, st, etc, must be used in body of letter.

Practise typing semi-blocked letter with subject heading

2 Type the following letter on A4 paper in semi-blocked style. Use full punctuation. Margins: elite 24–84, pica 15–75. Starting point for subject heading: elite 44, pica 35. Correct the word error.

Your Ref FL/CoSec/SY 6th March 1985

Our Ref JWDD/ACM

Jasper Teesdale Esq
Company Secretary
Videx Office Supplies plc
Hemming Road
LEAMINGTON SPA
Warwickshire
CV32 4LY

Dear Mr Teesdale

(Turn up 2 singles)

STAFF PENSION SCHEME

(Turn up 2 singles)

Thank you for your letter dated 28th February enquiring about a pension scheme for your staff.

GROUP SAVINGS PLAN

We are enclosing details of our savings plan which automatically gives life assurance cover to members. In addition, some of your employees may wish to take advantage of our unique life assurance option which doubles the amount of life cover for only 15% extra.

MODERATE CHARGES

An important part of our Group Savings Plan is the very low charges. Full information is given about this on page 4 of the leaflet entitled ADMINISTRATION.

We will be delighted to send our Norman Tracey to discuss our suggestions with you. Please let us know when a call would be conveneint.

Yours sincerely

J W DOSSETT-DAVIS

ENCS

See Typing Target Practice, pages 55 and 56, for further exercises on

FORMAT FOR OPEN PUNCTUATION

Up to this point in the book all the exercises have been displayed with open punctuation. This means that full stops have not been inserted after abbreviations, and letters have been typed with the omission of commas after each line of the address, and after the salutation and complimentary close. The modern trend is to omit punctuation in those cases as it simplifies and speeds up the work of the typist. However, punctuation is always inserted in sentences, so that the grammatical sense is clear.

FORMAT FOR FULL PUNCTUATION

It is also acceptable to insert punctuation after abbreviations and after each line of an address as well as after the salutation and complimentary close. Grammatical punctuation is always inserted. Open and full punctuation must NEVER be mixed: a document must be typed in either open or full punctuation.

ABBREVIATIONS

In typewritten work abbreviations should not, as a rule, be used. There are, however, a few standard abbreviations which are never typed in full and others which may be used in certain circumstances. Study the following lists, so that you will know when not to use abbreviations and when it is permissible to use them. You must always be consistent in their use.

(a) Used in the cases indicated:

Open punctuation	*Full punctuation*	
Ltd	Ltd.	Limited. Used only in names of private limited companies. It must be typed in full if that is how it appears in the printed letterhead.
PLC or plc	P.L.C. or p.l.c.	Public Limited Company. Used in names of public limited companies. It may be typed in full or abbreviated.
Co	Co.	Company. Used only in names of companies. It must be typed in full if that is how it appears in the printed letterhead.
OHMS	O.H.M.S.	On Her Majesty's Service. Usually abbreviated but occasionally typed in full.
PS	PS.	Postscript. Used only at the foot of a letter.
v	v.	Versus. May be abbreviated or typed in full. It is usual to follow the copy.
&	&	And, known as the "ampersand". Used in names of firms, such as Smith & Brown, and in numbers such as Nos 34 & 35 (Nos. 34 & 35).
@	@	At. Used only in invoices, quotations and similar documents.
%	%	Per cent. May be abbreviated or typed in full. It is usual to follow the copy.
Bros	Bros.	Brothers. Used only in the names of companies.

(b) Used with figures only:

am	a.m.	ante meridiem—before noon
pm	p.m.	post meridiem—after noon
in	in.	inch(es)
ft	ft.	foot (feet)
g	g	gram(s)
kg	kg	kilogram(s)
mm	mm	millimetre(s)
m	m	metre(s)
km	km	kilometre(s)

Note: Punctuation is NEVER used in metric abbreviations

FORMAT FOR SEMI-BLOCKED LETTERS

The following points should be noted when typing semi-blocked letters:

(a) Date—this ends flush with the right margin. To find the starting point, backspace from right margin once for each character and space in the date.
(b) Reference—type at left margin on the same line as the date.
(c) Body of letter—the first word of each paragraph is indented 5 spaces from left margin. Tap in and set tab stop for paragraph indent.
(d) Complimentary close—start this approximately at the centre of the typing line.
(e) Signature—as in fully-blocked letters, turn up a minimum of 5 single spaces to leave room for signature. Type name of person signing, starting at the same scale point as the complimentary close.
(f) Designation—begin to type official designation (if any) at the same scale point as complimentary close, ie, immediately below the name of person signing.
(g) Punctuation—semi-blocked letter may be typed with open or full punctuation.

FORMAT FOR SEMI-BLOCKED LETTERS WITH ATTENTION LINE AND ENCLOSURE

The ATTENTION LINE and ENCLOSURE are typed in the same position as in fully-blocked letters.

Practise typing semi-blocked letter with ATTENTION LINE and ENCLOSURE

1 Type the following semi-blocked letter using A5 portrait paper. Margins: elite 15–60, pica 10–55. Use open punctuation.

```
Our Ref FL/CoSec/SY          28 February 1985

FOR THE ATTENTION OF J W DOSSETT-DAVIS ESQ

David Jessop (Insurance Brokers) Ltd
Hanbury House
20 St Mary's Street
BRIGHTON
BN4 2EQ

Dear Sirs

     We have for some time been considering
the importance of a Staff Pension Scheme,
and we would like you to let us have details
of a suitable scheme.

     We enclose a list, giving names and ages,
of the staff we have in mind.

                    Yours faithfully
                    VIDEX OFFICE SUPPLIES plc




                    Jasper Teesdale
                    Company Secretary

ENC
```

Set tab stop for paragraph indents: elite 20, pica 15.

↑ Start approximately at the centre of the line of writing.

See Typing Target Practice, page 54, for further exercises on

(c) Abbreviations always used:

Open punctuation	*Full punctuation*		
eg	e.g.	exempli gratia—for example	***Note:*** There is no space in the middle of an abbreviation.
etc	etc.	et cetera—and others	
ie	i.e.	*id est*—that is	
NB	N.B.	*nota bene*—note well	
viz	viz.	*videlicet*—namely	
Esq	Esq.	Esquire	
Messrs	Messrs.	Messieurs—Gentlemen	
Mr	Mr.		***Note:*** Miss is not an abbreviation and does not require a full stop.
Mrs	Mrs.		
Ms	Ms.		

Practise typing abbreviations with open punctuation

1 Type the following sentences on A5 landscape paper. (a) Note the use of abbreviations. (b) Margins: elite 22–82, pica 12–72. (c) Blocked paragraphs. (d) Single spacing with double between each group of sentences. (e) Open punctuation.

Use the abbreviation Ltd in the name of a limited company (or PLC in a public limited company) if that is how it appears in the printed letterhead.

The book is printed in 3 volumes. Vol 2 has 600 pages, but Vol 3 is not so bulky, as it has only 400 pages.

The room measured 26 ft 4 in × 14 ft 2 in.

Mr & Mrs J F Browne arrived at 2 pm, ie, 10 minutes early.

Mr S V Gordon has addressed the parcel to Messrs Trent Bros instead of to Johnson & Co Ltd.

A top margin of at least 25 mm should be used when typing on plain paper.

Practise typing abbreviations with full punctuation

2 Type the following sentences on A5 landscape paper. (a) Margins: elite 22–82, pica 12–72. (b) Blocked paragraphs. (c) Single spacing with double between each group of sentences. (d) Full punctuation. (e) On completion compare with the previous exercise.
Note: One space after a full stop at the end of an abbreviation. No space after a medial full stop within an abbreviation.

Use the abbreviation Ltd. in the name of a limited company (or P.L.C. in a public limited company) if that is how it appears in the printed letterhead.

The book is printed in 3 volumes. Vol. 2 has 600 pages, but Vol. 3 is not so bulky, as it has only 400 pages.

The room measured 26 ft. 4 in. × 14 ft. 2 in.

Mr. & Mrs. J. F. Browne arrived at 2 p.m., i.e., 10 minutes early.

Mr. S. V. Gordon has addressed the parcel to Messrs. Trent Bros. instead of to Johnson & Co. Ltd.

A top margin of at least 25 mm should be used when typing on plain paper.

See Typing Target Practice, page 32, for further exercises on
Abbreviations

8 Type the following circular letter on A4 paper in single spacing and with full punctuation. Use margins of elite 22–82, pica 12–72. Correct the word error. This letter will probably run to 2 pages; if so, insert page number and "Date as postmark" on the continuation sheet.

Our Ref. SERVICE/PH/JMC

Date as postmark

(Turn up 8 single spaces)

Dear Customer,

SUPERCOVER INSURANCE AND SERVICE PLAN

A renewal notice for insurance cover will be sent to you direct from David Jessop Insurance Services. Please pay the amount due direct to them.

The premium wh y pay will cover the cost of insurance only - the charge for annual servicing shd be pd to our engineer after completion of service wh, as a "Super cover Contract Customer", y received at a reduced rate.

N.P. [Your insurance policy with David Jessop + us is, of course, conditional on our continuing to maintain + service yr boiler. (, we will replace faulty components,)

Run on: In the event of a breakdown occurring, as listed on the reverse side of the policy, + make the necessary claim on yr behalf to cover total cost of labour + materials.

l.c. [Our Engineers are at yr service 7 days a week, including bank holidays, from 0900 to 2100. As a "Supercover Contract Customer" y receive priority service. Please make sure that the person taking yr call is aware th y are a "Supercover Contract Customer".

[We encl. details of the new radiator thermostats wh, when fitted to ea radiator in yr home, wl prevent overheating and cd reduce yr fuel bill by 20%.

[These new thermostats can be fitted to any existing central heating systems.

[The average installation cost for 6 of these valves wd be £120 plus VAT. Additional valves fitted at the same time wd cost £12.50 ea. plus VAT. Please ask us to call on you and give a firm quotation.

[Thank you f yr custom. If you hv any queries, please do not hesitate to telephone us.

Yrs sincerely ← Turn up 2 singles

Mrs Pauline Hobart ← Turn up 2 singles

Service Department

See Typing Target Practice, page 53, for a further exercise on

FORMAT FOR PARAGRAPHING

Paragraphs are used to separate the different subjects or sections. This breaks the writing into short passages to facilitate reading and understanding. There are 3 different forms of paragraphing, viz, blocked, indented and hanging.

A Blocked paragraphs

Practise typing blocked paragraphs

3 Type the following on A5 landscape paper. (a) Margins: left 2" (51 mm), right $1\frac{1}{2}$" (38 mm). (b) Single spacing with double between each paragraph. (c) Blocked paragraphs.

```
As you have already learnt, in blocked paragraphs all lines start at the same
scale-point.

When single spacing is used, as in this exercise, you turn up 2 single spaces
between the paragraphs.

However, when double spacing is used you should turn up 2 double between each
paragraph.
```

B Indented paragraphs

When using indented paragraphs the first line of each paragraph is indented 5 spaces from the left margin. This indentation is made by setting a tab stop 5 spaces from the point fixed for the left margin. When using indented paragraphs, 2 single spaces only should be turned up between paragraphs, whether typing in single or double spacing.

Practise typing indented paragraphs

4 Type the following on A5 landscape paper. (a) Margins: elite 22–82, pica 12–72. (b) Single spacing with double between each paragraph. (c) Set a tab stop at 27(17) for the paragraph indentation.

```
     Insert the paper so that the top edge is flush with
the top edge of the alignment scale.  Then turn up 7 single
spaces.
———→
     You should then have a clear 25 mm margin above the
first line of typing.  It is incorrect to have a top margin
of less than 25 mm.
```

Return carriage twice on single

C Hanging Paragraphs

Practise typing hanging paragraphs

5 After reading through the exercise type it on A5 landscape paper. (a) Margins: elite 22–82, pica 12–72. (b) Single spacing with double between each paragraph. (c) Hanging paragraphs as shown.

```
A third type of paragraph is known as a hanging paragraph.
  This means that the first line of the paragraph starts
  2 spaces to the left of the second and subsequent lines
  as in this exercise.

Hanging paragraphs are sometimes used in display work to
  draw attention to particular points.
```

7 The first page of the letter to Bernard Holstein is fine; however, I have had to alter the second page. Please retype the second page using margins of elite 19–89, pica 13–73.

2

13 February 1985

B. Holstein, Esq.

(wh are being built by Graham + Co.)

NP I ~~We~~ enclose ~~notes~~ details of one of ~~these~~ the new flats, and you will see that the current price is much below that which other developers are asking.

NP Further to ~~a~~ contract, I would like to offer to purchase the flat numbered 705 in Carlton Towers at the price of £23,000.

I look forward to hearing from you.

Yours sincerely

EW BLACKHURST

Enc

FORMAT FOR CIRCULAR LETTERS

Circulars or circular letters are letters of the same contents which are sent to a number of customers or clients. The original is usually typed on a master sheet (stencil or offset litho) and a quantity is "run off". Alternatively, a circular letter may be stored on a disk and individual letters produced on a word processor.

Reference—in usual position

Date—typed in various ways; eg, 21st July, 1985

	July, 1985 (month and year only)
Follow instructions or layout	Date as postmark (these words are typed in the position where you normally type the date).

Name and address of addressee

(a) Space may be left for this and in that case the details are typed on individual sheets after they have been "run off". When preparing the master (or draft), turn up 8 single spaces after the date (leaving 7 clear) before typing the salutation.

(b) Very often the name and address of addressee are not inserted and, if this is so, no space need be left when the master is prepared. Turn up 2 single spaces after date.

Salutation

(a) Dear—the remainder of the salutation is typed in when the name and address are inserted.

(b) Dear Sir, Dear Madam, Dear Sir(s), Dear Sir/Madam.

Signature

The person writing the letter may or may not sign it. If the writer is signing, type the complimentary close, etc, in the usual way. If the writer is not signing, type Yours faithfully and company's name* in the usual position, turn up 2 single spaces and type the name of the person writing the letter, then turn up 2 single spaces and type the designation.

* If the company's name is not being inserted, turn up 2 single spaces after Yours faithfully and type the name of the writer, then turn up 2 single spaces and type the writer's designation.

6 Type the following on A5 landscape paper. (a) Margins: left 1½" (38 mm), right 1" (25 mm). (b) Single spacing. (c) Hanging paragraphs.

Open punctuation takes less time and space than full punctuation and it is therefore wise to adopt this method from the beginning of your typewriting training.

If a name and address appear in a heading or in one line in the text, and open punctuation is being used, it should be typed with commas between each item, eg, Mr J Appleton, 12 Grange Drive, Bury, BL8 2BG.

7 Type the following exercise on A5 landscape paper. (a) Margins: elite 22–82, pica 12–72. (b) Single spacing with double between each paragraph. (c) Make your own right margin. (d) Open punctuation. (e) Note the use of abbreviations. (f) Indented paragraphs.

When typing measurements always use the small 'x' for the multiply sign, and leave one space either side of the 'x', eg, 20 (space) ft (space) x (space) 10 (space) ft = 20 ft x 10 ft. The same spacing is necessary when using metric measurements, eg, 1 m = 100 cm; 1 m = 1000 mm; 1 m x 1000 = 1 km.

Note: Use of apostrophe for feet; double quotation marks for inches.

You can also use the sign for feet and inches, eg, 20 ft 10 in x 15 ft 9 in = 20' 10" x 15' 9". You will see that, when using the sign, there is no space between the figures and the sign, but there is one space after the sign.

Do not add 's' to the plural of ft, in, lb, m, kg, etc. In imperial measurements a full stop is used after an abbreviation when using full punctuation, but in metric measurements full stops are never used after symbols even with full punctuation, except at the end of a sentence, eg, 210 mm x 297 mm.

8 Type the following exercise on A4 paper. (a) Margins: elite 22–82, pica 12–72. (b) Single spacing with double between each paragraph. (c) Full punctuation. (d) Blocked paragraphs. (e) Locate and correct one word error.

As a typist in business, or in a typewriting examination, you wl be expected to remember and apply certain points of theory.

When writing to individuals a curtesy title is essential. If you do not know whether a lady is Mrs. or Miss, type Ms. A man should be addressed as Mr. or Esq., never both. If you use the courtesy title of Dr. or Rev., do not use Mr. or Esq.

It is usual to hv the left margin slightly wider than the right margin – except in display and tabulation work. When using A4 paper for business letters do not hv a left margin of less than 1" (25 mm) and the right margin shd not be less than half an inch (13 mm).

See Typing Target Practice, page 33, for further exercises on

2

5th February 1985

Mr. P. McDonnell

iii) A lump sum payment calculated at the rate of 25% of yr average earnings at termination, that you would have received between the date of termination and normal retirement age (up to a maximum of 25 yrs and reduced proportionately if yr service is less than 8 years). Yr entitlement wl be 47.67 weeks' pay.

On termination y wl receive

a) a lump sum of £15,108

b) a cheque to the value of yr pay in lieu of notice + severance pay. SEVERANCE

N.P. [Any payments due to y fr the Company Pension Scheme wl be pd separately + wl be sent to y as soon as possible.

I shd be grateful if y wd arrange to call at the Industrial Relations Department (4th floor) to collect yr cheque + sign the forms required by the Dept. of Employment in accordance w. the following timetable:

Thursday, 14th February	Friday, 15th February
0930-1200 OR 1330-1530	0900 - 1200 OR 1245-1500

N.P. [If y are unable to attend personally, y may send a representative, provided he or she brings proof of identity + written authorisation f y to receive the cheque. If y are cannot attend at the times indicated above, y may collect yr cheque fr the Industrial Relations Department at any time during the week commencing 18 February.

I wd like to take this opportunity of thanking you f yr past work f the company, + I extend gd wishes to y + Mrs McDonnell.

Yrs sincerely

D. R. Edwardes

Industrial Relations Manager

c.c. Personnel Manager

File

See Typing Target Practice, page 51, for further exercises on

FORMAT FOR HORIZONTAL CENTRING—ALL LINES CENTRED

Follow the points given for horizontal centring on page 33, but do not set a left margin, and centre every line, not just the longest one. For this purpose set a tab stop at the centre point of the paper and backspace one space for every 2 characters and spaces as before.

FORMAT FOR VERTICAL CENTRING

To centre the matter vertically on a sheet of paper, follow the points (a) to (f) as given on page 34.

Practise horizontal and vertical centring

1 Type the following notice on A5 portrait paper. (a) Set a tab stop at the centre point, ie, elite 35, pica 29. (b) Centre each line horizontally and the whole notice vertically

DAVID JESSOP (INSURANCE BROKERS) LTD
Hanbury House
20 St Mary's Street
BRIGHTON BN4 2EQ

P E R S O N A L   I N S U R A N C E S

2 clear spaces

SAVINGS
PENSIONS
LIFE ASSURANCE

MOTOR INSURANCE
(Business and Pleasure)

2 clear spaces

A PROFESSIONAL ADVICE SERVICE

2 Type the following notice on A5 landscape paper. (a) Set a tab stop at the centre point, ie, elite 50, pica 41. (b) Centre each line horizontally and the whole notice vertically.

CHRISTMAS FESTIVITIES 1984

IMPERIAL HOTEL
Station Place
Bournemouth

Christmas Day £35
Boxing Day - Dinner/Dance £15
New Year's Eve - Dinner/Dance £35

For enquiries and reservations please telephone
0202 291174

See Typing Target Practice, pages 34 and 35, for further exercises on

A long letter may require a second sheet. This is called a continuation sheet, and sometimes the name or initials of the sender are printed in the top left corner. Otherwise, always use a plain sheet the same size, colour and quality as the previous page.

The following details should be typed at the top of the second and subsequent pages: name of addressee, page number and date, starting on fourth single line from the top. In fully-blocked letters, all these details are typed at the left margin in double spacing in the following order: page number, date, name of addressee. In indented letters, the name of the addressee is typed at the left margin, the page number is centred in the typing line, and the date ends at the right margin (from right margin backspace one for one to find starting point). The letter is continued on the third single space below the continuation sheet details.

When a continuation sheet is needed, the letter must be so arranged that at least 3 or 4 lines are carried to the second page. On no account must the continuation sheet contain only the complimentary close and the name of the writer. Also, at least 2 lines of a paragraph should be left at the bottom of the first page. Do NOT divide a word from one page to the next.

If the reverse of the paper is used for the continuation sheet, then the margins must also be reversed, eg, first sheet: left margin 1½", right margin 1"; continuation sheet: left margin 1", right margin 1½".

When using a continuation sheet, leave one inch clear at the bottom of the previous page. To make sure that you do leave an inch, mark the sheet (lightly in pencil) about 1½ inches up from the bottom to remind you. As we have had to start the letter in the following exercise half-way down the page, you will get more on the first page than we have done.

Note: The word CONTINUED or PTO may be used in letters. A catchword is sometimes used, ie, the first word appearing on a continuation sheet is typed at the foot of the preceding page. None of the continuation sheet details (page number for instance) should be used as a catchword.

6 Type the following 2-page letter on A4 headed paper. Use margins of elite 19–89, pica 13–73. Mark the letter PRIVATE. Take one carbon copy for the File and one for the Personnel Manager. Type an envelope to the addressee and an envelope to the Personnel Manager. Correct the word error.

Our Ref. DPE/JR/195/ER

5th February 1985

Mr. P. McDonnell, 43 Victoria Terrace, LEAMINGTON SPA. CV31 3AL

Dear Mr. McDonnell,

I am confirming the information given to you by your Supervisor. The Company will accept your request for early retirement and your employment will terminate on Friday, 15th Februry (a), 1985.

On terminatin (o) you will receive:-

i) One week's pay in lieu of notice for each year of service, subject to a maximum of 12 weeks and a minimum of 4 weeks. Therefore, yr entitlement will be 12 weeks' pay.

ii) Severance pay at a rate of 1½ weeks' basic pay for each year of continuous service after the age of 18. Your entitlement wl be 57 weeks' pay.

FORMAT FOR HEADINGS CENTRED IN THE TYPING LINE

To centre headings in the typing line, find the centre point of the line by adding the 2 margins together and dividing by 2. Then backspace from this point, one space for every 2 characters and spaces in the heading.

Examples: Margins set at elite 22 & 82 22+82=104 ÷2=52 (centre point)
pica 12 & 72 12+72= 84 ÷2=42 (centre point)
elite 18 & 88 18+88=106÷2=53 (centre point)

Main headings centred
See guide given on page 36 for main headings. Centred headings are generally used with indented paragraphs. The heading is centred in the typing line.

Subheadings centred
See guide given on page 36 for subheadings. If the main heading is centred, it is usual to centre the subheading in the typing line.

Practise centring main and subheadings

3 Type the following exercise on A4 paper in double spacing throughout, ie, do NOT turn up extra spaces between paragraphs. (a) Centre the headings in the typing line. (b) Indented paragraphs. (c) Margins: elite 18–88, pica 15–72. (d) Make your own line-endings.

CABLE TELEVISION

Outstanding means of Communication

In the very near future your television set should be offering you a broader view of the world, and a broader choice of views and things to do.

Initially, systems are likely to have up to 30 chan-nels, and it will be possible to give specialist interests much more time than they enjoy now.

Cable television may also give you a greater say in your communities and the benefit of a 2-way, wide-band communication.

A viewer could buy a suite of furniture or sell a ward-robe via a classified advertising channel. Or Local Educa-tion Authorities may take advantage of cable for transmit-ting teaching programmes to all age groups and at all levels.

See Typing Target Practice, page 36, for further exercises on Centred Headings

FORMAT FOR FULLY-BLOCKED LETTER WITH FULL PUNCTUATION

Letter display is exactly the same as given on pages 56 and 57 for Open Punctuation. However, when using Full Punctuation note the following points:

(a) Full stop after the abbreviation Ref. but no other punctuation in the reference.
(b) "FOR THE ATTENTION OF ..." line does not have a full stop at the end.
(c) The points for typing the name and address of the addressee are the same as those for typing envelopes given on page 107.
(d) Always type a comma after the salutation.
(e) Always type a comma after the complimentary close.
(f) Always type full stop after abbreviations Enc./Encs.

BUSINESS LETTERS–SPECIAL DIRECTIONS

The words PRIVATE, CONFIDENTIAL, PERSONAL, URGENT, RECORDED DELIVERY, REGISTERED, SPECIAL DELIVERY, BY HAND and AIRMAIL are typed at the left margin, 2 single spaces after the last line of the reference or date (if typed at the left margin). FREE POST and POSTE RESTANTE (to be called for) are typed after the name of the addressee.

Practise typing a fully-blocked letter with full punctuation

5 Type the following letter in fully-blocked style using full punctuation. (a) A4 paper. (b) Single spacing. (c) Use suitable margins. (d) Correct word error. (e) Type an envelope.
Note: As the letter is marked PRIVATE and CONFIDENTIAL, the envelope MUST ALSO be marked PRIVATE and CONFIDENTIAL.

Our Ref. BD/DA

30 January 1985

PRIVATE and CONFIDENTIAL

A. J. Burnett, Esq.,
Personnel Manager,
David Jessop (Insurance Brokers) Ltd.,
20 St. Mary's Street,
BRIGHTON.
BN4 2EQ

Dear Mr. Burnett,

HARALD OLAF ADDISON

In response to our advertisement for a Management Accountant, we have received an application from the above-named, and he has given your name as a referee.

The person appointed will be responsible to the Chairman and duties will include:

(a) preparation and control of budgets on the basis of short, medium and long-range forcasts;

(b) controlling costs and highlighting deviations from budgets.

I should be most grateful if you would kindly let me have, in confidence, your opinion as to the applicant's suitability for the post.

A prepaid envelope is enclosed, and may I thank you in advance for your co-operation.

Yours sincerely, Joanne Johnson Director Enc.

See Typing Target Practice, page 50, for further exercises on

FORMAT FOR INDENTED PARAGRAPH HEADINGS

See guide given on page 37 for paragraph headings. The paragraphs may also be indented and the headings typed in either of the forms given on page 37. A full stop may also be typed after the paragraph heading, 2 spaces being left after the full stop.

FORMAT FOR SHOULDER HEADINGS

See guide given on page 38 for shoulder headings. The paragraphs that follow the shoulder headings may be indented.

Practise typing indented paragraphs with shoulder headings

4 Type the following exercise on A4 paper. (a) Double spacing. (b) Indented paragraphs. (c) Suitable margins. (d) Centre the main heading. (e) Type the shoulder headings at the left margin in capitals and underscored. (f) Locate and correct one word error.

STILTON CHEESE

"King of English Cheese"

Blue Stilton depends for its distinction on a delecate balance of flavour and aroma and is matured naturally. The blue veining is part of this natural process.

HOW STILTON IS MADE

NP Seventeen gallons of milk ~~like~~ & up to 4 months' careful attention go into each prime stilton. /uc

HOW TO CUT AND SERVE

Do NOT scoop out of the middle! The knife shd be drawn across (the surface of) the half cheese, leaving it, if possible, even more level than before.

FORMAT FOR ENUMERATED ITEMS

See guide on pages 43 and 73. As well as being blocked to the left, roman numerals may be blocked to the right with or without full stops. Full stops are never used with brackets. There are 2 spaces after the full stop, the bracket and after the figure without a full stop.

Example:

I (2	i. (2	(1) (2	1. (2	A. (2	(a) (2	***Note:*** No full stops
II spaces)	ii. spaces)	(2) spaces)	2. spaces)	B. spaces)	(b) spaces)	with open
III	iii.	(3)	3.	C.	(c)	punctuation.

5 Type the following exercise on A5 landscape paper. (a) Single spacing with double between each numbered item. (b) Margins: elite 22–82, pica 12–72. (c) Blocked headings.

A. G. ROBINSON PUBLIC LIMITED COMPANY

<u>Annual General Meeting</u>

SECTION IV - RESOLUTIONS

1. (a) Adoption of Accounts and Reports of the Directors.
   (b) Declaration of Final Dividends.

2. Re-election of John Bryden DFC as a Director.

3. (a) Appointment of Auditors.
   (b) Authorisation of Directors to fix the Auditors' remuneration.

See Typing Target Practice, pages 36 and 37, for further exercises on

FORMAT FOR FORMS OF ADDRESS WITH FULL PUNCTUATION—ADDRESSING ENVELOPES

The guide to the addressing of envelopes given on pages 62–63 applies with the exception of inserting punctuation after abbreviations and at line-ends. It should be noted that Miss is not an abbreviation and, therefore, does not require a full stop.

Mr. M. Scott   Rev. C. S. Howe   Messrs. Payne & Sons   Miss V. P. Hammond

Miss E. A. McBrian,
Fearnan,
ABERFELDY,
Perthshire.
PH15 2AA

P. Williams, Esq., M.A., B.Sc.,
56 John Street,
MERTHYR TYDFIL,
M. Glam.
CF47 0AB

Points to note:

(a) Full stop after an initial followed by one clear space.
(b) Comma at the end of each line except for the last line before the postcode which is followed by a full stop.
(c) NO punctuation in postcode.
(d) Comma after surname followed by one space before Esq.
(e) Full stop and NO space between the letters of a degree, but a comma and space between each group of letters.
(f) Notice recognised abbreviation for Mid Glamorgan.

Practise typing names and addresses with full punctuation

3 Type each of the following lines twice in double spacing. (a) Margins: elite 20–80, pica 11–71.

Mr. A. K. Smythe will call to see you next Tuesday at 3 p.m.

Address it to J. Ladd, Esq., M.D., B.A., at 69 Newtown Road.

Miss R. Y. Cruise will meet Mrs. Q. P. Carr at 9 a.m. today.

FORMAT FOR ENVELOPES—SPECIAL DIRECTIONS

FOR THE ATTENTION OF, PRIVATE, CONFIDENTIAL, PERSONAL, and URGENT are typed 2 single spaces above the name of the addressee. RECORDED DELIVERY, REGISTERED, SPECIAL DELIVERY, and AIRMAIL are typed in the top left-hand corner of the envelope. BY HAND is typed in the top right-hand corner. FREE POST and POSTE RESTANTE are typed on the line following the name of the addressee.

4 Address envelopes to the following. (a) Use blocked style and full punctuation. (b) Mark the envelope to Mr. Stone "PRIVATE" and the envelope to The Victoria Casting Co., "FOR THE ATTENTION OF MR. F. W.. NISBETT". (c) Do not copy the single quotation marks.

Mr. P. F. Stone, O.B.E., 21 Wessex Close, BASINGSTOKE, Hants. RG21 3NP

W. Craddock, Esq., 30 Bradford Road, BURNLEY, Lancs. B11 2DY

Ms. Wilma Pugh, 49 High Holborn, LONDON. WC1V 6HB

Mrs. S. Brennan, 17 Broad Street, WATERFORD, Irish Republic.

The Victoria Casting Co., 84 Ferry Road, BARROW-IN-FURNESS, Cumbria. LA14 2PR

Mr. John Jefferies, 47 Glasgow Road, MOTHERWELL, Lanarkshire. ML1 4EE

Miss H. Morgan, 23 St. John's Street, LLANELLI, Dyfed. SA15 1AA

Mrs. J. Whelan, 12 Woodford Way, EDGWARE, Middx. HA8 5ES

R. Cameron P.L.C., Kingseat, DUNFERMLINE, Fife. KY12 0TJ

U. V. Best & Co., 14 High Street, Kingsland, LEOMINSTER, Herefordshire. HR6 9QS

Rev. J. H. Haddington-Davis, 23 Daws Heath Road, LEWES, East Sussex. BN7 1AA

Sir Benjamin Winterford, Penrose, WADEBRIDGE, Cornwall. PL27 7TB

Ms. F. MacDonald, 17 Bridge Street, STORNOWAY, Isle of Lewis. PA98 2AA

See Typing Target Practice, page 50, for further exercises on

6 Type the following exercise on A4 paper. (a) Single spacing with double between each numbered item. (b) Centre the main heading. (c) Use suitable margins. (d) Indent the first paragraph, but use hanging paragraphs for those numbered with small roman numerals. (e) Block roman numerals to the right.

> ***Note:*** When blocking roman numerals to the right, always leave 2 spaces after the last number, full stop or bracket before the start of the text. This means that extra spaces are needed before the shorter numbers.

RECORDED DELIVERY

This service provides a record of posting and delivery and limited compensation in the event of loss or damage in the post.

Indent one space from margin ⟶ I METHOD OF POSTING

Indent 2 spaces from "M" in METHOD ⟶ i A recorded delivery fee must be paid in addition to the normal postage.

ii The address of the packet must be written on a special recorded delivery receipt.

iii The receipt form and the packet must be handed to an official of the Post Office.

Type at left margin ⟶ II DELIVERY

Indent 2 spaces from "D" in DELIVERY ⟶ i A receipt is obtained on delivery at the address on the packet.

7 Type the following letter on A4 paper. (a) Use suitable margins. (b) Take a carbon copy. (c) Type an envelope. (d) Correct one word error.

Your Ref PQ/EDH
Our Ref FL/SY

Today's date

Miss P Quinney [QUINNEY]
Betta ~~Sect~~ Selection Services
26 Piccadilly Arcade, West Street
EDINBURGH EH3 9HS

Dear Miss Quinney

Thank y for yr letter dated (insert suitable date) 11-11-1988 enquiring abt electronic typewriters. I enclose full details of the most advanced electronic typewriters on the market today.

For yr purposes may I recommend the SEL "X" model ELEG 23. This machine offers

l.c./ 1. File memory using interchangable mini-floppy disks;
l.c./ 2. Permanent memory for frequently-used phrases & formats;
l.c./ 3. Entry & recall display; 4. Interchangeable daisy wheels w. 10, 12 + 15 pitch.

If I can help you in any way, please let me know.

Yours sincerely

SECTION 41

See Typing Target Practice, pages 38 and 39, for further exercises on

Enumerated Items

Use the variable line spacer to ensure that the insertions appear just slightly above the dotted lines.

2 Type the following memo on an A4 memo form. (a) Use margins of elite 13–90, pica 11–75. (b) Take 2 carbon copies: one for Mr B Veck and one for File. (c) Use indented paragraphs and centre the subject heading. (d) Correct the word error.

MEMORANDUM

From P T Anderson .... Ref. PTA/JR/wp2

To Mr S L Rogers .... Date Today's date

WORD PROCESSORS

Following our discussion on Monday, I give below a no of points wh may help you to come to a decision

uc/ abt the purchase of Word Processing Equipment.

the ʌ 1 Manufacturers of word processors claim th ʌ typist's output can be increased dramatically. DRAMATICALLY

2 Benefits, such as higher efficiency & greater production, can only be gained if the office planning to

uc/ introduce Word Processing is well organised in the first place.

3 Staff hv to be trained; working conditions hv to be considered; & changes in career structure may be necessary.

~~4~~ 5 uc/ Some studies hv suggested th the display units of Word Processors can cause eye strain, although there has bn very little hard medical evidence to back up the theory.

~~5~~ 4 It is necessary to ensure th the new skills req'd are given adequate rewards & th jobs are graded to fit this overall careers' structure for secretarial staff.

6 It should be possible to increase the output & efficiency of this office by installing a word processer. Many of the repetitive tasks can be performed automatically by m/c, leaving the office personnel free to concentrate more on issues requiring human judgement & decision.

See Typing Target Practice, page 49, for further exercises on

A4 Memorandum

FORMAT FOR SIDE HEADINGS

These headings are typed to the left of the set left margin. Side headings are usually typed in closed capitals with or without the underscore, but lower case with the underscore may also be used.

The following steps should be taken:

(a) First decide on left and right margins.
(b) Set right margin.
(c) Set a tab stop at the point where you intended to set the left margin.
(d) From the tab stop set in (c) tap in once for each character and space in the longest line of the side headings, plus 3 extra spaces.
(e) Set the left margin at this point.
(f) To type the side headings, use the margin release and bring typing point to tab stop set in (c).

Practise typing side headings

8 Type the following on A4 paper. (a) Single spacing. (b) Set a tab stop at elite 18, pica 15 for the side headings. (c) Margins: elite 41–88, pica 38–72. (d) Centre the main and subheading over the typing line, ie, centre point, elite 53, pica 43. (e) Correct one word error.

INFORMATION ABOUT HOUSING

Rights of Tenants and Landlords

A series of booklets in question-and-answer form has been prepared by the Department of the Environment for home-owners, landlords, tenants and anyone seeking information about housing.

Three titles are:

THE TENANTS' CHARTER	New rights for council, new town and housing association tenants.
NOTICE TO QUIT	A brief guide to landlords and tennants.
WANTING TO MOVE	A guide for those wanting to rent or buy in another area.

You may obtain copies of any of these booklets from your local council, Housing Aid Centre or rent officer.

9 Type the following on A5 landscape paper. (a) Single spacing with double between each paragraph. (b) Centre the main heading over the typing line. (c) Set a tab stop at elite 18, pica 15, for the side headings. (d) Margins: elite 38–88, pica 35–72.

YOUR INTERVIEW

A Few Suggestions

When the interview day dawns, do not worry – it is natural to be nervous. However y shld prepare yourself.

BE ON TIME	Allow plenty of time to get there because arriving late cd lose y the job.
SUITABLE CLOTHING	Wear clothes th are appropriate to the job for wh y are applying.
HOMEWORK	If at all possible, find out everything y can abt the organisation.

See Typing Target Practice, page 37, for further exercises on
Side Headings

EXTRA CARBON COPIES

Follow the rules given on page 64 for the typing of carbon copies. It is quite often necessary to type more than one carbon copy, any extra ones being for the information of others concerned. If this is the case, the name(s) of these recipients are typed either (a) in the top right or left corner or (b) at the foot of the letter or memo. The names are usually typed one under the other (if more than one) and preceded by the words "Copy for . . .", "Distribute to . . .", or "cc . . .". When the completed letter is removed from the typewriter, the individual names are ticked or underscored. A carbon copy should also be taken for the file.

	1st carbon	*2nd carbon*	*3rd carbon*
OPEN PUNCTUATION	cc J Robinson ✓ Mrs M Rogers File	cc J Robinson Mrs M Rogers ✓ File	cc J Robinson Mrs M Rogers File ✓
FULL PUNCTUATION	c.c. J. Robinson ✓ Mrs. M. Rogers File	c.c. J. Robinson Mrs. M. Rogers ✓ File	c.c. J. Robinson Mrs. M. Rogers File ✓

FORMAT FOR MEMORANDA

Revise the points given on page 48 for the typing of memos. The layout of the printed forms used for memos varies considerably, but the same rules for typing them apply. Remember to leave 2 clear character spaces after the words in the printed headings before typing the insertions and to use the variable line spacer to ensure their alignment. Never type a full stop after the last word of an insertion, unless it is abbreviated and full punctuation is being used. Special directions such as PRIVATE, CONFIDENTIAL, etc, are typed at the left margin one clear space above the first line of the printed heading.

Note: A memo with printed heading is given in the *Teaching Notes and Solutions* and copies may be duplicated.

1 Type the following memo on a printed A5 memo form. (a) Use indented paragraphs. (b) Take 2 carbon copies. Mark the first carbon copy for Mr. G. Sumner and the second one for File. (c) Centre the subject heading. (d) Use full punctuation. (e) Mark memo confidential as in copy. (f) Type one envelope for Ms. Jean Reynolds and one for Mr. G. Sumner.

Note: As the memorandum is marked CONFIDENTIAL, the envelopes MUST ALSO be marked CONFIDENTIAL.

CONFIDENTIAL MEMORANDUM

From Leonard West Ref. LW/Staff

To Ms. Jean Reynolds Date 24 January 1985

Return carriage/carrier TWICE before and after subject heading.

JOHN COTTERIDGE, SALES ASSISTANT

Mr. H. Whitaker, Managing Director, H. W. J. Whitaker & Co. Limited, has telephoned me and complained about the rude manner in which our Sales Assistant, John Cotteridge, spoke to his Secretary this morning.

Mr. Whitaker's company place a great many orders with us and, no matter how difficult his demands may be, we cannot afford to upset him.

Would you and George Sumner have a word with John Cotteridge and let me have your report.

c.c. Mr. G. Sumner
File

Some characters, not provided on the keyboard, can be typed by combining 2 characters, ie, by typing one character, backspacing and then typing the second character, or by typing one character and then the second immediately afterwards. In a few cases the interliner must be used to allow the characters to be raised/lowered.

Study the following examples and practise typing them:

Asterisk	Small x and hyphen.	*
Brace (commonly called brackets)	Continuous brackets typed one underneath the other. (See exercise on next page).	( ) ( ) ( )
Cent sign	Type small c, backspace and type oblique.	¢
Dagger	Capital I and hyphen.	†
Division	Colon and hyphen.	÷
Dollar sign	Capital S and oblique (slash).	$
Double Dagger	Capital I raised half a space and another capital I typed slightly below; or capital I and equation sign.	‡ ‡
Equation sign	Two hyphens—one hyphen slightly above the other.	=
Exclamation mark	Apostrophe and full stop.	!
Feet	Apostrophe typed immediately after figure.	8'
Inches	Double quotation marks typed immediately after figure(s).	7"
Minutes	Apostrophe typed immediately after figure(s).	10'
Multiplication sign	Small x with a space either side.	4 x 5
Plus sign	Hyphen and lowered apostrophe.	+
Seconds	Double quotation marks.	10"
Square brackets	Oblique and underscore—see explanation below.	[ ]

On modern typewriters many of the above characters are provided. On many machines it is difficult to type the division sign and plus sign as combined characters. Where this is the case, it would be wise to insert these in matching-colour ink.

When the ASTERISK has to be typed in the body of the text (exercise 2 on the next page), it is typed as a superscript (raised character). Before typing the combination asterisk, turn the cylinder one half space towards you, type small x, backspace and type hyphen; then turn back to normal writing line. Where the asterisk is already fitted, DO NOT lower the paper before typing as the sign on the type face is already raised.

To type a SQUARE BRACKET take the following steps:

Left bracket:

(a) Type oblique sign.
(b) Backspace one and type underscore.
(c) Turn cylinder back one full line space and type underscore.
(d) Turn cylinder up one full line space, backspace once and continue with typing up to the right bracket.

Right bracket:

(a) Type oblique sign.
(b) Backspace 2 and type underscore.
(c) Turn cylinder back one full line space and type underscore.
(d) Turn cylinder up one single space, tap space bar once, and continue with typing.

Practise typing square brackets

1 Type each of the following lines 3 times. (a) Double spacing. (b) Margins: elite 22–82, pica 12–72.

[756 ÷ 12 = 63] [12 x 5 = 60] [200 ÷ 2 = 100] [10 + 15 = 25]

[20 + 6 ÷ 2 = 13] [200 x 2 ÷ 4 + 30 = 130] [40 + 6 ÷ 2 = 23]

See Typing Target Practice, page 40, for further exercises on

Combination Characters

FORMAT FOR SUBDIVIDED COLUMN HEADINGS—BLOCKED STYLE

If you use blocked-style tabulation, then it is not necessary to centre subdivided headings vertically or horizontally. Starting points for headings will be the left margin and the tab stops for each column. Each column heading will start on the same horizontal line which will be the starting point for the deepest heading. Exercise 13 below is an example of blocked style with subdivided headings blocked—compare the layout with that in exercise 12 on page 103.

Practise typing tabulation with subdivided column headings

13 Type the following table on A4 paper. (a) Double spacing. (b) Centre the whole table vertically and horizontally on the paper. (c) Use blocked style. (d) Rearrange in property number order.

COUNTRY COTTAGES - SELF CATERING

P R I C E   L I S T

Property Number	Number of Weeks	Low	Mid	High
		17 April to 20 May	21 May to 6 July	7 July to 3 September
		£*	£*	£*
139	1	62.25	84.55	186.00 /Trs
14	1	87.25	129.55	189.00
31	1	8~~7~~2.25	84.55	118.0~~0~~0
269	1	70.25	89.55	118.00
99	2	145.5~~1~~0	189.10	250.00
224	2	114.50	178.10	216.00
87	2	---	1~~5~~60.10	186.00

* The prices quoted include the rental fee, the booking fee, and VAT at 15%, where applicable.

FORMAT FOR FOOTNOTES

In the table above you will notice an asterisk after the £ signs. This refers to the footnote after the last horizontal line. The footnote reference in the body is always a superior character (superscript), see page 95, and may be a figure or sign (asterisk, etc). In the body of the document there is NO SPACE BEFORE the figure or sign. At the bottom (in the footnote) there is ONE SPACE AFTER the figure or sign. If there is no asterisk on your typewriter, make one with x and hyphen (combination characters, see page 93).

Proofreading: please turn to page 180 and complete exercise 3

Practise typing combination characters

2 Type each of the following lines 3 times on A5 landscape paper. (a) Single spacing. (b) Margins: elite 20–80, pica 18–78.

```
From afar there came to our ears the call "Cuckoo!  Cuckoo!"
They had spent $300 on presents and came home with only 90¢.
The asterisk (*) is used for a reference mark in a footnote.
250 ÷ 5 + 50 ÷ 4 = 25;  25 × 5 – 15 ÷ 2 = 55;  $125 ÷ 5 = $25.
```

BRACE

The brace is used by printers for joining up 2 or more lines. To represent the brace in typing, use continuous brackets as shown in exercises 3 and 4 below.

Practise typing brace

3 Type the following on A5 portrait paper. (a) Centre horizontally and vertically. (b) Double spacing except for bracketed items which should be in single spacing. (c) Leave 3 spaces between columns.

```
CLASS LIST

                Position    Marks

H Jones         1           78

A Adkins        2           76

F Foster        3)          74)
G Green         3)          74)

H Hopkins       5)          70)
L Jones         5)          70)
L Lawson        5)          70)
```

HANDWRITTEN OR PRINTER'S BRACKET

This has to be replaced by the round brackets used in exercise 3 above. Where lines of unequal length are bracketed together, the brackets are typed immediately after the last characters in the longest line. All the brackets in any one group are typed at the same scale point.

4 Type the following on A5 landscape paper. (a) Use the same line spacing as in the exercise. (b) Margins: elite 22–82, pica 12–72. (c) Leave 5 spaces between the columns. (d) Replace the written bracket with the round brackets.

SPACING BEFORE AND AFTER PUNCTUATION

Full stop	Two spaces at end of sentence
Comma Semicolon } Colon	No space before, one space after
Dash	One space before and one space after
Hyphen	No space before and no space after
Exclamation sign) Question mark)	No space before, 2 spaces after at end of sentence

See Typing Target Practice, page 40, for further exercises on

FORMAT FOR SUBDIVIDED COLUMN HEADINGS—CENTRED STYLE

Practise centring subdivided column headings

12 Study the following table and the notes given below. Then display the table on A4 paper in double spacing. (a) Centre vertically and horizontally. (b) Insert leader dots.

CANAL TRAFFIC - 1981

Commodity	Canal Traffic '000 tons		
	Atlantic to Pacific	Pacific to Atlantic	Total
Wheat	2,901	100	3,001
Coarse Grain	13,000	353	13,353
Sugar	1,934	3,536	5,470
Soya Beans	5,237	---	5,237
Pulp and Paper	815	2,475	3,290
Iron and Steel Manufacturing	1,650	7,248	8,898
Miscellaneous Ores	710	3,050	3,760
Coal	14,500	200	14,700
Chemicals	2,700	655	3,355

CENTRING OF SUBDIVIDED COLUMN HEADINGS HORIZONTALLY AND VERTICALLY

In the above table, the heading "Canal Traffic '000 tons" must be centred over the second, third and fourth columns. To do this, first find the centre point to these 3 columns as follows: (a) from the first tab stop tap in one space for every 2 characters in the longest line of the first, second and third columns; (b) then tap in half the number of spaces to be left between the 3 columns; this is the centre point; (c) from this point backspace one for every 2 in "Canal Traffic '000 tons". Then proceed as follows:

(a) Type the heading "Canal Traffic '000 tons".
(b) Type the horizontal line underneath this heading, and along this line mark the scale points for the vertical lines for each of the 3 columns beneath.
(c) Type the headings for these 3 columns.
(d) Centre the heading for the first column vertically on the headings already typed. Do this by counting the number of lines and spaces in the headings typed, in this case 5, and from this number take the number of lines to be typed, eg, 1 line from 5 lines=4. Divide by 2=2. With the alignment scale on "Canal Traffic '000 tons" turn up 2 spaces and type the heading "Commodity" centred over the longest line.
(e) Type the horizontal line below the deepest headings.
(f) The items in the first column (usually descriptive) all start at the same scale-point.
(g) In the figure columns, the longest line of figures is centred and other figures typed, so that units are under units, tens under tens, etc.

Note: When ruling vertical lines for the subdivided columns, only extend these as far as the mark you have made on the second horizontal line as shown above. Always type the deepest heading first.

See Typing Target Practice, page 47, for further exercises on

SUPERSCRIPTS (SUPERIOR OR RAISED CHARACTERS)

A superscript is a character that is typed half a space above the line of typing. To type a superscript, turn the paper down half a space and type the character to be raised. If your machine does not have half spacing, use the interliner. In the exercise below, notice the degree sign. On its own it is typed immediately after the figure, but when followed by C (Centigrade/Celsius) or F (Fahrenheit), there is a space between the figures and the degree sign but no space between the degree sign and the letter C or F. Always use lower case o for the degree sign, eg, 10 °C. Superscripts are used for typing degrees and mathematical formulae, eg, $a^2 - b^2$.

SUBSCRIPTS (INFERIOR OR LOWERED CHARACTERS)

A subscript is a character that is typed half a space below the line of typing. To type a subscript turn the paper up half a space and type the character to be lowered. If your machine does not have half spacing, use the interliner, eg, H_2O $C_{12}H_{22}O_{11}$. Subscripts are used for typing chemical formulae.

Practise typing superscripts and subscripts

5 Type each of the following lines 3 times. (a) A5 landscape paper. (b) Double spacing. (c) Margins: elite 22–82, pica 12–72.

Subscripts are used in typing H_2SO_4, $CaCO_3$, N_2O and CO_2.

Superscripts are used for typing degree sign 4 ^oC.

A right angle equals 90°; 1° equals 60', and 1' equals 60".

At 10 am the temperature was 4 ^oC; at 2 pm it was 20 ^oC.

$ax + b^2 = a^2 - bx$. $a^2 (a - x) + abx = b^2 (a - b)$. $x^2 - a^2$.

SLOPING FRACTIONS

When fractions are not provided on the typewriter, these should be typed by using ordinary figures with the oblique, eg, 2 fifteenths=2/15; 3 sixteenths=3/16. Where a whole number comes before a "made up" fraction, leave a clear space between the whole number and the fraction. DO NOT put a full stop between the whole number and the fraction. Fractions already on the keyboard and sloping fractions may both be used in the same exercise.

Practise typing sloping fractions

6 Type the following exercise on A5 landscape paper. (a) Single spacing. (b) Margins: elite 22–82, pica 12–72.

2½, 3¼, 6 2/5, 2 5/16, 3 7/8, 4 8/9, 8 2/9, 7 3/7, 6 3/10, 5¾.
The following widths are in inches: 7½, 4 3/8, 6¾, 7 1/10, 8¼.

ACCENTS

When a typewriter is used for a great deal of foreign correspondence, the keys are usually fitted with the necessary accents. However, when accents are used only occasionally, the following are put in by hand in the same coloured ink as the ribbon.

´	`	^	~
acute	grave	circumflex	tilde

Usually typed as combination characters are:

diaeresis and umlaut=quotation marks typed over letter, eg, Düsseldorf
cedilla=letter c, backspace and comma, eg, Alençon

7 Type the following lines on A5 landscape paper. (a) Double spacing. (b) Margins: elite 20–85, pica 11–76. (c) Take one carbon copy. (d) Insert the accents on the top copy and the carbon copy.

Franz Nüsslein, 18 Münchnerstrasse, Düsseldorf, West Germany.
André Brésilien, 25 av Galliéni, Alençon, France.
Señor Juan Garcia, Edificio Phoenix del Mar, Alicante, Spain.

See Typing Target Practice, page 40, for further exercises on

FORMAT FOR MULTIPLE-LINE COLUMN HEADINGS—CENTRED STYLE

Each line of a column heading is centred horizontally within the space allocated for the longest line in that column heading. The whole of the heading in any one column is centred vertically in the space allocated for the deepest heading. The headings MUST be typed in single spacing. When typing multiple-line headings using the centred style of display, proceed as follows:

(a) Turn up 2 single spaces after the main or subheading or, if a ruled table (as exercise 11 below), turn up 2 single spaces after the first horizontal line.
(b) Type the deepest heading first.
(c) Move carriage/carrier to tab stop set for column with deepest heading.
(d) If the longest line is in the column itself, then all lines in the column heading are centred on the longest line in the column.
(e) If the longest line is in the column heading, then that line is typed at the tab stop and all other lines in the heading centred on it.
(f) Find the centre point by tapping the space bar once for each 2 characters/spaces in the longest line. Make a note of this point.
(g) Backspace one for each 2 characters/spaces in the line to be centred. Type the line at the point reached.
(h) In this way, centre and type all lines in the heading.
(i) Move to the next deepest heading.
(j) Count the number of lines in this heading and subtract the number from the number of lines in the deepest heading just typed. Divide the result by 2. For example, in exercise 10 below:

Deepest heading	3 lines
Next deepest	2 lines
Difference	1
Divide by 2	$\frac{1}{2}$—turn up half a space from first line of deepest heading before typing "Gained".

(k) Turn the cylinder towards you so that the alignment scale is at the base of the first line of the deepest heading just typed. From this point, turn up half a space and start typing the next deepest heading. Use the same method as in (f) and (g).
(l) Continue with other column headings in the same way.

11 Display the following table on A4 paper. (a) Double spacing. (b) Centred style.

INTEREST RATES

Currency	Individual Bank Deposit or Currency Equivalent	Fund Bank Deposit or Currency Equivalent	Gained by Fund
	%	%	%
Sterling	$8\frac{3}{4}$	$9\frac{3}{4}$	1
Deutsche Marks	$4\frac{3}{4}$	$7\frac{1}{2}$	3
French Francs	15	19	4
Swiss Francs .	$3\frac{1}{2}$	$6\frac{1}{2}$	3
Japanese Yen .	$2\frac{1}{2}$	$5\frac{1}{2}$	3
US Dollars ...	$7\frac{3}{4}$	$10\frac{3}{4}$	3

Column headings are always typed in single spacing.

See Typing Target Practice, page 46, for further exercises on

FORMAT FOR FULLY-CENTRED TABULATION

In previous exercises on tabulation all the tables were blocked. You must also become proficient in centring column work. The following points should be noted:

(a) Refer back to page 39 for horizontal and vertical centring.

(b) The main heading and subheading (if there is one) are centred on the paper, ie, backspace once for every 2 characters and spaces from the centre of the paper.

(c) As in previous exercises on tabulation, backspace once for every 2 characters and spaces in the longest line in each column, plus half the number of spaces to be left between columns. Set your left margin at the point reached.

(d) Tap forward from left margin and set tab stops.

Note: Any one piece of tabulation must be BLOCKED or CENTRED—a combination of the 2 is unacceptable.

Practise typing fully-centred tabulation

1 Type the following exercise on A5 landscape paper. (a) Centre the exercise vertically and horizontally. (b) Double spacing. (c) Leave 3 spaces between columns.

SOME BANK SERVICES

Traveller's Cheques	Financial References	Loans
Night Safe Deposits	Mortgages	Credit Cards
Bridging Loans	Current Accounts	Tax Advice
Executors and Trustees	Savings Accounts	Budget Accounts

FORMAT FOR COLUMN HEADINGS—CENTRED STYLE

If the column heading is the longest item in the column (as in exercise 2 below) the column items are CENTRED under the headings as follows:

(a) Type the column headings at the left margin and at the tab stops set.

(b) Find the centre of the heading by tapping the space bar once for every 2 characters and spaces in the heading, starting from the left margin or the tab stop set for the heading. This will bring the carriage/carrier to the centre point of the heading.

(c) From the point reached in (b), backspace once for every 2 characters and spaces in the longest line under the heading. This gives you the starting point for EACH ITEM in the column. Make a note of the point reached, then cancel the tab stop set for the heading and set another tab stop for the start of the column items.

2 Type the following exercise on A5 portrait paper. (a) Centre the exercise vertically and horizontally. (b) Centre the column items under the column headings. (c) Double spacing. (d) Leave 3 spaces between columns.

ABBREVIATIONS

Open Punctuation	Full Punctuation	Word in Full
Ltd	Ltd.	Limited
viz	viz.	videlicet
g	g	gram(s)
ie	i.e.	id est

See Typing Target Practice, pages 41 and 42, for further exercises on

FORMAT FOR MULTIPLE-LINE COLUMN HEADINGS—BLOCKED STYLE

Where column headings consist of more than one line or are of unequal depth, they are always typed in single spacing. They are never underscored in a RULED table. The following procedure should be followed when typing multiple-line column headings and using a blocked style of display:

(a) Set margins and tab stops as usual.
(b) All column headings start on the second single space after the main or subheading. However, if the table is ruled, as in exercise 10 below, then the column headings will start on the second single space after the first horizontal line.
(c) The heading over the first column is typed at the left margin.
(d) Headings in other columns start at the tab stop set for the beginning of the longest line in the column. Each line in any one heading will start at the same scale point.

10 Display the following table on A4 paper. (a) Single spacing with double between each item. (b) Use blocked style of display. (c) Type in alphabetical order of vegetables.

VEGETABLES FOR FREEZING

VEGETABLE	PREPARATION	BLANCHING TIME	PACKING
1 Asparagus	Wash, trim, blanch and tie in bundles	2-4 mins	Polythene containers
5 New Potatoes	Scrape; cook until just tender		Polythene bags
4 Mushrooms	Only small button mushrooms. Wash and sauté in oil		Polythene containers
6 Spinach	Wash, blanch, drain well.	2 mins	Polythene containers
2 Broccoli	Wash, ~~trim~~ TRIM, blanch and drain well	3-5 mins	" "
3 Fennel	Trim, wash, cut into slices, blanch, drain + pack	3 mins	Polythene bags
8 Turnips	Trim, peel, ~~and~~ dice; blanch, cool, drain	3 mins	" "
7 Tomatoes	Skin, simmer for 5 mins. Rub through sieve; pack		Polythene containers

If the column heading is shorter than the longest item in the column (as in exercise 3 below) the column heading is centred over the longest item:

(a) Set left margin and tab stops as usual.
(b) Find the centre point of the column by tapping space bar once for every 2 characters and spaces in the longest column item, beginning from the point set for the start of the column. This will bring the printing point to the centre of the column.
(c) From the point reached in (b), backspace once for every 2 characters and spaces in the column heading. Type the column heading at the point reached.
(d) The column items will start at the tab stop already set for each column.

3 Type the following exercise on A5 portrait paper. (a) Use centred style of display. (b) Centre the table vertically and horizontally. (c) Centre headings over the longest item in each column. (d) Double spacing. (e) Leave 3 spaces between columns.

LONDON THEATRES AND CINEMAS

<u>West End</u>

<u>Theatres</u>	<u>Cinemas</u>
Lyric	Odeon, Leicester Square
Shaftesbury	Plaza
Piccadilly	Classic
Vaudeville	Warner
Royal Opera House	Prince Charles

4 Type the following exercise on A5 landscape paper. (a) Use centred style of display. (b) Centre the table vertically and horizontally. (c) Double spacing. (d) Leave 3 spaces between columns.

WEATHER FORECASTS

<u>The expected situation for 0600 hours today</u>

COUNTRY	GENERAL SITUATION	TEMPERATURE
Amsterdam	Showers	54
Barcelona	Sun	62
Dublin	Rain	50
Gibraltar	Fair	73
Las Palmas	Sun	77
Luxembourg	Cloud	50

See Typing Target Practice, page 42, for further exercises on

FORMAT FOR LEADER DOTS

(a) Leader dots (full stops) are used to guide the eye from one column to another. There are 4 methods of grouping but, for the moment, we will use only continuous leader dots.

(b) Leader dots must be typed at the same time as you type the horizontal line to which they apply.

(c) There must always be one clear space between the last word and the first dot or the last dot and the vertical line, ie, leader dots must never be typed right up to the preceding or following word or line. No word or letter must be allowed to extend beyond the last leader dot, although leader dots may extend beyond the last word.

(d) Leader dots must always finish at the same point on every line, although the longest line may not have any leader dots—all dots on the other lines finish at the last letter of the longest line.

(e) In the exercise below, the leader dots finish at the last letter of the longest line and, to ensure that you do not type them beyond this point, after typing the second horizontal line, move the typing point to the start of the figure column, backspace 4 and type one full stop. When you have typed the details at the left margin, leave one clear space and continue to type the full stops until you reach the scale point where the dot has been typed.

8 Type the following table on A5 landscape paper. (a) Single spacing. (b) Centre vertically and horizontally. (c) Use blocked style. (d) Insert leader dots.

FOR THE MOTORIST

Gift Ideas

Item	Item Number	Price
		£
Fog Lamp	26	6.95
Battery Charger	41	17.50
Steering Wheel Glove	110	2.40
Quartz Clock	53	12.50

£ sign is typed at the tab stop when using blocked style of display

9 Type the following table on A5 landscape paper. (a) Single spacing with double between each item. (b) Centre vertically and horizontally. (c) Use centred style. (d) Insert leader dots.

S A L E

Size	Item	Price
		£
36" - 48"	Men's Real Leather Safari Jackets	35.00
38" - 44"	Men's Full Length Suede Coats	39.95
34" - 40"	Ladies' Coney Fur Jackets	39.95
28" - 34"	Boys' Leather Bomber Jackets	16.95

£ sign is typed over unit figure in £ column when using centred style of display

FORMAT FOR HORIZONTAL RULING—TABULATION

A neat and pleasing appearance may be given to column work by ruling in ink or by the use of the underscore. An "open" table has no ruled lines. Its main use is for displayed columns of items in the body of a letter or report. A "ruled" table has the column headings separated from the column items by horizontal lines above and below the headings, and below the last line in the table.

When typing a ruled table proceed as follows:

(a) Find vertical starting point by calculating number of typed lines and spaces—remember to count the horizontal lines.
(b) In the usual way, backspace to find the left margin. Set margin and tab stops.
(c) From the last tab stop, tap space bar once for each character and space in the longest line of the last column PLUS 2 spaces, and set right margin at the point reached.
(d) Type main heading and subheading (if there is one) at left margin if blocked style is used, or centre for centred style. Turn up 2 single spaces and return carriage to left margin.
(e) Press margin release key and backspace 2. This gives you the starting point for the horizontal line which is typed by means of the underscore and finishes at the right margin.

Note: Turn up TWICE after and ONCE before a horizontal line, but turn up TWICE after the main or subheading before the first horizontal line.

TABULATION WITH COLUMNS OF FIGURES

When columns in a table contain figures, care must be taken to see that units come under units, tens under tens, etc. Thousands must always be marked by commas or spaces consistently.

Practise typing figures in columns

5 Type the following table on A5 landscape paper. (a) Centre the table vertically and horizontally on the paper. (b) Use centred style of display. (c) Double spacing. (d) Leave 3 spaces between columns. (e) Rule by underscore. (f) Turn up 2 single spaces before and after the £ sign.

COMPARATIVE DEPARTMENT TURNOVER

£ sign is centred over the longest line of figures

Department	1979	1980	1981
	£	£	£
Clothing	114,320	196,400	212,345
Furniture	1,100,450	2,368,500	2,432,546
Kitchen Utensils	800,000	909,120	345,625
Hardware	523,412	619,345	800,050
TOTAL	2,538,182	4,093,365	3,790,566

See Typing Target Practice, pages 43 and 44, for further exercises on

In addition to the horizontal lines, a boxed table has vertical lines and the left and right sides may or may not be closed in by vertical lines. The vertical lines between the columns must be ruled exactly in the middle of each blank space. It is therefore advisable to leave an odd number of spaces between the columns—one for the vertical ruling and an equal number on either side of the ruling. To rule the vertical lines, take the following steps:

(a) First set left margin for start of first column, tab stops for the remaining columns, and right margin as explained on page 98 (a–d).
(b) After typing main heading, return carriage to left margin and type first horizontal line as explained on page 98 (e). Then turn up 2 single spaces.
(c) Move to first tab stop and backspace 2; at this point make a pencil mark for the first vertical line.
(d) Move to next tab stop and backspace 2; at this point make a pencil mark for the second vertical line.
(e) Continue in the same way for any additional columns.
(f) When you have typed the horizontal line at the bottom of the table, mark in pencil the bottom of each of the vertical lines.

Note: When marking the top of the vertical lines, make a note of the scale point at which the vertical line has to be drawn so that when you have typed the bottom horizontal line you will know exactly where to make the pencil mark.

Vertical lines may be ruled by underscore or in ink. Horizontal lines may be ruled by underscore and the vertical lines in matching-colour ink. Do not allow the vertical lines to extend above or below the horizontal lines. They must meet precisely.

6 Type the following table on A5 landscape paper. (a) Centre the table vertically and horizontally on paper. (b) Use blocked style. (c) Double spacing. (d) Leave 3 spaces between columns. (e) Rule horizontal lines by underscore and vertical lines in ink.

HINDU, SIKH AND MUSLIM

Festivals and Anniversaries

HINDU	SIKH	MUSLIM
Ram Navami	Guru Gobind Singh's Birthday	Muharram
Janam Ashtami	Baisakhi	Ramadan
Dussehra	Guru Nanak's Birthday	Eid-ul-Fitr

7 Type the following table on A5 portrait paper. (a) Centre the table vertically and horizontally on paper. (b) Use centred style. (c) Single spacing. (d) Leave 3 spaces between columns. (e) Rule horizontal lines by underscore and vertical lines in ink.

COMPARATIVE FIGURES IN MILLIONS

	1982	1981
	£	£
Turnover	742	611
Profit before tax	16	26
Net Assets employed	142	137
Orders in hand at 30 June	1 810	1 688

With centred style, the £ sign is centred over longest line of figures if there are no pence in the column. If there are pence, the £ sign is typed over the unit figure of £ column

See Typing Target Practice, page 45, for further exercises on

SECTION 43 Tabulation— Horizontal and Vertical Ruling